SPIRITUAL

TERRORISM

(True life Experiences)

By Monica Tomtania

ISBN 13: 978-069254-452-5
ISBN 10: 0-69254-452-6

AUTHOR'S BIOGRAPHY

Monica Tomtania is an ordained servant of God with the Assemblies of God. She was called into the ministry at the age of 10, after a near-death encounter with Heaven and Hell. She was one of the leaders of The Tears of Jesus Evangelistic Association.

She and her late husband, Rev. Geoffrey Kwame Tomtania planted numerous churches in Ghana and Togo and ministered in Africa, Europe, the United States, and around the World. They shepherded the largest AG church in the country of Togo, and through their ministry many have come to know the Lord, experienced freedom, and are serving in the ministry around the world. Monica served as the National Women's Ministry Director in Togo for 15years, and mentored many in Togo for the work of the ministry. She is the author of GOD STILL SPEAKS and THE ENDTIME DAUGHTERS OF THE KING. She is also a Pastor and a mentor, marital and spiritual counselor, and a songwriter. She is currently serving as the senior pastor of *Family For Christ Assembly of God* in the Bronx, New York, as well as helping the diaspora from Africa.

DEDICATION

I dedicate this book to my Lord and Savior Jesus Christ, through whose sacrifice and the shedding of His precious blood, I have become the daughter of the Most High God. Through Christ Jesus, my Lord and Messiah, I have gained access into the presence of my Heavenly Father to obtain grace and mercy, strength and victory in this great combat He led me through.

The LORD is my Rock and my Fortress and my Deliverer, my God, my Rock, in whom I take refuge, my Shield, and the horn of my Salvation, my Stronghold and my Refuge, my Savior; You save me from violence. I call upon the LORD, who is worthy to be praised, and I am saved from my enemies. For the waves of death encompassed me, the torrents of destruction assailed me; the cords of Sheol entangled me; the snares of death confronted me. In my distress I called upon the LORD; to my God I called. From His temple He heard my voice, and my cry came to His ears ... He sent from on high, He took me; He drew me out of many waters. He rescued me from my strong enemy, from those who hated me, for they were too mighty for me. They confronted me in the day of my calamity, but the LORD was my support. He brought me out into a broad place; He rescued me, because He delighted in me (2 Samuel 22:2-6; 17-20).

ACKNOWLEDGMENTS

To my Heavenly Father: First and foremost, I would like to thank You, ABBA, my Heavenly Father, for Your great love for me. Had it not been Your mercies and grace, I wouldn't be alive today. Your abundant grace sustained me, and it is still sustaining me in my walk with You. Papa, it is all about You, and I will always give You all the glory due for the powerful work You've done in me and through me for Your glory. I did not deserve Your goodness, yet You carried me like a little baby through the storms and the fires, and through it all, Your Name was glorified.   You are the Conquering King!

To my late husband, Geoffrey K. Tomtania, who is now dancing with the Lord Jesus on the streets of gold in Heaven: Eternity will never be able to comprehend the love the Lord injected into your heart for me, as frail as I was. You were an amazing husband, a true friend, a dear brother, a great father, and a wonderful man of God. By His grace, we stood all the tests in time together, and the Lord fought all our battles for us. I thought I would be the first to see Jesus, but Abba thought it otherwise. It won't be long we shall see each other face to face, and fall at the feet of the One who brought us together.

To my dear children: Thank you so much, my little angels and prayer warriors, who cried and begged the Lord to spare their

Mama. You are the best gifts the Lord gave to me—the prophesied four sons, who became a reality! I love you so much.

I would also like to thank the staff of the Institute of Children's Literature. It was through its courses that I have been able to get this book together.

Great thanks and appreciation to Mrs. Pegi Deitz-Shea, my instructor and editor, whose patience in editing the manuscript, and especially her encouragements, motivated me to finish the book. May the Lord richly bless you. You are a blessing!

To the online Bible resource, Bible gateway <www.biblegateway.com/passage/search>, for making this important tool possible and easy for the servants of God and Christian writers.

Now to You, O LORD be all the glory, great things You have done!

TABLE OF CONTENTS

Forewords: Mrs. Pegi Deitz-Shea
Foreword: Pastor Richard Terherst (Harvest Church, California)
Attestation: Mr. Ernest Moses
Introduction: Spiritual Terrorism, What It Is.

FOREWORDS

Spiritual Terrorism is a harrowing personal account of one Christian family's struggle against evil forces such as fetish priests and people possessed by demons. Monica Tomtania, a minister in New York, writes compellingly about how she called on Jesus Christ to help her battle the devil in her native Africa, and how she continues to do so in her congregation in America. Given recent fatal attacks against Christians around the world, we need to follow Tomtania's recommendations for keeping evil at bay.

Author Pegi Deitz Shea, Professor, Editor & Author.
(Check out her social justice and multicultural books, awards, writing workshops, curriculum guides and editing services!)

We first met Pastor Monica Tomtania in 1988 while serving as missionaries in Togo, Africa. She and her late husband Geoffrey were pastors of Calvary Temple Church in Lome'. God joined our hearts together as fellow laborers in His Kingdom and as lifelong friends.

Pastor Monica's book, Spiritual Terrorism, telling her life's story, is a read you won't want to miss. It is laced with principles of success in overcoming spiritual opposition and overwhelming circumstances. It is a reflection of the power of the Holy Spirit moving through the lives of vessels totally yielded to Him. It is the real world story of struggling with the tribulations of life while experiencing the incredible faithfulness of our heavenly Father.

In a time when much of the church leadership has become glitzy and entitled celebrities, Pastor Monica Tomtania is the real deal. She is a minister of honesty, integrity and genuine Holy Spirit power known only to those who have experienced brokenness.

May God unfold to you the principles of intimacy with Him, which leads to spiritual authority, as you read the pages of this book.

Your fellow servant,
Pastor Richard Terherst – Lead Pastor, Harvest Church,
Concord, CA

ATTESTATION

Life is full of heartaches, pain and sorrows, but there is always a light of satisfaction and joy at the end of it, especially when you have the Lord Jehovah on your side as your Savior, Sustainer and Conqueror. That is exactly what I have observed and seen in the life of my dear younger sister Monica Tomtania, born Moses. She has loved and has devoted her life to knowing and serving the Lord ever since she was even below the age of ten (10) years.

Monica has been such a godly influence on me and on the entire family. Despite the pains and blows she has received in her life, like a hard hit of a soccer ball when we are on the side line watching the game, she has remained true to her faith and stood firm in her relationship with her Lord till today.

It was through her prayer and intercession that I came to know the Lord, and now serving an elder in an Assemblies of God Church in Italy.

It is my prayer that the Lord will continue to sustain her with much grace and mercy for the race, and divinely enable her to finish well with Him. May her life continue to reveal Christ to all who come in contact with her.

Ernest Elvis Moses, Verona, Italy (Unfortunately, Ernest passed away with a sudden heart attack last November 2012 in Italy before the book was published)

INTRODUCTION

Can you imagine a human being playing a double role of being at different places at the same time—getting out of the body and flying to places to cause havoc and still be sitting down with you eating breakfast? That is mind-boggling, isn't it?

What will you do if agents of terror become verbal and aggressive toward you? And how will you conduct yourself if witches and wizards demonically begin to manifest visibly, changing into different things in front of you? You will run and hide?

How will you react if Lucifer visits you and tells you that you have certain things in your house that belong to him? And that if you do not give those things back to him, he will be at war with you and destroy you and your family?

You see, from the time I saw the first light on this beautiful world God created for mankind, I began a difficult journey of spiritual terrors and unexplained encounters that led me to search for meaning, protection, and purpose. And for the fact that we, my husband and me, began to wage the same battle for our lives and that of our four sons, and the ordeal and moments of prayers and fasting poured into it for our victory, has inspired me to inform the world of the forces beyond our scope.

Life is really full of mysteries, unresolved issues, and oftentimes terrors in different forms. Some are man-made, planned and inflicted on the innocent and the weak. Others are instigated by unseen forces beyond our scope. In actual fact, what we are talking about is spiritual terrorism.

Spiritual terrorism, what does it mean? Terrorism is defined as the systematic use of terror, often violent, especially as a means of coercion. Terrorism is the use of violence and threats to intimidate or coerce, especially for political purposes; the state of fear and submission produced by terrorism or by any other means.

"'Terrorism' actually comes from the French word terrorisme[2] and originally referred specifically to state terrorism as practiced by the French government during the 1793–1794 Reign of terror. The French word terrorisme in turn derives from the Latin verb terreō meaning "I frighten".

In November 2004, a United Nations Secretary General report described terrorism as any act "intended to cause death or serious bodily harm to civilians or noncombatants with the purpose of intimidating a population or compelling a government or an international organization to do or abstain from doing any act".[3]

So, spiritual terrorism is a systematic use of terror, violent attacks or oppression that is incorporeal, non-physical or intangible to the human eyes. And although these phenomenal encounters are non-physical, they can be revealed to an individual through dreams and visions, or it could manifest in the physical.

In any way, God can choose to make it known to His children through the supernatural eye-opening into the invisible and the visible manifestation in a person being used by the demonic. And when it happens in that manner, God gives His

16

children the gift of discernment to know and understand what is going on.

It is said that there are five kinds of terrorism—spiritual, physical, psychological, emotional, and economical. And whatever form terrorism takes, it is always devastating. Terror in any form is unacceptable. Spiritual terrorism is an attack from the pit of hell that affects the physical nature, the spirit or soul (mind, will, and emotions), resulting in sicknesses and diseases. These acts of spiritual terrorism come in different forms just as physical terrorism.

I call it spiritual, because many of the terror activities committed by these demonic agents are ignored today by society. Some are classified as a natural phenomenon. For example, certain act of cold- blooded murders, suicide, and ritual murder of innocent people in different parts of the world, are instigated by demonic forces, yet we give them different names—mental illness, et cetera.

To some, these ongoing unimaginable acts of terror have become a normal lifestyle for them. But the worst of all terror acts are the ones the naked eyes cannot see. Spiritual terrorisms are nonphysical, bizarre, and unexplained, because they are perpetrated by demonic forces in different ranks. And their agents, operations and the acts they pose go beyond what anyone can even imagine. They cause greater havocs than any acts of physical terrorism combined.

Why? Because they work invisibly, and before you notice their invasion, they have already taken root. The demons secretly destabilize families, instigating division in homes in order for them to thrive in an atmosphere of chaos. They also use the 'divide and rule' tactics to gain ground and work against people. They have some power to kill and steal the health and joy of others (John 10:10; Matthew 10:28). They possess and oppress innocent folks, making them feel miserable, unloved, rejected, uncontrollable, and useless.

In fact, these spiritual terrorists are proud of what they do, because they have a mandate to destroy humanity created in the image of God. Their agents have been recruited by satan, and they faithfully do his bidding.

Spirits manifest in different forms. They have different names. They are sometimes called demons, powers of darkness, principalities and powers. And their recruits are called witches, wizards, psychics, and other different kinds of supposed "good" names. They work in every sphere of life. They are not afraid of anyone. They work in ranks, and they do not relent. They can penetrate into many lives in disguise. They destroy curious lives through numerous means, especially through ignorance. Because they know that ignorance is the number one weapon they can use to capture their victims.

These spiritual terrorists are not weaklings. They are a powerful group, bigger and stronger than al-Qaida, because they are spiritual. And they are bent on winning. That is why you need to be informed. And although they are strong and powerful, they are not greater than the Almighty, All-powerful, and the All-knowing God.

> *For though we walk in the flesh, we do not war according to the flesh. For the weapons of our warfare are not carnal but mighty in God for pulling down strongholds, [5] casting down arguments and every high thing that exalts itself against the knowledge of God, bringing every thought into captivity to the obedience of Christ, [6] and being ready to punish all disobedience when your obedience is fulfilled (2 Corinthians 10:3-6).*

[1]

THE BATTLE FOR MY LIFE

Growing up was like living in hell. My life in Ghana hung in the balance all the time. Daily fights with demonic forces and witches wore me out. Horrifying dreams of witches ripping my throat and tearing my clothes off my back became routine. All the while, my witch aunt, Mother's youngest sister, kept on bragging and taking responsibility for my ill fate.

"I will kill her," the possessed aunt would say, always boasting of her spiritual caliber. "She won't live long."

Who was she talking about? Me! It was scary. But no one dared to confront her. They were afraid of her, because she'd attacked others in the family numerous times. They knew they would be dead in no time if they ever confronted her.

On top of all the spiritual attacks I was facing, there was no sickness that didn't knock at my life's door. There was no death threat my little body didn't go through. It seemed I collected all the garbage of diseases that crossed my path as well—stomachaches, dizziness, migraines, painful rheumatism, and fevers of all types.

There was no outbreak of any ailment in the country that I didn't pick up. I couldn't eat much. I suffered terribly from head to toe. I had terrible sores and bleeding gums so bad that the teeth in my mouth were constantly shifting out of place. I would wake up in the morning with blood in my mouth.

The enemy was battling for my life. I could hear voices and whispers over and over, telling me I was of no good to God. And for that reason God wanted to destroy me. There were times I had to be carried on the back or crawl to school, because of the boils on both knees.

I was lanky and helpless. I was bullied and nicknamed. My schoolmates called me "Rotten Fish." My family nicknamed me "Trashcan" and "Crier." Hopelessness became my own adaptation of my name.

Although Mother was a staunch Methodist and a member of the Singing Band, she polluted her faith in Christ with ancestral worship and all kinds of beliefs. Since she was desperate to see me healed, she tried everything within her reach. And because the faith of my family was a messed-up faith, I was transported to different places for help—from one hospital to another; from one fetish priest to another 'supposed powerful' "fetish priest. I loathed it, but I was helpless and so was dragged to them.

There was a time, I remember so well, when Mother took me to this particular fetish priest, who was related to our family in this town named Kwesimintsim. Normally, the priest would go into his secret voodoo chamber and consult his fetish alone. Then he would come out and inform the seeker of what the powers told him. After which he would prescribe a goat, a lamb, or a few chickens and other things, depending on the problem the person presented or the caliber of the individual.

During this last consultation, the priest became so frustrated with me for no reason at all. Then he said something to Mother that disturbed me for a while. There was no way I could have understood his diagnosis.

"Oh my, I cannot get into her spirit," he whispered to Mother. "I see another super-power in this girl, who is more powerful and greater than what I have."

"What is that?" Mother was wondering, and gave a deep sigh. "Why do you want to get into her spirit?"

"Don't you know that is how we do our job? I need access to her spirit in order to work with the forces that are trying to destroy her. But this girl's spirit is covered. The Power in her is really beyond myself. It is over-shadowing her like a blanket. That is the reason why she is not even dead."

"What does that mean?" Mother asked, so perplexed and desperate.

"It means that this child might one day become a bigger fetish 'priestess' than I. But in the meantime, I need to snatch her away from the witches who want to kill her."

"What has she done to them?" Mother muttered. "I know my sister and her allies had openly vowed to destroy her, but they wouldn't have her. She's done no harm to anyone. And I know God will take care of her."

Afraid of losing me, Mother began to sob. I joined in, tears running down my cheeks. I feared for my life.

"They are fighting really hard, because she will become great someday. I see them all around her fighting to eliminate her," the fetish priest said emphatically. "I will come and visit you one of these days."

"Let me know when you will be coming. I may or may not be in town. You know I am a busy widow with eleven children."

"Don't worry, I will come and visit her later if possible. Do you understand?" He winked at Mother.

I sat trembling as if I was going to die in a minute, but overheard all their conversation. The man looked at me with such an evil eye that sank deep into my soul. He wasn't happy with me at all for a reason I had no clue of. He was a witch, a medium and a representative of the evil one, and he was proud of it.

On the other hand, I felt he was afraid to touch me. Yet wanting to get his money, he mixed up some stinking herbal potion and gave it Mother to bathe me in. Then I was left quivering in the cold with no dress on except my underwear.

After that, guess what? He asked Mother to buy two chickens from him, one white and one black for the atonement of my soul, as he explained, plus a big bowl of rice and the necessary condiments. The priest wrung the neck of the birds without severing it completely, and then he tossed them up in his compound.

Poor birds! They fluttered and flapped around, spilling blood everywhere and turned on their backs and died. Everyone at the convent clapped their hands and rejoiced, because they believed the ancestors had accepted the offering, which meant that if the birds had landed on their belly that would have signified that the offering was rejected.

The apprentice priests and shrine women picked up the birds. They cleaned and washed them up and cooked the meat with the rice Mother bought. While they were still cooking, Mother wrapped me with one of her African wrappers, because I was really shivering and feverish.

When they fished cooking, they poured the whole dish— rice, meat, and the stew into a big basin. All those living in the fetish house gathered around to feast on the food with the exception of me. They were given strict instructions on how the food should be eaten—no breaking of bones, and no hands washed with water after eaten. I was forbidden to taste the food.

After they had lavished themselves with the food, they all surrounded me. I thought they were going to tear me apart. They began to smear and bathe me with whatever was left on their hands—oil, tomato sauce, whatever. I hated it, but I had no control of my fate.

This ceremony, as the fetish priest explained to Mother, was to present me as a 'no good to be destroyed' to the devil in order to prevent the witches from breaking me into pieces. But was it true? Even after these ceremonies, I did not become well. I was still sick, fighting in my dreams with witches and demonic forces all the time.

Nighttime was a nightmare. Daytime fatigued me, because it was as if the clothes I was wearing were also choking me. My condition worsened day after day. I desired rather to die than to live, because I did not understand what was happening to me.

[2]

DIVINE INTERVENTION

On top of the physical pain and the spiritual battle I struggled with, I also fought with rejections, insecurities, and hopelessness. I felt I was of no value to anyone. I lived in fear all the time, and so I developed a strong attachment to Mother, although I was the 8th child. And since I was bullied so much at school, I always hid somewhere to avoid being hurt.

Different name-callings such as 'rotten fish' and 'scaly girl' now focused on dark spots I had on my neck and face, and also a big scar on my right side.

As a result, I had to always cover my entire upper body to my neck in order to prevent people from seeing my scars even when the weather was hot as Hades. I remember disturbing Mother numerous times to tell me where I got those blemishes and scars. She refused categorically for a while, but she couldn't keep it in any longer.

Her face sagged as if there was something haunting her. Then with mixed emotion, she began, "You were only nine months old. I had finished given you a bath," Mother said. "It was getting late. I was cooking plantain and cassava for fufu on one coal pot, and soup on another in front of the kitchen. The family dinner had to be ready before the 'troops' began to cry and howl here and there. And so, thinking of a quicker hands-free, back-free way of getting things done, I decided to attach you to your sister Jemima, who actually wanted to hold you. None of the older sisters were home, and it wasn't Jemima's first experience.

"Knowing the overall curiosity of Jemima," Mother continued, "I warned her not to try to get up with you, while I kept an eye on her. But unfortunately, Jemima decided to do otherwise when I moved away to get some condiments for the soup. Suddenly, a horrifying scream echoed. I knew immediately that you were in trouble. So leaving whatever I was searching for, I rushed to the scene. But alas! The unbelievable had just happened. Jemima stood up, and lost control of you. You fell on the cooking pots, which in turn flared open. That was it."

With tears running down her cheeks, she said gently to me, 'My pretty little thing was burned all over. It was really hard to believe. Maame, forgive me. And forgive your sister as well, okay?'

"No problem, Mother. It wasn't anyone's fault," I told her.

'Now, rushing here and there,' Mother continued. 'I began to use what I was acquainted with to heal you. But it wasn't giving you any relief. Finally, I rushed you to the clinic. When I arrived at the doctor's office, he told me you'd suffered a terrible deep degree of burns, and there was nothing he could do to save your life. He prophesied no hope of survival. Walking home with my baby lying feebly in the cloth, I turned my heart toward the God I had heard preached about at church. I cried out to Him, 'Oh God, are You the same God of miracles? Please, forgive me my sins, and heal my daughter. I know that there is nothing too hard for You. This baby belongs to You.' Even though I did not know the Lord as I should, I knew that He was a prayer-answering God, a God who could turn evil into good.'

Although Mother kept on crying and begging God to spare my life, the doctor's verdict still threatened her faith as well.

Suddenly, she heard someone call her from behind. "Auntie Aggie, Auntie Aggie." She turned around, and standing behind her was a tall middle-aged man.

"My first instinct was to ask him where he knew me from, and what he wanted from me,' Mother said. 'I didn't know him. But I kept my calm."

"'Why are you crying?'" the strange man asked.

"I explained the whole ordeal to him. But he seemed not to be disturbed at all. He interrupted me and said, "'Listen woman, I know this is hard on you. But you have to understand that what happened to this baby will not terminate her life. She will not die.'"

"She will not die? But the doctor has given up on her, and I don't think she will survive these horrible burns."

"'Do you believe in miracles?'"

"Yes sir, I do."

"'You see, the hand of the Lord is upon this baby. She is going to be a wonderful instrument in the hand of God. She will touch many lives and will bring many sons and daughters into the Kingdom of God. Your daughter will live.'"

"Oh my goodness," I mumbled, tears of hope now flooding my face.

"'However, listen to these instructions very carefully, and she will be made completely whole.'"

"Yes sir, I will do whatever you tell me."

"'Collect snail shells and burn them up in fire. Grind the burned shells into powder. Then mix the powdered shells with fresh palm kernel or coconut oil. Smear the mixture over her body frequently, and she shall recover.'"

Very much excited, Mother thanked the man and headed home. After taking a few step, she looked back to ask the man where he lodged. Her intention was to go back and really express her gratitude the African way when the baby recovered. But to her surprise, he was nowhere to be found.

Who is this man who just talked to me? Where did he go? She pondered. *Who is this person who was sent to encourage me and to show me what I was supposed to do for my daughter's recovery. Is he an angel or what?*

Maybe! Nobody knows. Goosebumps sprouted all over her. Fortunately, Mother had a trashcan full of snail shells from what she had cooked the day before. She already had a jar full of fresh palm kernel oil made.

Was it a coincidence? No! God will always use what you have to accomplish His purposes in your life for His glory. The widow at Zarephath had just a handful of flour and a little oil in a jar. And that was what the Lord used to make provision for her, her child, and the Lord's prophet. (*1 Kings 17:8-16; also 2 Kings 20:1-7).*

Mother hurried to the house, rehearsing over the supposed miracle prescription given to her by a mysterious stranger. There was no time to waste. She went to work as soon as she arrived. And the Lord miraculously healed me.

Although I survived this terrible hot water ordeal, it left a painful scar on my soul. I began to experience emotional traumas, and it went on for a long time. I cried for no reason, but no one in the family ever asked what the problem was. No one felt my heart's cry. I didn't know it either, but I felt out of place in my own little world. So I was nicknamed 'Crier.'

I would hide under the bed for hours when visitors were at the house. And Mother would search everywhere for me. If the visitors were there before I returned from school or wherever I was sent, I would wait outside or hide behind the door until they left. I was afraid of everything and everyone. I could hear Mother call out, "Maame, where are you? Come out from your hiding. No one will hurt you." But it wasn't possible.

Even though the whole family prayed every morning at five, no one specifically prayed for me. My little heart was craving for love and acceptance, self-worth and identity, and protection, and it wasn't getting it.

"After all, you are not the baby anymore," I heard over and over.

They don't get it! Oh my, how I wished they would also experience the pain in my heart and the longings of my soul. I felt miserable.

Strangely enough and without explanation, by the time I was five, I knew in my heart that there was Someone bigger or greater somewhere I should search for, and who may care more than anyone else. I began my search every day with a little prayer to God: *'Lord, if You are real and care about me, I want to know You. I want to see You, and I want to hear Your voice.'* I prayed that prayer almost every day including the Lord's Prayer. He didn't answer my prayers right away.

[3]

A STAB ON MY HEART

What I had been searching for, I had not found yet. The growing urge for joy, love and acceptance was intensifying. Even though I loved Daddy, he wasn't home much, sometimes for a week or two at a time. So I developed a strong attachment to Mother.

I really loved my mother. Mother was not mean to any of her children, only that she never expressed her love with the words, "I love you." It wasn't her fault, because she wasn't taught how. Rather, she taught all of us at a young age the basics of life. She taught us great lessons in life. Some of these I see it fit to mention.

Mother taught us to love God, to work hard, to live lives above reproach, and to respect the Name of the Lord. She emphasized on how to avoid evil companionship, and how to use one's time and talent for good things that will profit others.

Mother always stated the importance of loving everyone without discrimination. Prejudice wasn't a part of our family culture, rich or poor, blue or white, clean or dirty, sick or healthy. All were welcomed in our home.

Cooking and doing household chores were like breathing to most of the children. No clean up in the morning? Then, no breakfast. No shower? No food, except on Saturdays when we had to go to the farm. We began the day with prayer. That was our morning coffee. Then we took our positions to sweep or clean in the compound, inside the bedroom or in the kitchen, making it sure everywhere was clean and dirt free before we thought of putting food in our mouths. Mother's motto was, "Cleanliness comes with Godliness."

We were all equipped little by little for our own future lives at a young age. We were not pampered either, because Mother was very religious and a strict disciplinarian. But she was very loving in every way. Unless it was extremely necessary, Mother never disciplined or scolded any one of us in front of people. Her eyes were the watch guard for all of us. We just had to look at her face to understand what she wanted from us or needed us to do. And I thank God for giving me such a loving Mother.

As for Daddy Francis, he fought in World War II, and was the chief driver of his battalion. After the war, he got a job with Levantis, a French company, which later on became C.F.A.O., which was based at that time in Sekondi-Takoradi, Ghana's twin cities.

Sekondi-Takoradi harbored the first seaport of Ghana, which served the sub-region of West Africa. Daddy continued his job as the chief driver for this company, delivering goods to their stores in the nation, from north to south and from east to west. He built houses like crazy, and accumulated wealth.

However, Daddy's main problem was that he started breeding everywhere he went to deliver goods. He was really handsome, and drew the women to himself like a magnet. Although he had three wives with about twenty known children, he gave himself extra heavy loads with all the children he had everywhere. *How could he possibly divide himself to satisfy all these numerous women and children?* Only God knew what he was going through at that time?

As the hole in my heart became bigger and bigger, numerous questions clouded my mind. My dilemma increased, especially when I saw other children my age playing around with their fathers. *Why doesn't Dad stay and play around with us like other Dads do?* I questioned. I knew Daddy was a good father, but how come he wasn't around us all the time?

The answer was evident. Daddy was carrying his own problems. I loved him so much and needed to hear him say, 'Monica, I love you', *b*ut I never heard it from him. Maybe that wasn't his fault. I thought, perhaps most 'third-world' fathers hardly ever expressed their love to their siblings verbally.

Even then, he somehow demonstrated his love by the material things he provided for all his children. Anytime I asked Mother where Daddy was, she would say, "Your Dad is doing fine. He really loves you. Don't you see what he is doing for us? You have food to eat, clothes to wear, and you never walked barefooted like other children."

I knew that, but all I wanted was to see him often and hear "I love you" verbally from both of my parents.

Daddy loved people. He shared all he had with the poor. He was a good-deeder indeed! I remember the times Daddy would come back from his trip with a truck full of plantains, bananas, oranges, and whatever he found edible on his route back home. Mother would in turn share it among the neighbors and the family.

One particular morning, I got up with strong fear and anxiety. It began to envelope me little by little until I felt I needed to hide behind someone. But I couldn't figure out what was happening. I was only seven years old at the time.

I rarely saw Daddy, and although it felt strange to me that he hadn't visited for weeks, it wasn't a big deal to me anymore apart from the fact that I missed him that particular day. That day, the 21st day of September 1959, became the turning point of what our family would become in the future.

People were coming in and going out of the house. Mother was in the bedroom sobbing. I wanted to run to her, but we weren't allowed to be with her. An aunt had come from Sekondi and was talking to Mother. The moment the aunt saw Jemima and me peeping through the door, she sent us to the mini market by the main highway to buy her a few cooking condiments. I thought she was trying to help out since Mother wasn't feeling well that day.

Whilst leaving the house, I spotted a packed passenger truck a few yards away from the police station. A few relatives wearing traditional African clothes were standing by, faces sagging with grief. I got stuck by just looking at them.

"Hey, what are you looking at? Let's go!" Jemima yelled at me.

"What's happening over there?" I asked her.

"Has that got anything to do with you?" she shrieked.

"I think something is happening over there."

"Stop asking me questions, and let's go," Jemima said, pulling me away.

We rushed to the market and got the condiments. By the time we came back to the house, I saw the unbelievable. Our house was filled with mourners. Some were trying to hold us and to comfort us. Others were just wailing uncontrollably. I knew Daddy was gone. I wanted to escape to a far-away land, but it wasn't possible. I couldn't move. I was hi-jacked and sandwiched under the bosom of my half-sister, Alberta. I sobbed and trembled, but her arms became my comfort and security.

There it was! Another stab to my little heart! – A painful memory that would never leave my mind. The worst part of it all was that Mother had just had her eleventh child, Catherine, a two month-old girl, and Mother was also very sick. Imagine her pain. Her hopes had been shattered in just a blink of an eye.

When I heard the wailings of Mother and my family, I pondered, *how good is this God who will take my father away, a father who had many children to take care of? What is Mother going to do with all these children without a husband to help? Where do the dead go? What happens when people die?* These and many other questions flooded my mind. No one could read my heart in order to answer all my questions. Sheer confusion filled my mind.

When the cries died down for a while, I decided to hide. I figured out that if I could run through Daddy's room, which would actually give me access, an escape route to the outside. I sneaked into the room, the only way to the parlor. I had no clue of what I was going to encounter.

I stumbled over something that was really mind-boggling. There, in front of me, leaning by the wall, was the corpse of my Dad, eyes bandaged, nose filled with cotton, etcetera, *Oh, how frightening it was!* A scene that would become a thorn in my flesh.

Oh, how frightening it was! "Jesus!" I screamed. I screamed again and fell. That was it! I fainted. I woke up in Mother's arms with a shock that impacted my heart for years. And when I came back to myself, even at age seven, I felt as if the whole world was crumbling underneath me. I didn't have a clue. Who could help me?

I thought God had totally abandoned me, because I loved my Dad very much. No one knew what killed him. But now, he was gone for good. I wrenched in pain all the time. My dilemmas increased.

Before the funeral, Daddy's relatives came into the house that day. Mother was wailing in agony inside our bedroom. I did not know what was happening to her. Straightway, Ernest came out of the room weeping bitterly, banging at the door.

I sneaked into the room in my curiosity and stood at the corner behind the door, watching what was going on. It was a tug-of-war between Dad's relatives and Mother. Dad's relatives were asking Mother to give them the keys to the safe, the drawers full of clothes, his cars and trucks, and everything she and Dad had labored for. She was pleading with them to leave, but they weren't moving away without what they'd wanted.

Finally, Mother caved in after much pressure and gave them the keys. They opened the drawers one by one, removing everything my Dad had owned out of the room. They took everything—from clothes to pins, even his underwear. His minibus and truck were all taken away within seconds. Nothing was left for us. It was a horrible sight. They carried all his belongings, packed them in one of the trucks, and left with the corpse.

Oh no, how can people be so cruel and inhuman? Mother spent the rest of the day wailing in despair, with baby Catherine in her arms. Ernest followed the truck where Dad's body was and kept on screaming, weeping, and banging on top of the truck as it made its way to the main road.

In tears and agony, we all wondered what actually happened to Daddy, and why he died in a fetish convent and not in a hospital. Interestingly, rumors of demonic involvement in Daddy's death began to break out even before the burial. Frictions between the families were evident. We were too young to dig into it. But a few years later, the confessions of a dying cousin of Daddy brought to light all who were involved in killing Daddy with witchcraft. Their reason? Daddy was wealthy and more blessed than them.

After the funeral, Mother had to sell whatever she could lay hands on to take care of us. Since she was well-informed in catering, she really put herself and all of us to work in order for us to have an education. She would knead the dough for bread in the evening, and by morning it was ready to bake.

At the same time, Mother would be frying her doughnuts, or cooking 'kenkey' (boiled corn meal) to sell. In addition, she created a farm on a family property near Grandma, which yielded corn and beans, cassava and peppers, tomatoes, okra and garden eggs (smaller white eggplants). She cultivated sugar cane on another family property. Those foodstuffs were really heaven-sent during harvest time. We had coconut plantation as well, because the placentas and umbilical cords of each child was used to plant coconut trees. This was an old tradition.

Mother struggled day after day to help ends meet. During school sessions, Mother went to the farm alone. We, the children, did our best to help on Saturdays. On holidays however, we all chipped in in full force to help her with the farms as well as her sales. So at a young age, I knew what hard work was all about.

In order for all of us to have good education, pretty clothes and good care, Mother acquired different kinds of fast consuming goods and household items from wholesalers at the Market. Each one of us sold something door-to-door during the holidays and the weekends. She made small moneyboxes for each one of us, and engraved our names on it. That was our piggy bank, and the money each one of us saved, served to pay for our school fees, uniforms, and personal items.

The first retail items I sold were loaves of bread and bars of 'Key soap.' Then I sold kerosene by measure. In due course, I began to sell corn meal, uncooked and cooked rice, beverages, cooked and roasted peanuts and chickpeas, as well as many others. When mango season arrived, I sold mangoes. When orange season came, I switched to oranges. I swapped from one thing to the other in order to gain more money to help pay my school fees, and have a little leftover for clothes and whatever I needed. We all did the same, both the guys and the gals. That was life for us. But because of my health, my allotted selling areas were limited.

Even in those times of desperation, the more frequent I communed with God, the clearer my mind became. During those moments, I could literally hear angelic voices singing the most beautiful, melodious hymns to me all the time. Those songs were so soothing I knew I was no longer alone. I felt God was literally singing over me. I could also hear the Lord speaking to me in a sweet and gentle voice, expressing His love to me. Yet, the enemy kept on telling me how miserable and rejected I was. It was a battle for my mind.

[4]

A NEAR-DEATH ENCOUNTER

A few months after Dad's death, I joined the local Methodist choir at the age of 7. I was the youngest choir member. Music always gave me joy and a sense of belonging. And thank God, He has given me the talent to write over 600 songs. I'm hoping to make an album soon. Some of the songs and choruses I wrote are now being sung in Africa and around the world.

In the third year of my involvement in the choir, something strange happened to me. This was the time of the year the Methodist choirs normally held a competition to rank the best choirs in the sub-region of Sekondi-Takoradi. Our home choir participated in one of those competitions held in Sekondi. And for the first time in my life, I sang, "A Mighty Fortress is our God"

That day, I rushed with excitement into the vestry to remove my choir robe. The moment, I opened the door of the chapel, I saw my witch aunt standing in the middle of the pews. She gave me a hateful twitch with her eyes and then said something. I really didn't understand what she said.

What was she doing in the house of God at that time?

Just then, I felt a sharp pain in my throat. *Hmm, this is awkward,* I talked to myself. I complained about the pain to Mother as soon as I got home, but Mother wouldn't believe me, because it didn't look like I was in any kind of pain.

After pressuring her for a while, she said, "Maame, I think you might have swallowed a fish bone earlier today."

"No, Mother, I haven't eaten fish today. We just came back from Sekondi, and we didn't eat anything there." But she really didn't pay much attention to what I was saying.

"Drink a lot of water," she said casually, and went back to the kitchen.

I understood Mother's actions, knowing she was surrounded by her nine hungry children at the time. She assumed the supposed-bone in my throat would drift away with the quantity of water I would drink. I drank, but it didn't help. Mother's prescription had worked many times for all of us, but this time, the more water I drank, the worse it became. That was weird.

By the following morning my throat was swollen. Mother tried everything she could think of for one full week. None of the herbs she used for treating sore throats helped. The swelling grew bigger and more painful. Then a strong fever followed.

When she came to her wits' end, Mother asked Jemima to take me to Dr. Sagoe's clinic at Takoradi. The old Doctor Sagoe was known to be the best physician at that time in that sub-region. His diagnosis was final. If Dr. Sagoe said that someone would die, it would happen exactly as predicted. He was trusted and feared by all; he had no friendly demeanor—too serious, too strict.

I was terrified to death when we arrived at the clinic. The look on his face wasn't friendly at all. Upon careful examination, Dr. Sagoe told Jemima that he was going to try something very important, which will determine my fate. "She may have a boil in her throat," he said.

A boil in my throat? Can that be possible? Where did it come from? I contemplated. I wanted the boil out, because it was too painful.

"Young lady," Dr. Sagoe said to me, looking straight into my eyes, "I will try to insert the tip of a teaspoon inside your throat, okay? If it is able to penetrate the boil easily, it means there is the possibility of giving you medication to prevent untimely death. Do you understand? However, if the spoon doesn't penetrate through, I cannot do anything for you. You may not survive, and you will die. This kind of boil is very dangerous and is fatal. Do you understand, eh?"

I nodded, scared to death.

Jemima and I were ushered into a small room. As I sat on the bed, my mind raced, thinking on the doctor's final statements, *"You may not survive. You will die."* Then Dr. Sagoe came into the room holding his teaspoon. He asked me to prop my head backward. It was practically impossible. My neck was swollen. I was in severe pain and could not move my head.

Being impatient with me, and not knowing the gravity of what I was going through, Dr. Sagoe turned my head brusquely to examine my throat. I screamed in pain, tears flooding down my face. The pain felt like an intense electrical shock that went through my entire body. It was too severe to contain! I could not even turn my head, but he was bent on doing what he intended to do. Then he took his turn with the spoon.

"Ouch!" I cried. What an excruciating pain! I began to cry and gasp for breath. My throat was bleeding. *This is ridiculous. Is there no other method he can use to examine me other than the tip of a teaspoon and twisting my head around?*

When Dr. Sagoe saw the blood, he stopped what he was doing and propped my head forward, very angry. He looked intently at me, shaking his head. After a while, he walked us outside the room into the lobby and left. The pain was so unbearable that I began to shake uncontrollably. It felt as if someone was ripping my head off. Jemima covered me with the cloth she was holding.

Dr. Sagoe came back to us and stood by the door looking at me sadly for a while. He shook his head in regret. Jemima understood his body language and beckoned me to follow her back home.

Although Jemima had taken me to the clinic, we weren't all that close. There was a little tension between us. And I believed that was due to the offense she took when I got burned. I loved her, but somehow, I felt my death would benefit her more, because she wasn't moved an inch with what the doctor had said. *Maybe my nonexistence would give her a sense of worth.* I convinced myself.

Since we had no car, and we couldn't walk back home on the three-mile trail, we boarded the public transportation back to the nearest station and walked slowly home. I was in shock. My head was spinning so fast, I thought I was going to die. I was feeling dizzy. My heart was racing, and my head pounded hard, as if someone was cracking my head open.

What was the benefit of going to the clinic? Anyway, I was feeling sicker when we arrived home that afternoon than when we left the house.

Once at home, and Jemima gave them Dr. Sagoe's diagnosis, everybody became discouraged and alarmed, but not Mother. She had received a prophetic word a few years back over me when I should have died with the hot water burns. So she was not willing to give up. Trying everything she could lay her hands on to help me recover, she continued to use all the different kinds of herbs she had known in her life. But my condition worsened as the days went by. I could not even turn my head or neck.

At that moment, I began to reminisce on all the stories in the Bible I'd heard in Sunday school. I was told Jesus could heal every disease. I was told He could raise the dead. I was taught songs about Heaven. So I sang silent hymns about Heaven that I was familiar with, songs like, "In the sweet by and by" and "Jesus loves me". I contemplated on what the Lord was preparing for His children in the hereafter, but I still had no peace.

I had heard in Sunday school that children are God's, and they are taken straight into paradise after they die. But I did not know whether I was ready at that time to meet the Lord. In actual fact, I did not want to die! I wanted to live. I wanted to grow up and support Mother when she grew old. But here I lay suffering and dying. *How can that be?*

I'd heard about Heaven, but I wasn't all that sure I was going to go to Heaven if I died. Somehow, I knew there was more to life than just going to church and believing in the Bibl. There was something about eternity that bothered me, but there was no one around me at this crucial moment of my life to show me the way to God and His Heaven. There was no one to help me to know the Jesus I now know as my Lord and Savior. Those surrounding me were all religious folks who were as lost as I was.

How does a person know Christ? I asked myself. I did not know it either. I knew He had died for me. I knew He was buried, and He rose up again and went back to Heaven. But I had not been taught to receive Him in to my heart. *Is there a process? I had no clue.* But this thought continued to sound harder and harder in my spirit. I had memorized most of the stories in the Bible, including the Ten Commandments and the Sermon on the Mount, but I knew not the way to Heaven. In my own mind, I prayed and asked Jesus to heal me.

Finally after three solid weeks of not drinking or eating, something tragic happened. My heart began to race rapidly one morning. I knew I was dying at that moment. I wrenched in pain, and I felt my heart stop. I passed out. And this is what happened.

In a flash, I was out of my body. I could see my body lying on the mat, and the real Monica, my spirit, standing by watching all the activities going on. Jemima yelled and called out to Mother. Everybody was running for something and crying. I heard Esther telling Ernest to bring a certain medicine called "Oku."

Why didn't they bring the "Oku" earlier? Now it seems it is too late.

Suddenly, I found myself in a different realm. This place seemed to have been placed in-between two environments. Turning to the left, I saw this horrifying, dark, unexplainable place. It was like a crushed mountain filled with volcanic lava, churning and burning up people, yet they were not dying. I could see and hear people crying and wailing in agony, begging for water to quench the thirst of their undying souls. It was a horrifying scene. I began to cry for help. The horror of the place was indescribable to the human mind.

A giant angelic being was holding on to me, ready to throw me into the horror-filled pit. I asked him, "Is this place for me?"

"Yes," he said. "No, I don't want to go there.

"Please, help me! Help!"

As I was screaming for help and sobbing uncontrollably, he said to me, "Monica, this place is for those who have not given their life to Jesus. This terrible place is for those who do not believe that Jesus is the only way to the Father. It is for those who have not been forgiven of all their sins and washed in the blood of the Lamb of God that was shed at Calvary. It is for those who have chosen to live their lives without God. This terrible place is for those who have no time to serve God. It is a place of everlasting torment" *(Isaiah 33:14; Daniel 12:2; Luke 16:19-31; Matthew 25:41-46; Revelation 14:9-11; Revelation 20:1114).*

An unusual force surged within me, and I cried out, "Jesus, save me." Without a chance for me to say anything again, the angel turned around with me to another place better than what I had seen earlier. Yes, this place was quite different. It was beautiful beyond description, and too soothing to explain. I could see shining gates of pearls and hear the most beautiful echo of heavenly music. The flowers were beautiful beyond my ability to explain. Everything seemed perfect. I knew immediately this was Heaven. I was extremely happy I had escaped that horrible place, and wanted to stay in this awesome environment.

The angel said: "Monica, this is Heaven. Heaven is for those who have accepted Christ Jesus as Lord and Savior. It is for those who have given their lives to Jesus and are living for Him. It is for those whose sins have been forgiven and are washed in the blood of the Lamb of God, who is Christ, the Lord. He is the Only Way to Heaven. Many do not believe there is a Heaven and a Hell. They are all very real. Go and tell them."

That was my commission to the world—to tell the world about Christ, about the existence of Heaven and Hell. This, I reasoned, must be my reason for living.

Oh what a wonderful place! I was no longer suffering. I wanted to stay, but the angel wouldn't allow me to. At that moment, someone else took my hand and led me through another gate. I was lamenting and saying to my escort, "No, no, leave me here. I want to stay."

That was the best place ever. There was nothing like it. The place was so glorious and beyond imagination. At that instant, I felt a sharp pain in my throat. Then I regained consciousness.

When I opened my eyes, I saw Mother and Ernest standing by my side. There were others who were crying around me. All eyes were filled with tears. I began to cough and vomit blood. The boil had burst. It was really very painful, but I knew the Lord was healing me. At that instance, I remembered what I was told. I prayed and gave my life to Jesus Christ and professed Him as Lord, asking Him to wash me in His precious blood.

This first out-of-the-body experience became the starting point of who I am today and how I shall spend eternity. This is the driving force of my relationship with Jesus Christ, my Lord.

Although it took a while for the sore to heal, I was glad I wasn't sent to hell. I continued to wonder what would have happened had I died. From that moment, I was enveloped with such godly fear no one knew of. I literally lived in this atmosphere, afraid to speak, or do anything that could send me to hell.

Mother told me later on that Grandma had ordered a casket, and they were preparing for my passing when the Lord gave me this glorious miracle. I knew at that moment, that God holds the bigger picture of my life in His hands, and nothing can snatch me out of His hands, unless He permits it.

I could not share the near-death experience with anyone except Mother and Jemima after my recovery. Then later on, I shared the whole encounter with my future husband, Geoffrey in

1976 at the Bible School. Others got to know it after I wrote it down during one of the writer's seminars held at the West African Assemblies of God Theological Seminary in Togo with the late Robert Cunningham of the Gospel Publishing House, USA, and Missionary John Weidman, who was the then President of ALM—Assemblies of God Literature Ministries, Togo. My story was turned into a tract entitled, "I DON'T WANT TO DIE," and was translated into French and other languages.

God indelibly wrote this near-death experience on my heart. It was hard to forget. I felt very miserable anytime I was tempted to do something contrary to the Word of God. I could not understand the reason. I still remember the times when we were very hungry. However, Mother had all her coins in the little 'superstitious' sack she hung at the back of the bedroom door. I knew that idols or anything dedicated to Satan had no power to harm me, but whatever I took from that sack, although I was hungry, meant thievery to God.

Now that I know the Lord intimately, I know the nudge was from the Spirit of God, who was convicting me and guiding me to live a life well-pleasing to Him. He gave me grace to live for Him, because, after you've had such an experience with Hell and Heaven, it must definitely leave a mark on your life. I have pledged my allegiance to Christ and the Word of God that I will never allow anything to hinder me from going to Heaven. I know His grace will always guide and lead me.

A few weeks after the Lord brought me back from the dead, the miracle of my survival sent shockwaves to the kingdom of darkness. My witch aunt could not keep her evil intentions any longer. She confessed to Grandma in the presence of Mother about the curse she placed on me.

"I hated Maame," she said, "and I didn't want to see her excelling in anything."

"But what has she done to you?" Mother asked her.

"I just don't like her. I wanted her dead, but I guess my curse didn't work." She expressed in disappointment.

Mother was somehow shocked, because she did not connect the boil in my throat with her sister. However, she thanked the Lord that although the enemy used my witch aunt to place a curse on me, God turned it for something glorious, a personal call to the ministry. The Bible says in Romans 8:28, *"And we know that all things work together for good to those who love God, to those who are the called according to His purpose."*

The best part was that our choir won the first place in the competition! Halleluiah, the Lord won on both combats! But as for me, the struggles and spiritual attacks continued to terrify me from all angles.

[5]

TAKING A FIRM STAND

Once I gave my life to the Lord Jesus Christ, I begged Mother not to take me to the fetish priest again. She also told Grandma not to mention my name before any fetish shrine, which was part of the custom. Each child in the family's name was mentioned in the pouring of libation for the ancestors to protect them.

Grandma became so furious. "You are ignorant," Grandma said to me. "Don't you know of all the sacrifices and the blood you see in the Old Testament? Didn't God ask His people to bring these things to Him to pacify His anger against their sins, so that He would preserve their lives? Is it not the same thing we are doing to preserve your life?"

Maybe I was ignorant, but my spirit didn't like it. "Please Mother," I would beg her. "I don't need any dead relative and demons to protect me. I have the Creator of the universe residing in me. He will take care of me. And even if I die, I know I will go to Heaven."

"Be very careful," she cautioned me. "These people are vicious. They know how to get to your spirit."

I understood her concerns. But my dilemma increased. *Why is my family mixing Christianity with witchcraft and idol worship?*

49

Why should we go to church on Sundays to worship the Almighty God and then from Monday to Saturday worship the devil and consult witches? Didn't the Bible say God is jealous, and that we should not bow down to images and idols? Isn't the Bible against such practices?

> *"No one can serve two masters," says the Word of God. "For either he will hate the one and love the other, or he will stand by and be devoted to the one and despise and be against the other. You cannot serve God and mammon (deceitful riches, money, possessions, or whatever is trusted in)" (Matthew 6:24 Amplified Bible).*

I was so perplexed, confused, and without answers. I felt like an idiot. And now that I have rejected everything in connection with the devil and the fetish priests, the battle with everyone intensified. The fact is, when you reject the offer of my Grandma and the other relatives, they have various means to connect you to the demonic world.

One of the means by which they can get you to participate in their ceremonial incantations with the witch doctors is to take anything belonging to you, such as your everyday clothes, underwear, scarves and so forth, to inquire from the mediums. In our modern society, a new name has been given to it – the DNA in our clothing. And the devil and his agents knew it even before the DNA findings came out.

It wasn't all that easy for me, because I trusted in what Christ did for me at Calvary. I knew that taking such a firm stand would result in rejection and persecution from the entire family, especially, my own Grandma. Yet I had to stand for Christ for my own spiritual wellbeing.

I remember Grandma saying to me one day, "You don't have legs to stand on. You look like a chicken that has fallen into water. And you are placing a restriction on me not to do what? Tell me if you know better than I do." She really meant it. And their terror plots continued as well.

Jemima, my older sister, thought I was a nuisance to her, and she wanted me dead. She had said it many times. "I hate you. Mother loves you more than me, and she always compares me with you? But the good and respectful girl is the 'Trashcan', sick and tired of being sick, eh?" she would mock. "Then why don't you die and let Mother leave me alone?"

Albert, my younger brother, would ridicule me for not being strong and healthy. And Cathy would say, "I crack you with my fingers like the lies in my hair," while the fetish priest also kept eyeing me very closely. As for Philip, the second after me, we were really good friends, but he was deaf and dumb (hearing and speech impaired). Philip loved me so much.

Grandma came to our house one afternoon with the fetish priest. I was sitting at the corner reading my New Testament. "I have come, and I will come again, you stubborn kid." Grandma pointed to me. "Behave."

Although I didn't worry much about what my own siblings were doing, I was concerned about the other guy who was eyeing me. I felt my life was in danger. Fear gripped me. I had nowhere to run to than into the arms of Christ and pray. I began to pray in my mind, *pleading the blood of Jesus over me.* After looking around the house for a while, Grandma and the fetish priest left, not very happy.

Hmm, I breathed in a big sigh of relief thinking it was over. I stood up and walked to the kitchen where Mother was preparing her dough for bread. "What did they come to do, Mother?" I asked her the minute they walked out. "Was that the visit he talked about when we went to him about a year ago?"

"Maybe. He said he came with Grandma to check out and see who in our house was opposing him. He expressed his inability to operate in our home anymore."

"Oh, oh, that is exciting. There is someone opposing him from our house? Who can oppose such a person?"

"You don't want to know. Do you?"

"Yes, Ma. I do."

"He said you are the one opposing him, but I know better. He's promised to come back and visit us again, but I don't know when."

"Mother, how can a frail sickling like me oppose such a person?"

"I know. I guess he is afraid of you. Didn't he say that you have someone over- shadowing you?" Mother said. "There is something peculiar about you. I knew it when you had the hot water burns in your ninth month, and what the "angel guy" told me about you. You are God's special gift to me."

"Thanks, Ma." I smiled and began to walk out of the kitchen.

"Shhh, don't tell anyone."

"I won't, Ma."

"Hey, come here. Did you find your missing items?"

"No, Ma. I don't know where they went."

"You know, Grandma told me today that she came here the other day and took your slip and blouse to go and consult with the priest."

"I don't like that. Why is Grandma doing that to me?" I felt violated.

"She said she wanted to understand why you were sick again, but it did not work. But she said the gods wouldn't answer the fetish priest. That's the reason both of them are mad at you."

"Thank God," I said. "Why are they concentrating on me and not on the others? I am not the only child in the family."

"I know. But what's in you that they are mad at?" Mother wasn't all that excited this time. "Don't you understand my fears as well? I wish I knew exactly what is in you too."

"Ma, I am a child of God. It's not me opposing him in anyway. It is the Holy Spirit in me. I know the blood of Christ is covering me, and they cannot kill me."

"Don't be saying that. You need to be very careful and take care of yourself," she cautioned me. "Go to bed, it's late."

By the time we were about to go to bed at nine, it began to pour heavily. Yet there was no lightning and no thundering as there normally is during rainy season. Then it stopped before ten o'clock. I fell asleep so quickly after prayer and woke up abruptly between one and two o'clock. Suddenly, I saw a frightening lightning, flashing through our window. It was like there was someone holding a fireball flashlight, trying to poke through our window.

This is unusual. I woke Mother up. I wanted her to see what was happening. But her eyes were heavy. Being tired of all the different jobs she was doing for our survival, she told me it was just the lightning, and rolled back to sleep. My younger sister, Cathy, was sleeping deeply. I was not satisfied with Mother's answer, so I sat up and continued to bother her to take a look at what I was seeing again.

"Oh Maame, I am tired," she grunted and sat up. But when she looked over this time, she jumped out of bed and said, "O my God, what is this? This is very strange."

"Yes Ma, it is really scary. Please, shall we pray?"

Both of us prayed seriously, *"O God protect us. Preserve us from the evil one...."* By this time, I was convinced it was pure witchcraft, because it was now penetrating into the room. I got scared. My heart was pounding hard with goose bumps and chills all over me.

"I plead the blood of Jesus over us." I whispered it over and over. I wanted to go under the covers.

Suddenly, something rose up within me. I crawled out of bed and said, "I send the fire of the Holy Spirit against you. I rebuke you in Jesus's Name. Get away from here, right now in the Name of Jesus. You cannot have me, you witch! I am the child of the living God. I am covered by the blood of Jesus Christ."

In a few seconds, the strange fire flickered so rapidly and dwindled down. At that moment, I heard a squeaky groan at the back of the window. It was bizarre and frightening. I turned and looked at Mother. She had her jaw dropped and mouth wide open.

Then it vanished completely. The fear in me melted away. "Thank you, Jesus."

"Really, that was a witch?" She was stupefied. "Hey, how did you manage to know it was a witch?" She shook her head in dismay.

I was speechless. I had no comments and no taking of credit.

"But that prayer, how powerful it is!" Mother expressed.

"Jesus gives us power to overcome evil forces that terrorize us," I told her. "And when the Holy Spirit resides in us, He gives the child of God the gift of discernment."

Mother nodded in approval. We prayed again and went back to sleep for couple of hours before daylight shone through, because

Mother was supposed to leave at seven in the morning to visit Grandma.

"There is a funeral going on in the village, and I need to attend. I will return in the evening. Pray for me too," she told me and left.

A few hours later, I saw Mother rushing to the bedroom door. *Something is wrong. Isn't she supposed to return in the evening? Why has she come back now?* I asked myself.

She opened the bedroom door and called me into the room. She looked terrified and confused. Her facial expression revealed what she might have seen or experienced. She beckoned me into the room.

I ran to her and asked, "Mother, is there anything wrong? Please, what happened at Grandma's house?"

"Hmm, Maame, listen to this. The world is so strange. (Here is Mother's story in her own words as narrated to me). As soon as I got to the village, I saw the fetish priest entering Grandma's house. I was eager to see him, since he is part of our family. But he seemed very angry with me. I went to him and asked why he was so mean to me. But he wouldn't respond to my greetings."

"'Don't disturb me,'" he replied and turned away from me.

"Please, tell me what I did wrong to anger you, and I will ask for your pardon," Mother said and followed him outside. "I didn't want to have any problem with him. Everyone in the village is afraid of him."

The moment we walked to the back of the house, the priest said, "'Shhh, okay, listen. Don't tell anyone what I'm going to tell you.'"

"Don't worry about that. No one will know it."

"'Promise me first.'"

"Okay, I promise."

"You see, I came last night to visit you as planned in order to check on you and the children, but that your daughter, your crazy daughter chased me away."

"Oh my God, I didn't know you came to visit," I shook my head.

The fetish priest interrupted, still lamenting over his dilemma, 'I am so mad. I don't know what kind of power she has to do that to me. Look at how I'm burned. She sent fire on me.' He showed his arm and back, and part of his neck to Mother.

"Oh, I am so sorry. Please, forgive her."

I wanted to laugh when he said you chased him away, but I had to use tact to pacify his anger, I was really afraid of him.

"'Look, I am no longer coming to your house again. But don't tell anyone about this,'" the fetish priest said emphatically, warning me of severe punishment if I did.

"No problem," I assured him and left. (End of her story)

"Mother, don't you believe the guy was coming to kill me?" I asked her.

"Yes, I believe with all my heart that he came to harm you, but God fought for you. He is evil, but thanks to God for the victory."

"Praise the Lord!" I said. Mother and I laughed, and I left to the kitchen. From that day on, mother held me dear to her heart. We had a secret with God, but the battles continued.

[6]

THE TRANSITION

After graduation from high school, Mother asked me to go to Accra to help Flora, one of my oldest sisters, who was going to have a baby. She was in her 6th month. I accepted to go, because I hadn't traveled outside our region before. I was very excited and wanted to experience life outside our home.

Flora came to visit and we left Takoradi very early in the morning with the first bus. As we journeyed to Accra, I thought I was going to a paradise somewhere. I was so naïve and daydreamed of a better life somewhere outside our home. I enjoyed every bit of the journey, and imagined how Accra would be a paradise on earth.

We arrived in Accra at 11a.m. And my first impression of Accra was quite different from what I'd heard. Accra was a normal African city like Takoradi. Anyway, I was happy to be away for a while. I was treated like a little princess until Flora resumed work the second week after my arrival. Her attitude and reactions made me to understand that I had not followed her for pleasure but to work hard and endure lots of pain.

In the months that followed, I went through a Calvary-like experience I would never forget.

Flora would leave the house very early in the morning without giving me any money or food until she arrived home in the evening. This went on for several months. One morning, before she left for work, I politely said to Flora, "Sister, would you kindly give me some money to buy food? I ate nothing yesterday, and I am really hungry. ---"

She interrupted me angrily. "What are you saying? Did you die for not eating? Wait until I come back! Do you understand me?"

I thought she would be home around noon. But I waited and waited until 7p.m. From that moment, it became a routine. She ate at the canteen at work, but I went two to three days without food. Once in a blue moon, she would give me supper in the middle of the week.

I became weak and sickly. But Flora didn't care to ask whether I had eaten or not. She would often come home and go straight to bed, because she had eaten on her way home. I prayed and read my Bible faithfully, which was my spiritual food.

Flora never cooked a meal since I arrived. I was the sole cook. Weekends were the only time we cooked in the house, so I would run from Asylum Down to Nima market in order to finish cooking at the exact time given to me.

My predicament was when I had no right to taste any of the food I had cooked until she had finished eaten first. If none of the food remained, then I had to go to bed hungry. It also meant I'd had to either go out to buy food by the roadside if she so decided. Walking out alone late at night to buy food was un-called for when I'd cooked sufficient for both of us each time she asked me to.

The Dirty Meal

Knowing perfectly well how dangerous it was, I chose to go to bed hungry than risk my life in the hands of rapists.

Due to the ill treatment I was receiving, I developed stomach problems. I could not understand the reason for her behavior towards me, but I prayed for her every day. One particular day, Flora left for work as usual without anything in the house. I had drank water all day until I felt I was drowning in my own fluid.

I wanted real food, but it wasn't going to be possible. A tenant, who was a single police officer, asked me to help her with her dirty dishes before she left home. She promised to give me a treat at the end of the month. By the time I finished my personal chores and remembered the officer's request, it was almost three in the afternoon.

Hurriedly, I opened her door and began to clean up before she arrived by 4.30 p.m. When I got to one of the heavy cooking pots, which was halfway filled with water, I set it aside to finish it last. While stirring the pot, I saw that it was full of rice mixed with dirty water. I knew it was not good to be eaten, but I was dying of hunger. I washed the soap off my hands and prayed. Slowly, I drained the dirty water from the rice, and stuffed my empty stomach with the 'delicacy'.

At the first gulp, I felt a sharp pain go through my chest to my stomach. To me, it was normal, since I hadn't eaten anything prior. I drank a cup of water over my 'supernatural provision', and finished the officer's chores before she arrived home. And without exaggeration, the dirty rice was my meal for that day. I cried many times and asked the Lord what I did to merit such ill treatments.

"Yuck!" you may say. But a hungry person, who is really desperate and dying, will not care about the taste of the food. All you want is to survive. That's exactly what I did that day. Flora arrived home at 7p.m. as usual and went to bed right away. For me, I was grateful for the provision God made that day—rice in dirty water. It wasn't the best, but I didn't die.

The Enemy's Lures

On top of what I was going through in Accra, the enemy also began to use different means to lure me to sin. I faced dire challenges numerous times. The constant offer to sell myself for money, food, or sex was really appealing. *How many times didn't the young men in the community asked me to offer myself in exchange for money or food? How does one survive such temptation if not by the grace and power of God?*

In one particular time, our neighbors, a Lebanese family, invited me to their home. They gave me a Lebanese flatbread filled with meat and veggies. The meal was really yummy. They repeated their hospitality once a week for about three weeks. The week that followed, one of the young men held on to my clothes and said, "Monica, you only want free food, eh?"

"Did you want me to pay for the meal?" I asked him.

"Yes! Don't you know that?" he replied.

"Why didn't your family tell me?" I asked, frustrated with myself.

"What do you want to give in exchange?" he said.

"What kind of exchange? I don't have anything to give you."

"Don't you know what you are supposed to do? Nothing is free like that ---."

Being so innocent and harmless, I asked him again to tell me what he really wanted.

"Come, let's go to bed, and you can enjoy our food every day," he said. "I will take good care of you.

"Sex? No! No exchange for anything," I said to him. "Take your food. I'd rather go to bed hungry than sell myself. My God will take care of me."

He left disappointed. It was a difficult decision I made when I knew I would go hungry again. So I threw myself into the hands of the only One who is able to sustained me—GOD.

Hunger is not an easy route for anyone to take. Anyone can sell themselves for a piece of bread to satisfy their hunger. I had the opportunity to steal or cheat, yet my heavenly Father's still small voice was always behind me saying, *"Monica, it shall be all right. Just hang in there. Be faithful to Me, and your faithfulness shall be rewarded."*

That was all I needed to know. I prayed and waited for His intervention. I believe those were the precious moments the Lord used to strengthen my walk with Him. In fact, trials, hunger, and rejection, led me to knock at Heaven's door for more grace to live a life well pleasing to Him day by day without faltering.

The Angelic Assistance

Though I still couldn't understand Flora, I prayed for her every day without fail. Finally one day, she busted out her hatred and said, "Hey, listen, stop praying in my house. As long as you are staying with me, keep your mouth shut, you hear?" I didn't say a word. I stared at her face.

"Your prayers are destroying everything I've been doing here. I burn my incense and candles, yet the 'saints' are not responding to my prayers. It is because of you." She grew very angry. "If you want peace, then stop praying the kind of prayers you do, okay?"

I knew better. No child of God can survive in this wicked world without the powerful weapon of prayer. I understood the negotiation the enemy was trying to make with me in order to find a loophole somewhere to attack me. Those threats could not stop me from praying. But the more I prayed, the worse my condition became.

On one February night, Flora delivered a beautiful baby girl at the Korle-Bu Teaching Hospital—a drama-filled delivery. The next morning, since I did not have money for transportation to the hospital to visit her, I walked about three miles from Asylum Down to Kaneshie to inform our paternal aunt, Mrs. Catherine Avevor, hoping that together we would go the hospital.

Arriving at Kaneshie, I took the only route I was familiar with through the Awodome cemetery. I saw some people going back and forth and thought it was safe. In the middle of the road, I felt the presence of evil and prayed. Something prompted me to look behind one of the largest tombstones that wasn't far from where I was. I saw two men hiding behind it. I got scared and continued to walk hurriedly.

Just then, something stirred up within me to check behind me. Oh my, the two men I had seen earlier behind the tombstones were striding fast toward me. I took to my heels, but I was too weak to run as fast as I desired. They doubled the efforts to get me.

I prayed and asked the Lord to protect me. Just as they were about to lay hands on me, a taxicab showed up from nowhere and stopped in the middle of the road close to where I was. The moment they saw the cab, the two men ran back into the cemetery. I trembled in fear, and tears flooded my face. I thought I was done.

The cab driver said to me angrily, "What are you doing here? Where are going?"

"Sir, I am going to see my auntie," I told him.

"Why did you come through the cemetery? Don't you know that this is a deadly spot?"

"Please, I didn't know that," I sobbed.

"What is the name of your aunt?" he asked.

"Her name is Mrs. Catherine Avevor. I came to her house one time with my older sister."

"I know her very well," the cab driver replied. "She is one of my friends." The sternness in his face changed into a sweet, beaming smiles, as if he had known me for a long time. "Okay, let's go," he said.

The driver took me to Aunt Catherine's place, and waited until she came to the door to let me in. By the time I turned around to say thank you to the cab driver, he and the car were nowhere to be found.

"Oh my goodness!" I exclaimed to my Aunt. *"Did you see the cab driver? The cab driver who just saved me from the hands of evil men?"* Chills!

"No, what cab driver, Monica?" my Aunt replied.

I was emotional and still in shock from what I had just witnessed that I could not immediately utter any word. Once inside the house, I told her what I had just experienced.

Auntie Catherine was very happy to see me and to hear how God delivered me from the hands of those evil guys. She said to me, "Monica, don't ever venture through there again. Awodome cemetery is the worst point in Accra. Reports of rapes and murders are really rampant here." I promised her I wouldn't take that risk again in my life. But when I told her about the taxi driver, Auntie Catherine told me she did not have any friend who was a taxi driver.

Who am I to be favored with such a heavenly protection? I contemplated. It was a deadly venture I took that day, but the Lord was with me. The Scriptures declares: *"This poor man (girl) called, and the LORD heard him (her); He saved him (her) out of all his (her) troubles. The angel of the LORD encamps around those who fear Him, and He delivers them"* *(Psalms 34:6-7 emphasis mine NKJV).*

Aunt Catherine sent me away to the hospital with food for Flora and enough money for transportation to Korle-Bu and back. Three days later, Flora came home with her beautiful baby girl. I was excited to see them but was very reserved. I guess that's how I was fashioned. I do not harbor resentment for long. It doesn't go well with me. Bitterness and unforgiveness make me sick.

However, despite all the sacrifices I made for her and the baby, nothing changed my sister's heart. Although Flora had rheumatism, and she couldn't do anything for herself for over a month, the verbal and emotional abuse rather intensified. Three months after delivery, she resumed work.

The Stranger and the Timely Word

One evening, Flora came home as usual, having already eaten from the canteen at her work- place. She changed her clothes and came back out holding a ball of ice cream. (This was a special kind of ice cream that was imported from Great Britain in the 60's). She sat by the kitchen enjoying every drop of her ice cream while I sat at the corner of the garage with her baby on my lap hungry and almost fainting. After she had enjoyed about two-thirds of the ice cream, she gave what was left to a tenant's son who was standing by.

What is that? Don't I deserve to be treated well? I have sacrificed months to take care of you and your daughter and you treat me like that? I pondered and waited, tears running down my cheeks. I waited for Flora to say something about my food. My stomach was churning. I had become pale and weak, feeling dizzy. At about a quarter till nine, when she was about to go to bed, she called me and gave me money to go out and get me something to eat.

How am I going to do this? I asked myself. Going to buy food at that time of the night alone was dangerous. I was really scared when I left the gate. I prayed the Lord to be with me. Each step I took was filled with tears. I could not figure out why I should suffer all my life. But I entrusted my life into God's able care.

I had walked a few yards from the house when out of nowhere, two men approached. I intuited they might be among the bad guys, who raped girls around that area. An inner voice warned me to be very careful. I had to listen to my gut. I wanted to turn and ran, but I had no strength to venture, for by that time, I had lost about twenty-five pounds. I prayed, "Oh Lord, please, send your angels to protect me. ---"

Suddenly, a strange car sped towards where I was. The car's headlight brightened my path and blinded the guys until I swerved to the corner of where the vendors were. Oh how grateful I was! It was like what the Lord did for the children of Israel by the Red Sea when Pharaoh's army pursued them.

And the Angel of God, who went before the camp of Israel, moved and went behind them; and the pillar of cloud went from before them and stood behind them. [20] So it came between the camp of the Egyptians and the camp of Israel. Thus it was a cloud and darkness to the one, and it gave light by night to the other, so that the one did not come near the other all that night (Exodus 14:*19-20*).

Now, I had my food—a ball of cooked cornmeal, a piece of fried fish and grounded pepper sauce. But going back home was now a nightmare. I prayed for His protection again. The moment I crossed the street, I heard someone call out my name, "Monica, wait for me."

When I turned, I saw a certain middle-aged man pacing very fast towards me. His face was beaming with smiles, as if he had known me for a long time. *Who is he? How did he get to know my name?* I wondered. I had no confidence in any man whatsoever. I glared at him with skepticism.

"Have you forgotten who I am?" he asked, seeing the expression on my face.

I couldn't figure out where I'd met him. Yet he insisted that he knew me, and that he was my next-door neighbor, who was coming home from work. *Okay, I could use his company.* I was too shy to talk to women much more to men, so I couldn't say a word as we walked toward home.

About a few yards away to the house, the neighbor broke the silence and said, "Monica, I have been watching you closely, and I know you are worried about your life. I understand what you are going through. Do not be discouraged with what is happening right now. The hand of the Lord is upon you, and no one can destroy that. The Lord is going to bless you. He will give you a wonderful husband, a man after His heart, and He will also give you four sons. The Lord will use you and your husband to impact many lives.

Then He will take you farther away from your people to a faraway land. There, the Lord will cause you to forget your own family, because He will give you a whole new family. You will be blessed and your family will be a blessing. You are a chosen vessel to the nations of the world ---" (Summary).

I listened attentively as he spoke until we arrived at our gate. Then, he finally said, "Monica, if you will believe and not doubt, you shall see the fulfillment of what the Lord has promised you. Don't give up. Remember that God will use your pain to bring healing to others. Bye and have a good night."

"Thank you very much, Sir," I said, and ran inside the house. I felt so blessed. However, being so hungry, I only wanted to eat my food and go to bed. I ate fast and went to bed. It wasn't until the next day that I began to think about what I was told.

Within the week, I tried to see if I could find the "next-door neighbor," but to no avail. *Who is this guy? A next door neighbor or an angel, because the message seem too personal. I will see.* I felt in my heart that he might be the same angel who had been watching over me since I was a child.

Now, you may ask, "If your mother was so loving and really trained all of her children well, what went wrong with Flora?"

According to Mother, Flora was very young when one of my paternal aunts came to take her. And according to other sources, Flora was treated like a slave without mercy. She was terribly abused verbally and emotionally, and the inner wounds she incurred had not been healed until I went to her. As a result, she treated me just the way she was also treated.

As you know, abused people will always abuse something or somebody. When a child lives in an abusive situation for a long time, he or she may think of abuse as the norm. When a person is always bombarded with acts of terror or brainwashed that terrorism is okay, the possibility is that they may turn out to be terrorists.

To me, those moments of sufferings drew me closer to search for the heart of God in order to receive grace to persevere. And indeed, the Lord kept me from fallen into the snare of the enemy. His able hands kept me from selling my birthright for food. The Lord made me to understand that when I remain devoted to Him despite my questions and trials, I will definitely find peace and joy in His presence.

Sometimes when we pray, we feel as if God isn't within our reach. Let me assure you. He is always there for us. He cares about us. But He allows those moments of despair and silence to build in us godly character. The Word of God offers us hope and encouragement, comfort and assurance that God hasn't forgotten us.

The Lord says, *"---Do not fear, for I have redeemed you; I have summoned you by name; you are mine. When you pass through the waters, I will be with you; and when you pass through the rivers, they will not sweep over you. When you walk through the fire, you will not be burned; the flames will not set you ablaze. For I am the LORD your God, the Holy One of Israel, your Savior..." (Isaiah 43:1-3).*

[7]

MOVING FORWARD

The month in which I arrived at Takoradi was the peak of the campaign for the census and the elections. The nation of Ghana was in transition from military rule after the coup in 1966, which ousted the former President Kwame Nkrumah, to civilian rule. I was very happy to be counted as part of the human race in Ghana. Mr. Busua won the election.

Soon after the elections, Georgette arrived from Accra one Friday evening with the baby and left her with us without prior notice. So instead of beginning the school year at the Takoradi Polytechnic in the morning, I had to go with the evening classes. Mother and I took turns to take care of the baby until I finally switched to the morning session.

That same year, an evangelist, named Rev. George Appekey of Takoradi Assembly of God Church, came to the school to preach the gospel. This was the first time I had seen someone preach with such an anointing. His message was so powerful that before the altar call was made, many students ran to the altar to accept the Lord Jesus as their Lord and Savior. I also went forward to renew my commitment to the Lord and not to accept Christ as Savior again.

The first time I accepted the Lord Jesus into my heart was when He brought me back from death. But this time, my going to the altar had such a powerful, spiritual significance in my life; especially when I identified myself publicly with Christ before all my mates.

From that day on, a deeper passion to know more of the power behind the evangelist's preaching was stirred in me. I knew that God had a higher purpose for me other than being trained as a stenographer secretary.

Soon after that, the presence of the Lord overshadowed me in a tremendous way anytime I went to classes, insomuch that it became evident to my class mates that the Lord was with me. That gave me such a resistance against sexual sins, which were rampant among the students.

My passion for God continued with deeper revelations and visions. Many times in the middle of the night, I would hear someone calling out my name, "Monica, Monica." I would wake up to find everyone sleeping soundly. Each time I heard my name, I would go to Mother and ask if she called.

Having disturbed her a few times, she gave me a different response and said, "Maame, anytime you hear the voice call out your name, say, 'Speak Lord, for Thy servant is hearing.'"

Mother's piece of advice reminded me of Samuel in the Bible. *Oh, I should have known better.* I was still an immature Christian taking baby steps one day at a time in faith and obedience to the little I knew from the Word.

The night after, I heard the same familiar voice calling out, "Monica, Monica."

I sat up and responded, "Lord, speak, for Thy servant is hearing." I heard nothing else, so I went back to sleep.

Suddenly, a sweet and awesome presence enveloped me. It shrouded me as if I was being wrapped with a warm blanket. Then, I heard a small soft voice,

"Monica, Monica, I am the Lord your God. I chose you to be My servant even before you were born. I have great plans for you. I have loved you deeply with an everlasting love that will never be altered. Will you consecrate your life wholly to Me and to My service? You are Mine. Will you give Me all your heart? Do not be afraid. I will be with you always in all the days of your life. I chose you for My service. ..."

I sat up on the bed shivering, not knowing what to say or do. In the morning, I rehearsed what I had heard to Mother.

"Monica," Mother said, "I know you are different from all my children. And I know that one day you may turn out to be a 'Mary' or something else for God, maybe a nun or a minister of the gospel, who knows?"

From that day on, I settled it in my heart to be what He wanted me to be. But what? I did not know. My prayer life intensified from that day onward.

The Stacks of Destiny

It was the month of April 1971. The weather was warm but breezy, so I set a mat on the floor by the front door leading to the living room to read my textbooks. The moment I closed my eyes to pray, I had an incredible vision that made me shudder. I saw the Lord Jesus being nailed to the cross. He was in such a terrible agony, screaming and shaking. He was soaked in blood. As they lifted up the cross, the blood dripped from His head to His feet.

All of a sudden, the same pain and anguish enveloped me. I wept and sobbed uncontrollably. Then a voice thundered behind the thick cloud that had formed behind the cross and said: "Monica, this I did for you. I loved you so much so as to die for you. Would you consecrate all your life to Me and for My service?"

"Yes Lord, I will do whatever You ask me to." I responded without hesitation. At that instant, the presence of Lord hovered over me. Then, I woke up abruptly. That day, His death on the cross, had a deeper meaning to me, because it has now become personal—HE DID IT FOR ME (MONICA), BECAUSE HE LOVES ME!

How precious that revelation was to me—to have the affirmation of His love! To understand that Christ Jesus, the Son of the Most High God, did all that He did because of His love for me in particular was what I could not fathom. But how painful His death was! The vision was engraved in my spirit. It is as fresh today as it was when I first saw it.

A few days after, while relaxing on the same spot and contemplating on His love, His presence overshadowed me again. This time it didn't lure me to sleep. The response I had given the previously kept on ringing on my mind. "Yes, Lord!" *But what does He require from me? What does it mean to be consecrated to His service?* I had no clue. I prayed for understanding.

Suddenly, I fell into a trance, and the heavens opened. I saw stacks of books coming down from heaven. The books were laid flat on each other touching the sky. Starting from the bottom, the label on the first three books shone clearly. The fourth was incomplete, and the inscriptions on the remaining books were faint.

The first book on the bottom had this inscription: **S.U**, the second, **A.G**, the third was **S.G.B.I.**, the fourth book **MISSION TO ...**, et cetera. Unexpectedly, Mother entered into the room and called out my name, and I came to myself.

What on earth are all these books and signs? I prayed but couldn't figure them out. I questioned for a while. I had no response, and there was no one to help me understand what the Lord was actually saying to me through those inscriptions in abbreviation. Since I could not identify the inscriptions on the remaining books, I wrote down what I saw and kept it in my Bible.

The Unfolding Of The Books

One morning while I was reading the Psalms, I tumbled over this passage again in Psalms 139:16-18, which read: *"... All the days ordained for me were <u>written in Your book before</u> one of them came to be. How precious to me are Your thoughts, O God! How vast is the sum of them! Were I to count them, they would outnumber the grains of sand. When I awake, I am still with You."* These verses reassured me of God's preplanned recorded events of my life before I was even conceived in my mother's womb.

Fortunately, John Quaisie, one of my cousins, came home for vacation. John was attending the Cape Coast University and was a strong Christian. Even though I wasn't a talker, I had a strong urge to approach him to ask for some insights into those books and signs the Lord had revealed to me, given that he was more advanced in the things of God.

John said to me, "Sister, I believe the first book, S.U. represents a group I have come in contact with at the college of which I am a member. We have a chapter here at Takoradi, which meets at the Central Presbyterian Church. Do not worry. The Lord will give you peace concerning each inscription when you come in contact with them."

The following Sunday, after the usual service at our local

Methodist church, John invited me to go with him to the meeting. Some of the young people at the church also came with us. Although I was excited at first, I felt very anxious as we rode along on the bus, not knowing what the Lord meant by those inscriptions.

The moment we entered into the Takoradi Central Presbyterian Church, the inscription on a banner they was displayed at the altar caught my attention was. It read,

> WELCOME TO S. U. (SCRIPTURE UNION). MAKE YOURSELF AT HOME AND MEET JESUS. HE LOVES YOU, AND SO DO WE.

I was moved to tears, asking myself why He loved me that much to give me His directions. I couldn't wait to experience Jesus that day at the meeting. I understood Psalms 23 in a different way—a personal way. The Lord is really my Shepherd.

The LORD is my shepherd, I lack nothing. He makes me lie down in green pastures, He leads me beside quiet waters, He refreshes my soul. He guides me along the right paths for His name's sake. ... Surely Your goodness and love will follow me all the days of my life, and I will dwell in the house of the LORD forever" (Psalms 23 summarized).

The entire session was awesome—the song service, the prayer time, and the message given were really uplifting. But there was one chorus, which kept on ringing in my heart for a long time.

He lives, He lives,
Christ Jesus lives today
He walks with me and talks with me
Along life's narrow way
He lives, He lives,
Salvation to impart
You ask me how I know He lives
He lives within my heart.

I concluded that maybe the Scripture Union (S.U) might be the place the Lord was going to use to help me know Him better. And it was true. From that day, I became very active in the Scripture Union. Even when I had no money, I would walk the three-miles from Effiakumah to Takoradi central to attend the meetings. In addition to the Bible study and worship time, all night prayer sessions also went on every weekend. But Mother wouldn't allow me to go to Takoradi alone for the all-night prayers.

The Second Book Unveiled

A few weeks after the Scripture Union encounter, I was informed about a special all-night prayer meeting that was going to be held at a church opposite the Takoradi central police station. I was very much excited about this particular all-night prayer meeting. I could not wait to be there I prayed so hard, and Mother gave me permission to attend. What a treat it was to me!

Cousin John came, and we set out to find the location and visit with them for the first time. When we arrived at the church, the inscription on the front door stunned me. The second sign on the book cover, **AG** was printed just as I saw in the vision. The excitement I had dwindled down, and fear invaded my mind.

What on earth is God going to take me through? Does He want me to join that church? No, this can't be possible. I have been raised a Methodist, and a Methodist I will die. I told myself. Oh Lord, please help me to trust Your judgment, because You knows best, I prayed. I went back home filled with more questions.

[8]

A GLORIOUS BAPTISM

Day after day, as I contemplated on the stacks of books and the inscription I had just seen, I felt in my spirit that God might have a surprise package waiting for me at this church too. What? I had no clue.

Although I was gripped with fear, a strong craving for more of God was stirred in me. I had never prayed with such a passion before, and I could not wait to be back at the prayer meeting again.

The next Friday seemed to be the longest day of the week for me. It wasn't coming as quickly as I wanted it to. But when it finally arrived, I tried to finish my chores in order to avoid any conflict with my sisters.

John had gone back to Cape Coast, so I attended the meeting with three other friends from our church. Prayers had already begun when we arrived. My friends walked in and sat in the front row. They had no problem of shyness, but I was still struggling, so I sneaked silently into the back of the church and joined them to pray.

I had not visited any Pentecostal church prior to that. I had been told Pentecostals were fanatics, and I should be very careful of them. But I was eager to know why the Lord revealed that particular church to me.

The people were unbelievably loud as they prayed. *Are they fighting with God? Is God that far away that they had to scream and yell for Him to come down?* I thought. I wasn't used to screaming when praying. But somehow, whatever those people were screaming for or at, brought down the presence of God. God's presence was tangible and real. I felt it.

After a long praise, worship, and prayer on our feet, we sat down while the leader, Evangelist Lt. John Yamoah, prepared to speak. He welcomed all first-timers and announced his theme: *The Baptism of the Holy Spirit.*

The moment Mr. Yamoah lifted up his head and saw me, he stopped in the middle of his introduction and asked the participants to give a clap offering to the Lord. They became really hysterical with hard claps and shouts of Halleluiahs and Amens!

Then Mr. Yamoah said, "Praise the Lord! Last night while I was praying for today's meeting, the Lord gave me a revelation of a young lady who was going to come into the meeting today. The Lord told me she is a chosen vessel to the nations. He said He was going to baptize her with the Holy Spirit in a powerful and unprecedented manner, and that He is going to use her in such a way that people will marvel at His power to transform. She will be changed into a different person and do the impossible for His glory. The Lord showed me the dress, and even the head-kerchief she was going to wear. And praise the Lord! That is the lady over there at the back."

Hand claps and screams echoed everywhere. I felt out of place. I was not very much excited in that kind of atmosphere. *Me, a chosen vessel for great things? I don't think so.* I said to myself. *This guy doesn't know who I am.* I got scared.

Why me? I could not comprehend why God had to reveal me to someone I had never met before, except that I knew He told me to be there in that particular church. So, if God said it, then I will wait to see what He wants to do with me. That was my comfort.

Seeing the doubt in my face, Mr. Yamoah pointed at me and insisted, "Sister, you are the one I saw, and I believe the Lord is going to baptize you with the Holy Ghost and with fire today!"

The congregation turned to look at me again. Oh my, how wanted to run and hide! But it wasn't going to be possible. I said to myself, *Hey, Monica, be calm. There is nothing good in you that the Lord could use to help others. That vision he saw may not be true. He might have seen someone else other than you... blah, blah...* I protested in my heart.

Then Mr. Yamoah started to preach. His preaching on the Holy Spirit was like a mirror to my soul. It cut through my heart, my mind, and the very core of my being. I'd never heard such a message on the Holy Spirit before. I did not know who or what the Holy Spirit Baptism was all about. But Mr. Yamoah's explanation on the baptism of the Holy Spirit was so simple and clear to the point—the Holy Spirit is a Person, He was GOD, and He helps every Christian to be a faithful witness of the Lord.

I thought the Holy Spirit was something else other than being God, or just the breath of God. That night, the Holy Spirit was made real to me, and I knew from that point He could be touched.

By this time, Mr. Yamoah had wet my appetite for the baptism in the Holy Spirit. I wanted Him with everything about Him.

When the call was made to receive Him, almost everybody went to the front. I stood up, but didn't go farther than two steps forward. When the participants sang this particular song, the entire room began to shake.

> *They were in an upper chamber*
> *They were all with one accord*
> *When the Holy Ghost descended*
> *As was promised by our Lord*
> *Oh Lord, send the power just now*
> *Oh Lord, send the power just now*
> *Oh Lord, send the power just now*
> *And baptize every one*

Oh my, those people sang with such an enthusiasm and hunger for God, I thought the roof was going to cave in on us. The presence of the Lord filled the temple and many spoke in different languages as explained by the leader. It was so beautiful when the people began to sing and pray in their heavenly language, while others prayed with fervency. I prayed silently for a long time, crying and pleading with the Lord for the baptism of the Holy Ghost.

After a long session of travailing in prayer till two in the morning, the leader asked everyone to find a place and wait alone on God. There was such stillness and a holy hush for a while. Then suddenly, the room became charged with the groaning of the saints. But Mr. Yamoah was sitting alone at the corner, his face buried in his hands. *Is he disappointed because his vision hadn't come to pass at the time?*

I was still sitting at the back, not knowing what to do. Suddenly, I heard, "Monica, go to the altar and pray." I looked around to see if someone was standing behind me. There was no one. The voice came again, "Go to the altar and pray."

I knew it was the Lord. I looked around to see if no one was watching before I obeyed. I tiptoed to the front and knelt at the altar praying silently, asking the Lord to baptize me with His Spirit. As I prayed, I felt as if my heart was literally vibrating so hard on my chest. Then in a flash, the Lord opened my spiritual eyes. The sky was clearly opened for me to see the incredible glory of the Lord. The vision was as clear as the day and very awesome.

I saw the Lord sitting on His throne. He was highly exalted. Around the throne, were huge and powerful angels, each had six wings. The train of the robe of the Lord was so beautiful and awesome—transparent, crystallized white. It filled the throne, and descended down into the temple in which I was. All of a sudden, the six-winged angels flew around in harmony, worshipping His Majesty. With two of their wings, they covered their faces. With another two, they covered their feet, and with the other two, they flew around crying in a loud and a glorious voice, "Holy, Holy, Holy is the Lord."

The moment the robe of the Lord touched my feet, the presence of the Lord enveloped my entire being. A strong urge to sing along with the angels surged within me. I busted out with the same magnitude of praise singing, "Holy, Holy, Holy is the Lord!" Suddenly, the Holy Spirit descended powerfully on me while I sang in tongues and prophesied at the same time. Then I fell into a trance.

Like Isaiah of old, the Lord gave me a glimpse of His glory. It is written,

In the year that King Uzziah died, I saw the Lord sitting on a throne, high and lifted up, and the train of His robe filled the temple. Above it stood seraphim; each one had six

wings: with two he covered his face, with two he covered his feet, and with two he flew.[3] And one cried to another and said: "Holy, holy, holy is the LORD of hosts; The whole earth is full of His glory!" (Isaiah 6:1-3).

I didn't know exactly what happened to me and around me again. I was completely lost in the Spirit, speaking in an unknown tongue. A few of the brethren carried me home. The rest was history.

I came back to myself hearing the most beautiful song being sung behind me. I wondered who that was. Unknowingly, my older sister's son, George, was lying beside me on the bed I was resting on. Without exaggeration, the song I was hearing was on the lips of the baby! He was singing praises to the Lord, proclaiming God's majesty and greatness in a language I could understand so clearly.

That was unimaginable. I can't explain it. Others heard just a sound. But I believe it was the baby language syllables and giggling that the Lord opened my ears to understand! And what I heard from the lips of the baby added more weight to the experience I had a few hours prior. My nephew was literally glorifying the Lord in a way I had never heard before. So weighty and beautiful! The Bible says:

O Lord, our Lord, how excellent is Your Name in all the earth. Who have set Your glory above the heavens! Out of the mouth of babes and nursing infants You have ordained praise, because of your enemies, that You may silence the enemy and the avenger (Psalms 8:1-2).

But when the chief priests and the scribes saw the wonderful things that He (Jesus Christ) did and the boys and the girls and the youths and the maidens crying out in the porches and courts of the temple, Hosanna (O be propitious, graciously inclined) to the Son of David! they were indignant. [16] And they said to Him, Do You hear what these are saying? And Jesus replied to them, Yes; have you never read, Out of the mouths of babes and un-weaned infants You have made (provided) perfect praise? (Matthew 21:15-16 Amplified Bible).

This supernatural act of understanding babies, birds and animals, and even nature praising the Lord, was impossible in the natural realm. But the spiritual level the Holy Spirit of the Lord took me to that night, filled my life with such incredible experiences I would never ever forget and trade for anything in this life. Blessed be the Name of the Lord! Even today, I still hear whispers of heavenly music in the atmosphere.

As for Mother, she was very worried about me. I saw her standing by the bed when I regained consciousness. She questioned and questioned me on what might have happened in that prayer meeting. *What should I say?* I had no explanation to give that could satisfy her inquiries.

I couldn't explain it to anyone either, because the experience itself was beyond myself. Later that day, I tried to tell Mother what I saw—the Lord and the angels with six wings singing, 'Holy, holy, holy.' But that worsened the whole situation. She thought I was losing my mind. Her face sagged in disappointment for a long time.

As for Grandma, she hated me the more and sent news to all the Methodist churches in our area that her grand-daughter, Monica, was now insane. I wasn't insane, but rather infused with the glory of the Lord! From that moment, the Lord began to use me in all the nine gifts of the Holy Spirit. Time will not permit me to tell all of it. The Bible declares:

There are diversities of gifts, but the same Spirit. [5] There are differences of ministries, but the same Lord. [6] And there are diversities of activities, but it is the same God who works all in all. [7] But the manifestation of the Spirit is given to each one for the profit of all: [8] for to one is given <u>the word of wisdom</u> through the Spirit, to another <u>the word of knowledge</u> through the same Spirit, [9] to another <u>faith</u> by the same Spirit, to another <u>gifts of healings</u> by the same Spirit, [10] to another <u>the working of miracles</u>, to another <u>prophecy</u>, to another <u>discerning of spirits</u>, to another <u>different kinds of tongues</u>, to another <u>the interpretation of tongues.</u> [11] But one and the same Spirit works all these things, distributing to each one individually as He wills (1 Corinthians 12:411 Emphasis mine).

Coincidently, the day the Lord chose to baptize me in His Spirit was my birthday. No one celebrated the birthday, because they were all upset. But I was the most blessed person on earth. The best birthday present I ever received from my Heavenly Father was the baptism in the Holy Ghost, a baptism of glory!

Whatever might have happened that day, I was a different person. It seemed I was overloaded with weapons to fight the enemy. The emptiness in my heart disappeared immediately. The Lord inundated my heart with His unspeakable joy and peace! What a treat from Heaven!

Also, the love of God was poured over my whole life in a good heavenly dosage. I could see people differently like never before. He clothed me with Himself that I loved and served people in a much better way. And it has not left me since. I was a changed person, change for eternity.

[9]

THE DEMONIC EXCHANGE

One night when I was almost 18, something unusual happened. "Jesus, Jesus," I screamed, shivering under the shock of what I had just seen. The presence of the demonic in the room was horrifying. I could not understand why I was the only one to see those things.

"Shut up. Are you the only one in the house?" Effua, another older sister, shouted. "Leave us to sleep!"

Prior to this experience, Effua had come to visit the family that week with her two little children from Accra. She had at that time become a member of the Jehovah's Witness community because of her in-laws. She'd heard also that I had become a Pentecostal.

The first three days of Effua's visit was hell for me. "Hi, Monica, I learned you speak in tongues, the devil's language. Is that true?" she mocked. Because of Effua's criticism and ridicules, I became a mockery to everybody. She told me that the baptism in the Holy Spirit was demonic. And since my family had known me to be the 'Crier', they continued their mockery about Pentecostal people seeing demons everywhere and in everything. It was hard to swallow.

Mother cautioned them to stop their ridicule to no avail.

She tried to explain what she'd seen and the reality of what I'd been through. "Stop what you are doing. That is not right. One day you will regret it, because what she sees is real." They gave her a deaf ear.

"Explain yourself," Effua and Jemima would say. "Where are the demons and witches? How do they attack you and not us?" Bla, bla, they tormented me.

They knew I wouldn't respond, because I was very respectful and had a hard time defending my case before people. So, I would usually cry and beg them to stop their ridicule. But thank God, I was a different Monica now. I did not cry, but prayed for them.

The night of the fourth day of Effua' visit, something unusual happened. At about 2 o'clock in the morning, I felt a tap on my shoulder, and I woke up abruptly. I thought it was Mother. But there was no one there. Everyone was sound asleep. I knew it was the Lord, and so I began to pray silently.

I sat up praying quietly in the Spirit for about a few minutes, when I felt an evil presence coming through the door of the living room into the bedroom. The demonic figure walked towards me, and within seconds I was in a strong fight for my life. I cried out, "The blood of Jesus rebukes you. You have no power over me. You cannot have me. The One in me is greater than you. You are a defeated foe, in Jesus's Name." I fought, but the moment I said, "The blood of Jesus defeats you. The blood is my covering, in Jesus's Name," the spirit lost its grip on me.

Then the Lord opened my eyes. I saw the demonic figure in the form of a woman standing by the door. She looked evil, really beyond the word scary. "Jesus, Jesus, in the name of Jesus, get out of here. The blood ...," I screamed, speaking in tongues involuntarily.

My family woke up very angry, especially Effua. "Stop that! We want to sleep!" she whined and rained insult on me.

I couldn't blame them. They were not seeing what I was seeing. The presence of the witch was still hovering in the room.

It was the scariest thing I'd ever seen in my life. There are no words to describe the figure. I couldn't force any of them to believe what I was seeing. So I started pleading the blood of Jesus over myself again.

I knew I was safe. Because with the exception of where I was, everywhere in the room became as dark as darkness itself due to the presence of evil that was hovering around. All of a sudden, the demonic presence moved away from where it was standing and took off in the form of a whirlwind toward my sister Effua, who was sleeping by her baby.

Jesus, Jesus, I was whispering, because I couldn't pray aloud. It was so scary. But I was afraid of my sister's reaction. Soon after that, I felt a fresh breeze of the Spirit all over my body. The fear died out, and God's presence lured me into a deep sleep. That was really unusual for me.

In fact, I cannot tell exactly what happened the next, only that I woke up abruptly at the sound of a shriek. "Oh God," I cried, when I saw the most terrifying scene. Effua was dying. She was jerking, groaning, and foaming. Everybody was up crying. Mother was praying in her own way and was about to send Jemima to bring the fetish priest.

How can satan cast out satan? I asked myself. No, that is not possible. I felt that if nothing was done, Effua could be dead in a few minutes. Without anyone's permission, the Spirit of the Lord came powerfully upon me, and I said, "Please, Mother, let me pray first." I began to cast out the spirit of witchcraft and death from my sister. "You foul spirit of witchcraft, leave her alone. I take authority over you in Jesus's Name. Get out of her right now. You cannot have her. You will die your own death. Effua will live to testify of God's greatness. I plead the blood of Jesus."

Suddenly, the demonic force lost its grip over Effua, and she began to breathe normally. Effua came back to life and was freed by the power in Jesus's powerful Name. Yet, it took her at least a few more days to fully recover out of the spiritual shock she received.

Later that morning, as I was narrating the episode to Mother and describing to her what I had seen and the attack Effua received, one of my cousins, Bosomefi, came in. She had come to announce the death of a family member to Mother. The announcer said that the dead family member, whose name has escaped my mind, confessed to coming into our home to exchange herself with one of us. But this time, a greater power struck her down.

"What?" Mother exclaimed. "She came to my house to exchange herself with one of my children?"

Effua then gave me a nifty look, and went back into the room to rest.

Everyone got scared, although the witch was already dead. Why? Mysteriously, it had been known in the whole village that anytime that particular lady had to die, she would exchange herself with another person. But this time, Jesus stopped her! She was not God!

In fact, there are some mysteries in this world we won't be able to understand until we see the Lord Jesus face to face. He may explain them to us, who knows? But for the meantime, we must be in close relationship with Him and learn to be prayerful at all the times.

From that moment, Effua stopped making mockery about the Holy Spirit. But the more the Lord showed Himself to me in different ways, the more the enemy intensified his attacks and persecutions to destroy me.

[10]

GRANDMA'S BARGAIN WITH THE DEVIL

Soon after the death of the other witch who came to exchange herself with one of us, Grandma came to the house one early morning to collect some money from Mother, and left. She returned in the afternoon with the same fetish priest who wanted to kill me. The fetish priest was holding a medium earthen pot filled with some herbal concoction. He dug a hole in front of the door that led to Mother's bedroom. Then Grandma put the pot in the hole and placed a lid on top of it. They instructed Mother to pour water into the pot every day to keep it alive and effective.

While they were doing their enchantment, Grandma told Mother to ask me to leave the house. "I don't want her around here. She will destroy the good thing we are trying to do for the family." The fetish priest also didn't want to see me around. He said that my presence would destroy all their plans and effort to keep our family safe.

Protect our family? What a lie! As for me, in order to avoid having another conflict with Grandma, I went outside the house and sat on the veranda, praying and reading my Bible. I went back to use the restroom before they left. But the moment

Grandma saw me, she said to Mother, "Don't ever leave that thing dry and uncovered. It is your life and that of your children." Then swinging her finger at me and looking very angry and mean, she said to me, "And you, be very, very careful. And stop playing with fire. Do you hear me?"

Oh my, what have I done to my own Grandma? I had no clue. It was really frustrating. Soon after they left, I asked Mother, "Please, Ma, why does Grandma hate me like that?'

"Don't say that. She loves you. Maybe she doesn't know what she is doing," Mother said, trying to defend her mum.

"Okay, but what did they bury inside the ground? I overheard Grandma instruct that you should keep it watered all the time," I asked Mother.

"I don't know what it is, but Grandma said she was doing that for our protection," Mother told me. "You are too curious."

"Please, Mother, are you sure of what Grandma is doing? I am scared that this thing will go against us."

"Maame, I just don't know that."

"Mother, Jesus is our protector," I said politely. "He takes good care of us."

"I know that. But what should I do? Tell me."

"Please Mother, why can't you take a stand for Christ? You know who He is."

Mother left me and went into the room. I followed gently behind her. She sat on her usual chair and gave a deep sigh. "Oh, my God, what should I do?" she rumbled. I felt she knew something wasn't right with what the priest and Grandma had just done.

"Mother, why should our family mix everything up—half of God and half of satan? Please, this is not right. And God hates it."

"I don't like what they are doing, but I can't object to Grandma's ideas. She is very controlling. It is impossible to resist her. Haven't you learned that yet?"

"I know," I whispered and left the room. As for me, I determined that I needed no other spiritual protection from demons other than the mighty hand of the Lord that is upon my life. But as I crossed the verandah that night to go to bed, I had an unusual feeling in my spirit that the implanted pot wasn't for our protection but rather to destroy us one after the other.

That same night, the Lord spoke to me. He said, "Monica, your Grandma's juju is going to eliminate all of you one by one if nothing is done about it."

I sat up abruptly and began to pray. I did not hesitate to tell Mother the next day what the Lord told me. She wasn't happy, because she did not believe her own mother would join a fetish priest to eliminate her children. But nothing was done about the pot. I continued to pray.

A Great Loss

Two months later, I had a dream that Esther had died. I told Mother the dream, and we fasted for three days asking the Lord to spare her. I was confidently sure that my prayers were answered at the end of the fasting.

Esther was too dear to my heart to lose. Esther was the oldest of all of us, and an officer with the Ghana Fire Service

Department. All my expectation was on her, because she had promised to support me in my Theological training. She had already put my name on her will, both at work and in her church group named, Christ Little Band.

Two weeks after this dream, the Tears of Jesus, the evangelistic group I was a part of, organized an evangelistic outreach at our town's market. I was on stage singing with the group when I saw Esther coming down from a taxi. She was pregnant and looking tired, but she was still working. When she saw me, she stood there watching the drama we were presenting on hell fire.

At the time Brother Yamoah, the Evangelist, gave the altar call, Esther walked forward and accepted Christ as Lord and Savior. I was very excited for her that day, but I was a little bit disturbed as well. *How can someone be in the church all their life and haven't accepted Jesus Christ as Savior and Lord?* Anyway that day, my prayers for the salvation of my family began its course.

When I arrived home after the meeting, Esther gave me a very big hug and said to me, "Monica, I'm really proud of you."

I was thrilled. Esther's comment did me well because that was the first positive remark I'd received for a long time.

Six days after, Esther came back from work very early, because she went in for a maternity check-up. She set a mat at the corner of her verandah and lay down to rest. What happened later shook me to the very core of my being.

Suddenly, I heard a loud scream, "Jesus, Maame, please, come and help me." Esther was the one calling for help. I was at that time playing with her children outside. By the time I got to the door, she'd already gone into labor. In pain, she was telling Mother, "Please, help me get up. Someone hit me on the abdomen. Someone hit me with a club on my stomach."

"What are you saying?" Mother asked her.

"Help, help, it's painful. I'm dying. Someone hit me hard on the stomach. I saw a dark demonic hand hitting me." Esther believed a demonic force or witchcraft power hit her on the stomach.

We prayed and rushed her to the Maternity clinic close by us. A few minutes after, she delivered a stillborn beautiful baby girl. That was a mystery, because the baby was still alive and well thirty minutes earlier. But Esther continued to bleed profusely. She was then transferred to the general hospital after three hours of bleeding at the clinic.

Why did they keep her in the clinic for that long? Oh God, please, don't let my dream come true. Please, save Esther. I asked and prayed. Only God knew the reason the midwife kept her for that long.

Once at the General Hospital, the doctors stabilized her and gave her blood transfusion. She gradually regained her strength back. Mysteriously, that same night, my witch aunt, who wasn't even informed of Esther's condition, appeared at the hospital to visit her. That was the turn of events to the worst in Esther's life.

Soon after the aunt disappeared, Esther called for one of the nurses and narrated what she had just seen. She insisted that she wanted to see me. I had no idea, because I was taking care of her four children. By the following morning, Esther was gone, because the witch aunt went to finish what they had begun earlier.

A mysterious death none of us have understood. But why did God permit it? The dream had come true and Esther was dead. And although I argued against the buried pot, Mother was so afraid of Grandma that she left it as is. That began the trend of mysterious deaths in my family—Florence followed, Agnes (Effua), Mother, Phillip and others followed later.

Years after the burial of this demonic stuff, I also began to experience serious combat and attacks. The daily demonic whisper of me being the next to follow was crippling. Geoffrey and I fasted and prayed with no effect. However, immediately after Philip's death, the Lord spoke to me while I waited upon Him at church.

The Lord said to me, "Monica, do you not understand what is happening to your siblings? Unless you confess the sins of your forefathers and break the curses placed over the family as a result of your Grandma's disobedience, the whole family will be destroyed one by one. The 'serpent spirit in the pot' will bite all of you one at a time till you are all destroyed from the face of the earth. I visit the iniquities of the fathers to the third and fourth generations of those who hate Me. But My blessings also reside with those who love Me for thousands of generation. I have given you power in My Name to change the course of your generation. If you obey Me, I would change your DNA and that of your descendants forever."

Wow, what an insight! I've been taught that once someone becomes a Christian, they do not need to break down the curses and demonic connections in their family. But this was new to me. *Thank you, Lord.* I was really grateful to the Lord for His love and mercy toward me. But when I contemplated on what I heard, **"the serpent spirit in the pot"** and **"the iniquities of my fathers,"** I gained more insight into what Grandma and the fetish priest did years earlier. I now knew that what was killing the family was a demonic snakebite connected with witchcraft! And although I argued against it, I did not denounce it personally and destroy its effect on my life. Now, I had to do something about it.

Without wasting time, I sent a letter to my sister, Jemima, and asked her to call for a fast, asking the Lord for forgiveness for our family, and then uproot the demonic pot from the house.

Geoffrey and all the children also joined me to fast and pray. We wept before the Lord for the sins of my forefathers and Grandmother's.

Jemima and the family did exactly what I asked them to do with the exception that something strange happened the first night of the three-day all night prayer meeting. She said that in the course of the prayer, about 1 o'clock in the morning, a literal serpent appeared in their midst. But because they were gripped with fear, they were unable to kill it, and the serpent disappeared.

When Jemima called, I said to her, "Call for another prayer, if possible. And if the demonic serpent appears again, confront it with the blood of Jesus, kill it, and burn it."

It happened again. Jemima brought in one Pastor to pray with them. As they began to pray, a huge snake appeared in their midst again. "In the Name of Jesus, the blood of Jesus rebukes you," they cried out. The snake couldn't move. It became powerless. And this time, they gathered courage, killed and burned it.

We praised the Lord for what He did, because His power broke all the curses against me and is sustaining me today. I came to understand that confessing and repenting of generational sins, cutting down of all bondages and past bridges, exhuming all known buried stuff instigated by the enemy (*occult practices, witchcraft, Ouija boards, blood covenants, ancestral or family practices which were not in conformity with the Word of God, etc.*.), and bringing them into the light of God's presence, is the only way a Christian can have complete victory over the enemy.

[11]

THE CALL TO THE MINISTRY

My desire after graduating from Takoradi Polytechnic was to find a good job and support myself instead of depending on Mother's support all the time.

I had the call of God upon my life, but I did not know how to go about answering it. Even though I had been traveling with the Tears of Jesus Evangelistic Team for a while, I still felt there was more to it. At the same time, I also knew that life wasn't going to be easy for me if I did not find a job to support myself. I believed I had been trained to work to support myself and Mother as well. Deep down in my heart, I wanted to reward Mother for the hard work she had done in educating all of us without a father or a husband by her side. At least I wanted to make her proud of me.

As I was contemplating all these facts, I received a letter from my school of an opening at the Regional Office in Sekondi. The school had already sent my recommendation to the office without my knowledge. How exciting! I prayed, needing that job.

One early morning, I went to the office of the Director for the interview. Amazingly, I was hired on the spot. The only problem was that the office was a bit far for my home. Nevertheless, I accepted the job as from the Lord, especially since I hadn't applied for it.

Mother supported me with transportation to and fro during the first month until I received my first paycheck. Then, all seemed to be going on very well. The first office I worked in was a conference-room type setting. There were as many as four or six of us, but since I was timid, I never conversed with anyone other than saying the normal greetings.

By the following month, my boss changed my office. I was given a separate office. I worked directly under him at the Loans Department. I was very much enthused about the whole idea of being a working lady. My boss also liked me very much. But the Word of God says, *"For My thoughts are not your thoughts, neither are your ways My ways," declares the LORD. "As the heavens are higher than the earth, so are My ways higher than your ways and My thoughts than your thoughts" (Isaiah 55:89 summarized).*

A few weeks after I moved into the new office, strange things began to happen. I went to work one morning very excited. It was raining very hard. Lightning and thunder were flashing and clashing. My boss hadn't come to work before it started raining so there wasn't much to do. I decided to read my Bible.

Coincidently, I opened the Word of God, straight to Jeremiah 1:5. It read, *"Before I formed you in the womb I knew you, before you were born I set you apart; I appointed you as a prophet to the nations."* Trying to read it over and over, I felt a sweet presence and began to pray. I trembled under the power of God. I couldn't really understand what was happening to me.

Suddenly, the atmosphere in the room changed. The presence of the Lord filled the entire room, and I heard His voice, "Monica, what are you doing here? This is not your place. You are a chosen vessel to me. You have a higher calling."

It was the voice of the Lord, which I had heard before. The Bible says, *"He calls His own sheep by name and leads them out. I am the good Shepherd; I know My sheep and My sheep knows*

Me" (John10:3-14). But I couldn't figure out why He wanted me to leave the job I thought He had given me.

"Lord, didn't You say in Your Word that those who do not work should not eat? Why do you want to take this job from me?" I told Him all the consequences my resignation would entail as if He knew nothing about human affairs. I was becoming apprehensive concerning the choice I had to make, either to obey or disobey.

I went home that day overwhelmed. It wasn't that I doubted the Lord's word. The outcome of my obedience was the burden I was carrying. I was scared. I had no way of telling anyone. I continued to go to work and negotiate with Him, and the Lord continued to speak to me. Within the entire month, He spoke about three times and stopped.

Yeah! I was very happy. I thought the Lord had understood my dilemma. Soon after that, I developed unusual eye problems— blurred vision, watery eyes. I couldn't see well at all. It was unusual. Mother couldn't understand it either, because I had not informed her of the call to resign. The mysterious thing about the whole eye problems was that when I would be reading my Bible or any other book at home, I had no problem seeing. But the moment I went to work, I could hardly see anything on the papers I had to fill out for people needing loans.

I informed my boss concerning the problem with my eyesight. He gave me permission to see an ophthalmologist. I was prescribed reading glasses to correct my vision. But the problem persisted. I knew this was the Lord's doing—He was calling me into a full time ministry.

"But Abba, I dared not quit my job now after all that I had already gone through with the change of denomination and the baptism in the Holy Spirit," I told Him. He said nothing. I continued to work until He got hold of me.

One morning, I had gone to the office very early to finish the work I had left undone the day before due to the same eye problems. My office was on the third floor. I sat down to pray and work as I normally did after cleaning the office.

Suddenly, I felt the presence of the Lord with a heavy chill all over me. In a moment, I felt a hand in mine. That was all I could remember. The next thing that happened was really terrifying. I found myself at the last step of the 1st floor holding Someone's hand. As He was removing His hand from mine, I saw the nail print on His wrist. At that moment, He said to me, "Monica, this is not your place. You have a higher calling. My hand is upon you to use you to touch many lives for the kingdom." And He was gone. It was like a dream.

When I saw myself downstairs, I began to sob. I knew in my heart that it was the last warning. I rushed upstairs with fear and trembling, waiting impatiently for the day to end quickly. The minute I left work, I went straight to my pastor, Rev. Appekey, and narrated all the incidents to him. He knew it was the Lord, but he was worried about the persecutions I would be going through.

To me, that was it! Obedience is better than sacrifice. I couldn't go back to work again. Who wouldn't be scared of such an encounter? You want to behave like Jonah and be swallowed by a whale. As for me, I didn't want to spend even a minute in the belly of a whale!

Then the entire family heard the news via the officials of the school who got me the job. Oh my! Everyone went nuts. Some went into shock to hear I had resigned, because I'd heard a voice calling me in to the ministry.

"What kind of God will call such a shy, timid, soft-spoken person to the ministry? How is she going to survive? Nobody is going to support her. Heaven help those who help themselves. Those who don't work shouldn't eat, blah, blah," they fussed.

They meant well, but they did not really know the One who created the human mouth, and who owns the whole universe. He can use anything for His glory. The cases of Moses and of Balaam's donkey are self-explanatory. If God could make Balaam's donkey talk, can't He do anything with anybody today? *(Numbers 22:22-34)*. If God could use a stammering Moses to deliver His people from Egypt, is He less inferior to the One I am serving? *(Exodus 4:10-12)*. If He commissioned Peter to get money out of the mouth of a fish, isn't He capable of supporting me? *(Matthew 17:24-27)*. He makes a way where there is none for His Name sake.

I tried in my own way to explain to my family all that the Lord was doing in my life and the way the call came to me, but no one was ready to listen, except my older sister Esther and Mother. Mother understood as well. No amount of explanation appeased anyone.

Some days, I felt like ignoring His call because of numerous persecutions and ridicule. I went to bed hungry, because I was told, "Those who do not work do not have to eat." My sister and sister-in-law would be singing me out in plain mockery of my faith and my "silly choice." And they were preventing Mother from saving food for me. Mother had to hide food in order for me to eat. What a divine provision it was!

"How can God call someone like Monica to the ministry?" They chanted again and again. "Does God call women to work for Him? Is God this blind to call such a person to the ministry?"

You see, terrorism comes in different ways—emotionally, physically, verbally, as well as spiritually, to demoralize a person. I was really being terrorized in every way, because the devil wanted me to disobey the call of God on my life. It was really frightening. Should I quit, or should I obey? I had no answer for anyone other than to pray for more grace to survive. The call itself was and is still a mystery to me too, but the Word of God brought me comfort.

> *For you see your calling, brethren, that not many wise according to the flesh, not many mighty, not many noble, are called. But God has chosen the foolish things of the world to put to shame the wise, and God has chosen the weak things of the world to put to shame the things which are mighty; and the base things of the world and the things which are despised God has chosen, and the things which are not, to bring to nothing the things that are, that no flesh should glory in His presence (1 Corinthians 1:26-29).*

I was desperate for a breakthrough in order for me to leave for the Bible School. But the more I waited, the more painful the Christian life became as a result of the persecutions.

[12]

TRANSPORTED OUT OF TIME

The most crucial time of my life was between the time of waiting on the Lord and the preparation to go to Bible school. All hell turned loose against me—either to break me, destroy me completely, or prevent me entirely from fulfilling my purpose in life. My family turned against me. The Holy Spirit was sustaining and strengthening me for the difficult times ahead, but I needed a double dosage of divine and physical strength more than ever.

I decided to engage in a week of prayer and fasting to know the mind of Christ and to find direction for what He was calling me to do. Since I couldn't pray efficiently at home, I had to walk three miles to the church every day to spend time in His presence from morning till evening. I normally spent five to six hours on my knees, waiting for His intervention.

I prostrated myself underneath the pastor's desk, groaning in the Spirit for an answer from the Lord. Tears of despair and discouragement flooded my face. I wanted to give up. The burden of rejection, of hunger, and ridicule was too much to carry. The heartaches were unbearable and crippling. Oh, how my situation gave me glimpse of the agony my Savior, Jesus Christ, went through in Gethsemane!

My Evangelistic group knew my dilemma, but no one in the church knew my suffering. I never shared my problems with anyone. After all, it was not their fault. I am the one who received the call, and I am the one who resigned. I wept until there were no more tears, waiting for Him to do whatever He wanted to do with me.

At some point, I cannot recall the exact time, someone entered the Pastor's office. This wasn't a vision or a dream. If was far beyond both. I was transported beyond the realm of the Spirit.

I felt the presence of the Lord Jesus. It felt as if I could touch it, and I did. His presence filled the entire room. I knew He had come to comfort and strengthen me. Then He tapped me on the shoulder and said, "Monica, get up and let's go."

I lifted up my head, and there was the Lord Jesus. He was staring at me with a loving smile that penetrated my soul. His presence was beyond description. His presence was awesome, yet very peaceful.

Then He said to me again, "Monica, rise up and follow Me." He gave me a helping hand and stood me on my feet.

As soon as we stepped outside the pastor's office, the scenery changed. Holding hands, we began a long journey together through different routes. Together, we walked through a plateau of pleasant and unpleasant landscape. Part of it was dry, some was water locked. Part of it was fruitful and beautiful.

We passed through valleys that were deep and very dark, awfully fearful and rocky. Darkness overshadowed me. It was very difficult to walk. We tunneled to climb steep mountains that were very gorgeous, overlooking green grass and different kinds of flowers beautifying the meadow. I wanted to stay there and enjoy myself with nature, but He wouldn't allow me to stop.

He took me through storms of rain, sleet and snow. Frightening lightning and thunder scared me to death. The ground was so slippery that I slipped and fell. He gave me a helping hand and we continued our journey.

He took me along sandy beaches with beautiful blue water splashing over our feet. We also passed through thick forests that blanketed the ground with thorns. The harsh thorns pricked my weak and weary tender feet.

As I bent over to pull the lacy thorns from under my feet, He stooped to wait for me and with a soft voice whispered, "Monica, remove the thorns and keep on following Me. You can make it. We have a long way to go." It sounded like a loving instructor, who was trying to get the best out of his trainee.

We kept walking up and down, over the mountains, down through the valleys, and the plains until we began an upward climb of what seemed like ranges of iced glazed mountains, very beautiful beyond description.

Suddenly, like the sun rising out of its hiding, a beautiful city with gates made of jasper rose beyond the Glacier Mountains. Oh my, how gorgeous the brightness and beauty was! Like the flash of lightning, the Lord Jesus went ahead of me and leaned on the gate facing us, keeping an eye on me.

The climb was really tiring and hard. But the Lord kept on smiling encouragingly at me saying, "Come on, Monica, you can make it."

Weary and tired, I crawled to the gate. Hands and feet bruised, barely surviving the pain and the wounds I had incurred on our journey, I dragged my feet just to get to Him. I knew it would soon be over. Gasping now for breath, I breathed a deep sigh of relief the moment I got to the gate. I was somehow celebrating my own arrival at Heaven's gate in my heart.

"Please Lord, kindly open the gate so I can enter," I said.

"No, Monica, you can't come in now."

"Please Lord, I am tired. I can't live in this world any longer. The journey is too harsh." I whined and complained, as if He had no clue as to what I was going through. I was bargaining and pleading with Him to allow me to enter, because I could no longer bear the trials and persecution.

Then He gently said, "Monica, can you wait until I come?"

"Can I wait until You come, Lord? When? How am I going to?" I spoke softly. Looking in His eyes, I felt His profound love, a deep concern and care.

With His eyes fixed on me, He said in the sweetest and calming voice I've ever heard, "Monica, My grace is sufficient for you. I will never leave you or forsake you. All will be well." He was like a caring mother who was comforting her wounded child.

I whispered, "His grace is sufficient for me. His grace is sufficient for me." Suddenly, I came to myself, and knew I was transported beyond time.

I understood immediately that the Lord had brought me on this special journey to show me the rest of my life's story in a nutshell. He gave me a glimpse of what I would go through in my walk with Him. But He made me aware that no matter what I would go through, He will be there with me. He also showed me that I could and will make it to Heaven by His grace.

Without the slightest doubt, I perceived that these were the things I would go through—the valleys of despair and unanswered questions—the mountains of deep spiritual experiences and breakthroughs, the forest of confusions and hopelessness—the beaches of life's joys, hopes and blessings—the thorns of painful goodbyes and betrayals. The slippery ground of spiritual warfare and life's countless challenges.

Yes, I may falter. I may not see my way out of many things, but one thing is sure, His presence will always be there, and His grace would sustain me.

I got up from the ground, wiped off my tears and continued my walk with Him with sufficient grace to live for Him the rest of my life.

I walked back home in full assurance that day that no matter what would happen to me, no matter what I may experience—good or bad, sweet or bitter, I would never be a quitter, because My Lord will be there any time I needed His help the most to carry me in His arms.

Defying The Odds

Against all the odds, the Lord opened the door for me to go to the Southern Ghana Bible School at Saltpond for an interview. There were about twenty of us from all the corners of Ghana. Some were accepted, but others were not. Thank God, I was admitted to the school without the scrutiny many others went through. The Lord caused His face to shine on me, and His favor was already on my side.

My Pastor, Rev. George Appekey, asked the church board to support me, since there were four of us leaving for the same school. Unfortunately, the deacons decided to support the three men, Asare Minta, Archibald Brown, and Kwarteng, and left me out. Their argument was that I wasn't going to be profitable to them in the future as a woman. I was left to my own fate. It seemed as if that was my lot in life, rejection. But I refused to be discouraged.

It was certain that I didn't have what it took to support myself at the Bible School. Thank God, I left for the school that week with four church dresses and two casual wear for classes. Mother gave me a few cedi's (Ghana currency) for the road and some cakes of soap, sufficient enough to keep me afloat.

Finally, I stepped on the soil of Southern Ghana Bible School at Saltpond to continue my education for the work of the ministry. But to be in the School of the Bible was not fun. It was a time of great challenges. It was really intense. My food was the Word, and my water was prayer. The Holy Spirit was my Sustenance and Counselor. These were the essentials in my survival kit. They were the weapons the Holy Spirit gave me to survive the negative pressure from my mind and my colleagues.

I fasted every week and called upon Him to sustain me. Out of the seven days in the week, I fasted three of them. I didn't know why, but I enjoyed it a bit.

I desired deeply to be used by God. The Lord was my Father and Companion, and I addressed Him as Daddy. We chatted like a father does with his children, especially the one he so loves. I did not want to call Him someone else's God, like the God of Abraham, of Isaac, and of Jacob. I yearned to know Him intimately and personally, so that I could call Him ABBA, Monica's God. And the Lord became very close to me. He talked with me and instructed me on what to do, and how to live for Him. He gave me such a sharp memory to memorize difficult assignments. I received an A+ after a hard work of sleepless nights of praying and studying. But life at school was really hard for me. Principal Bronny Stroud and his family were such a blessing and an encouragement to me in many ways.

Personal problems and the spiritual challenges I was carrying were up to my neck. I cried all night for weeks, and felt I needed to quit. So early one morning, I packed all my belongings and went to Rev. and Mrs. Kessler, the new Principal, to announce my intentions of leaving. I had no desire of staying there any longer. Somehow, it was evident that they knew the heart of my problem. And through their counsel, I was encouraged to stay, fight, and wait on the Lord for His will to be done in my life. What a challenge! A real painful test of my loyalty and obedience to the Lord!

[13]

A TRUE LOVE STORY

One morning, at exactly about two o'clock, I heard the Lord speaking to me again in my sleep, "Monica, if I send you to Togo, will you go?"

"Yes Lord," I answered. I didn't even know where Togo was.

"If I send you to Niger and anywhere around the world, will you go?"

This time I was quiet, not knowing what to say.

The question was repeated, "Monica, if I send you anywhere around the world, will you go?"

After a little pause, I replied. "Yes Lord. Whatever You want me to do, I will do it wholeheartedly with Your grace. You know me better than myself."

Then the Lord ceased speaking. His questions sounded similar like Peter's moment of truth with the Lord Jesus after His resurrection in John 21:12-19. But I did not even know where Togo was at that time. It was no big deal to me. But it was going to be a big deal to the One who would send me to those places mentioned.

By morning, Mrs. Mercy Mills, the other pastor's wife, with whom I was sharing the same room, called me and asked of whom I had been talking to all those times at night.

"I have been talking to the Lord."

"I could hear a voice speaking to you, and you responding, but I didn't hear a word of what was said," she said.

Although Mrs. Mills might have been scared of my conversation with the Lord, she knew I didn't orchestrate it. I counted myself privileged to have a conversation with the Most High. Oh, how I loved to be in His presence!

Even though I had all these powerful encounters and confirmations from the Lord, I went to the Bible School with my own agenda—a one-year Bible training to be an evangelist and travel with the Tears of Jesus. But the Lord had other plans.

On top of personal agendas, I found myself in a terrible struggle for help—dealing with the students. As the only unmarried lady at the campus, I became the center of the conflict.

One day, after class, one student handed me a letter. It was about "LOVE." *I am not in love with anyone, so why should I reply to a 'so-called love' letter?* I asked, ignoring it. That opened the door for many other "LOVE" letters. But while every one of the young men who left a letter tried to convince me "God spoke to me about you," I had nowhere to lay my head. It was really funny and frustrating at the same time.

Another phase of my own problem was the fact that I had a strong desire to be like the famous evangelist, Kathleen Kuhlman and preach the Word under God's powerful anointing. Since I saw Kathleen Kuhlman as a single woman, I thought that God wouldn't like me to marry, and that God could never use a married woman.

Here, the Lord asked me to resign from my will, my passion, and my perceptions, and allow His will, His plans, and purposes to soak up my life completely. That is where I could experience the true joy of serving Him and being satisfied in doing His will. For me, that was hard to do, but it was a battle He won all the time, because God never loses a battle. He is the Commanding Officer of my life. It's not about me, but Him. But it is not easy to say that you've given all to the Lord, and still think you have to control the outcome.

A few days before the end of the school year, the Lord began to deal with me about my decision not to marry. I had struggled with Him for quite a year. So I decided to wait in His presence in order to be sure I was hearing right. Although I was fasting and praying, I was still hanging on to the other end of the rope, telling the Lord what I wanted from Him and not what He wanted from me. And since fasting and prayer don't cancel free will, I continued my negotiation with the Lord, giving Him all the reason for my unwillingness to marry. He said nothing to me throughout the week until the last day of the fasting.

At about eleven o'clock that night, immediately after the "Deeper Life" Friday evening service at the school, the Lord spoke to me and said, "Monica, I have My best for you. He is a man after My heart. I prepared him for you even before you were born." It was like a whisper in my ears.

I began to laugh. In my mind I was thinking, *who could that person be?* And since I didn't care much about who the person was, I prayed and went to bed. Suddenly, the moment I closed my eyes and began to doze off, I began to see an incredible vision:

A small light like a dot or the tip of a ballpoint pen was shot into the atmosphere. It was like a small star in the galaxies that was targeted on something particular. Me! The closer it came, the brighter it shone, until it expanded into a huge beautiful light blinding my eyes. Then in the star-like light, I saw a face. It was the face of one of the students, named Geoffrey. At that moment, I felt like screaming on top of my voice to say "No." Then I heard the voice of the Lord as clear as day, "Monica, this is My best for You."

Wow! What is that? I was dumbfounded. I began to sob saying, "Oh no" to myself and wept all night until daybreak.

After all, you do not even know him very well. Why should you ever think you know him better than his Creator, the Lord God Almighty, who is revealing this to you? I heard, in my subconscious. I knew the vision was coming from the Lord, but my ego was fighting against it. Why? I did not understand. I began to search for clues for my own behavior.

As I knelt beside the pew and began to reminisce on what the Lord had just revealed to me, I remembered, maybe, a piece of the puzzle. I remembered that when I sat at the corner of the cafeteria praying and contemplating on what the Executive Presbyters would say to me during the interview, one of the students passed by and said, "Hello." I responded with a "hello" as well. He walked to the chapel. A few minutes later, the guy passed by again and smiled on me. At that time, I wondered about what he was doing, because I didn't know him personally. So I didn't talk or say a word to him. *Was that part of the puzzle, Lord?* Maybe, who knows? But I was frustrated.

What was your problem, Monica? You may ask. I didn't know it either, but I supposed I was carrying a deeper problem than just not wanting to marry—insecurity, fear, and whatever was piled up inside my heart. And instead of dealing with my own doubts and fears about the one the Lord showed me, I was crying my heart out, trying to find a clue as to whoever this individual is or is not. In my mind, I speculated on everything that could possibly be wrong with Geoffrey.

My eyes were all puffy by the morning. Concentration in class that morning wasn't possible.

First of all, I was afraid of being abused, since my life had been centered on all kinds of terror. Pastors were not exempt from being abusive. Secondly, I had not fallen in love with any man before in order to know what true love really felt like. I had never had a date before. The culture and the church were strictly against dating. Third, I was brought up with a cultural bias concerning other tribes.

Without being a scientist to figure it out, Geoffrey had a big tribal mark on his face, which meant he was from another tribe other than mine (The Fanti tribe). The Fantis rarely had a mark.

To my Grandmother, marrying someone outside our tribe was somehow an abomination or a crime. All other tribes would not work for her grandchildren. She had probably forgotten how mixed we already were in her own family and that of my Dad's. Dad even had a Caucasian wife in addition to all the multiple women in his life.

Thinking about some of her reasons, Grandma didn't want our inheritance to be transferred to other tribes. Grandma thought Biblical, but acted quite differently, like a pagan. She was acting out senselessly without consulting the God of the Bible. But unfortunately, what my family hated was what God was leading me into in His Sovereignty. It was like Moses marrying an Ethiopian and Mariam throwing a fit! But what about Joseph marrying an Egyptian?

I knew it wasn't going to be easy, because I felt Geoffrey might be a Gā or from another tribe altogether. Despite all the confusions, I had such an inner peace beyond imagination. It wasn't the enemy talking me into something that would bring glory to the Name of the Lord. The devil doesn't promote God's agenda. He aims to destroy God's plans and purposes for humanity.

The Bible says, *"The thief comes not, but to steal, to kill and to destroy, but I (Jesus) came that you may have life and have it in abundance. ... I am the Good Shepherd; I know My sheep and My sheep know Me – just as the Father knows Me and I know the Father ... My sheep listen to My voice; I know them, and they follow Me" (John 10:10, 14-15, 27 – emphasis mine).*

On the other hand, I contemplated. Where did mother get her fair-colored skin from? What about the British blood in my ancestry line? What about my aunties, uncles, cousin, and all the half-breeds in my family, the Bonny, Moses, et cetera? What is the difference in marrying a white from far away beyond the oceans and marrying a fellow African, who is close enough that one can travel easily to meet their relatives? All those reasoning and many more raced through my mind.

Funny though, the more I reasoned with my own insecurities and inadequacy to be what He wanted me to be if I married, the stronger the Holy Spirit dealt with me to surrender. Surrender again and again! This is not an inner impression, because each instruction He gave me was in line with His Word. Finally, I agreed, but I placed a few fleeces before the Lord.

Place a fleece as a child of God? You may ask. Yes. I did. I was acting like a silly child really, and I believed Daddy God was and is still My Father. The Lord really understood my dilemma, and had patience enough to work with me through it.

Someone said, "Placing a fleece before the Lord is a sign of unbelief and immaturity." That may be or can be true. However, God deals with each of His children in the level of their relationship with Him, and He is even more understanding than any human being. God judges our motives behind our fleeces.

Without using the word 'fleece' or sign, almost every child of God has at least one time in their lifetime prayed, "Father if this is You" or "Lord, if this is your will." It all sums up the same. I wasn't the first to place fleeces before the Lord. There were many God-fearing men and women in the Bible who placed fleeces and asked the Lord for signs concerning specific issues. And God gave them their answers.

In Exodus 3, we see Moses standing before the Lord on Sinai, giving excuses why he wasn't the perfect guy for the job. Over and over, God gave him assurance with new signs and numerous wonders to confirm His call on his life.

God said, "I AM," meaning: "Moses, there is everything within Me that can make you effective in your calling. I AM is all you need, and without Me you cannot accomplish anything. I AM The Past, The Present, and The Future." Here were my fleeces.

Fleece number one: Lord, if You are really the One who wants me to marry Geoffrey, please, have him tell me that You said he should marry me. Then I would know this is from You.

Fleece number two: Lord, You know that it is a taboo in my culture for a girl to propose to a man, and moreover, I don't think I know anything about loving any man. I have never dated before, so Lord, I would like Geoffrey to actually come before the end of the school year to talk to me about it.

Fleece number three: Lord, You know who my Grandma is. Her ideologies and beliefs are different from Yours, and she controls the family. If this is really You, then speak to her and Mother, or do whatever You want for me to marry Geoffrey. Your will, I will gladly obey, if You answer my prayers, in Jesus's Name.

The Lord understood my heart. However, since Alex, a paternal cousin and a student, had been my prayer partner at the school, I confessed to him my doubts about what the Lord was asking of me. Alex prayed with me and promised not to let anyone know about it.

Now, who is this guy the Lord is bringing to me to become my future husband? I did not know much about him, but at least I can connect some dots down here for the mean time. *Was Geoffrey not the guy who said "Hello" the first time I came in for the interview? Did he know something about me before I came to the school?*

Geoffrey had never started a chat with me in any way. The only conversation he threw at me sometimes was a casual "Hello, sister, how are you?" he would say, when we crossed the route to the chapel. But did he know something I didn't? In some way, I imagined that my fleeces weren't going to work, knowing Geoffrey was never that close to me.

To my surprise, the opposite began to happen. I made my way to the chapel one afternoon after the normal work chores to practice on the piano. The moment I sat behind the piano and began to play gently, I felt a presence behind me. I did not bother to turn at first, thinking it might be Alex Nortey or John-Mark Arhinful, two of the students, but that was unusual. Alex would just walk to the front and begin to sing. As for John-Mark, he would just yell out my name.

Okay, this is strange. Turn and look, Monica. The moment I turned around, here was Geoffrey standing by the chapel door, watching me fiddle with the piano. As soon as our eyes crossed, I wobbled. Talk about fidgeting! I said to myself, *O God, what are You doing to me now?*

I stood up hastily, wanting to run out of the room. Geoffrey smiled and said, "Oh please, do not leave. I only passed by to listen to the one playing the piano. It sounded wonderful. I'm sorry to have disturbed you. Continue to play. I am going back to the classroom." He turned and left.

Hmm, what did he say? The music sounded wonderful? I thought Geoffrey might have been flattering me. I wasn't even good at the piano. I had just started learning how to play, but if he could find something good about that gibberish music and sound, then he could be an exceptional man of God!

Trembling, I sat back quietly in awe and respect for the Lord as never before. I was touched, because I had never heard people commend me. And if this is the kind of husband Geoffrey is going to be, then the Lord has a great sense of humor. The Lord knew I would need a very big dose of encouragement rather than criticism.

From that day onward, I watched Geoffrey closely but always from a distance. He was a very jovial and caring guy. His sense of humor and love for all the students radiated from the prayerful guy he was. He wasn't among the guys who troubled me earlier with their visions and dreams of marrying me.

Now, my fear of Geoffrey coming to talk to me about marrying him also dissipated, because he did not even bother to raise a subject that day. I felt weird about my own attitude. I prayed and repented the same day again and again. Then I prayed an unusual prayer. I asked the Lord to baptize me with His own Agape love in my heart, if Geoffrey truly was the one He showed me.

Be careful of what you pray for. It will come to bite you. Because this time, it was not a joke. That very moment, I began to fall in love with Geoffrey as if we were already dating. The response was so quick and powerful. *Lord, I have not even talked to him, so how can that be so fast?*

It was incredible. I felt half of my heart had been transferred to him. Anytime I saw him walking through the walkway to the chapel, my heart raced. I wanted to hide, because I could not make out what was happening to me now. Each day as I watched Geoffrey around the campus, I felt as if I was walking on a magnetic field of love. The Lord was winning my heart for Geoffrey.

Then the most wonderful thing happened. Missionaries Peggy Scott and Bonnibel Roll organized an end of year drama entitled "What is in thine hand." Each student had a role to play. Geoffrey's role was Moses. And imagine this. My maiden name was Moses. Was it a coincidence? Anyway, Geoffrey played his role perfectly well. I was hypnotized as he sang this particular song, tears flooding down his face.

> Jesus use me, and O Lord, don't refuse me
> For surely there's a work that I can do
> And even though it's humble
> Help my will to crumble
> Though the cost is great I'll work for You

At that moment, I knew I had truly fallen in love with Geoffrey without being connected, so to say. I could not get rid of him from my heart. Unbelievably, the Lord was ripping my heart in two with such a love I had never known was there. My Heavenly Father had stolen my heart for Geoffrey! A student nicknamed him "Weeping Prophet," because that's who he really was, a prophet of God, a man of God, full of deep love and passion for the Lord.

Soon after that, the school planned a three-day evangelistic meeting at Ewutu (Central Region) to plant a new church. It was in conjunction with our mid-term holidays. We had to leave the school on Wednesday at noon in order to prepare for the meeting that night. Sister Mercy and I were in charge of literature. The tables of books and cassette were set at the corner on the field. A few people were coming towards the meeting ground when we began to sing.

I became preoccupied with intercession more than the sale of books and lost somehow, the consciousness of why I was there—

to sell books and tapes. In the meantime, someone handed me a book and said something. I could not recollect who it was and what was said. I was lost in my own little world, praying in the Spirit.

Out of the blue, I felt a pull on the back of my blouse. I turned around and it was Alex.

"Hello, my sister, did you notice the guy who handed you the book?"

"Which book? Where is it?" I asked.

"You don't know where you put the book? You better find it. This could be what you wanted from God," Alex said, laughing out loud.

"A book? Someone slipped a book into my hand?"

"Yes, day-dreamer! I was watching you from afar, ha, ha, ha," he chuckled again.

It was really annoying. "But who was that?" I questioned Alex.

"Guess who? Were you sleeping or what? I suppose you went into a trance with your two eyes wide open."

I became so frustrated and questioned, "Oh no! Alex. I don't think you talked to Geoffrey about our conversation." I wanted to cry, thinking he might have said something.

Alex interrupted me, "You don't think what? Believe me, sister. I have nothing to do in this, okay? Don't you trust me?"

"But how did you know he was the one who gave me the book you were talking about? Let's get this straight." I frowned. *Alex might have betrayed my confidence.*

"Please, don't take me wrong. You know me well. I cannot betray you in any way. I happened to be watching both of you closely. I don't know what happened, but I believe something went well in the realm of the spirit, because I know I have been praying for the two of you. And you've been praying too, eh," Alex affirmed, laughing out so loud.

All the students turned to look at us. I felt embarrassed! I couldn't understand Alex. I searched through the boxes in front of me to see if there was a particular book, which might be quite different from the ones we were selling. I couldn't find it. Soon after the meeting, Alex came back to encourage me to make another search for the book. He suggested I look into my handbag.

"How can you predict that I have a book in my handbag, Alex?" I asked him.

"No one knows exactly, but anything can be possible."

It took just a glance and there it was. It looked like a dream, but I felt like a stupid fool. I had taken a book and kept it inside my handbag without thinking. I pulled out the book and guess what? The title of the book caught my attention right away: "I LOVE A YOUNG GIRL" by Walter Trobisch.

My gracious! I froze for a while and then turned over to the first page. Guess who? It was from Geoffrey! "To the One I Love," he had written.

Oh, I understand. He could only tell me what was in his heart through a book? Was he a coward like me or what? I asked myself. I couldn't resist the chills that soaked me up. Maybe that was his way of expressing himself. How can I judge him like that? Whatever it was, it seemed God had given me a semi-answer to my first fleece. But I wasn't satisfied.

Although I had the book, I complained to God that the book wasn't the fleece I placed before Him, because I love specifics. I wanted Geoffrey to speak to me personally. Although I was drawn to him as never before, we did not talk to each other before the meetings ended. But as we were about to board the school's minibus the next morning back to the school, I noticed something strange. Geoffrey was leaning on one of the students, William AduAmponsah. He brought Geoffrey to the bus and carefully helped him lie down on the last seat.

"What is happening?" No one answered me. I had no idea what might have happened to Geoffrey in the night. Soon, we arrived at the campus, and were all dismissed to our respective dorms. By the next morning, the campus was almost empty with the exception of four of us—Babanawo, William Adu-Amponsah, Justice Hayford, and me. I didn't hear of Geoffrey.

Maybe he was doing better and left for his station. I contemplated.

Brother Justice walked to me and said, "Sister Monica, did you hear of what happened to Geoffrey?"

"No. What's the problem?" I asked.

"He had another sudden stomach attack last night and was rushed to the hospital again. He is really sick, and we need to pray for him. He looked like a dying person."

"Lord, why do you want to give me somebody who is as sick as I?" I asked the Lord over and over again, but He did not reply to my inquiry. *Maybe Geoffrey needed someone who understands pain.* I thought. If so, I accept it.

Curiously, since the school was on vacation, there was noone to take care of the sick left behind. Miss Peggy Scott, one of the resident missionaries, came to me and asked if it was possible for me to help Geoffrey with his meals.

I laughed quietly and answered, "Yes, Ma."

She couldn't figure out the reason for the laughter and asked, "Is there anything wrong, Monica?"

Shaking my head, I replied, "No, Ma'am," but I knew my reason for the laughter. *Doesn't the Lord have a sense of humor? Why should I be the one to take care of my would-be, if God wills? Das!*

With the little money Miss Peggy gave me, I hurried to Kromantse, bought some fresh fish, went back to the campus and prepared him light soup. I did my best to serve him with whatever he needed. Within three days, Geoffrey recovered and was faring very well. Everybody was surprised.

Wasn't there a cause? Things happen for a reason. Maybe, that may be my test or it could be Geoffrey's fleece as well, who knows.

It was about three o'clock in the afternoon. The entire campus was quiet. The other three students were in their respective dorms. I was happy, but I felt lonely. I missed Mother so much. I wanted to be at home for the holidays, but the circumstances around my calling and the financial problems I was facing, weren't favorable for me to travel home. Not wanting to throw a pity party alone in my dorm, I decided to go in the chapel to pray.

I had spent about forty-five minutes on my knees before the Lord when a song a brother taught me in my former church exploded in my heart.

> Ao, Ewuradze (Oh, Lord). Ao, Ewuradze,
> Me resu frɛ wo (I am crying out to You)
> Ao, Ewuradze, me re twɛn Wo
> (Oh Lord, I am waiting on You)
> Me nyim dɛ Ewuradze n'enyi wɔ mo do
> (I know Your eyes are upon me) Ntsi,
> meyi n'ayɛw daa daa
> (That's why I will worship You)

I sang and wept in His presence for a while. Then afterwards, I went behind the piano and started fiddling with the same song over and over, tears dripping down my face. His presence filled my entire being.

Somehow, in the middle of this beautiful spiritual atmosphere I was enjoying, someone opened the chapel door unexpectedly. I tried to wipe the tears off my face to see who the intruder was. To my surprise, there stood Geoffrey by the door, about six feet away from me. He was standing there, head bowed, watching me wipe the tears off my face and the drops off the piano.

I wanted to disappear that moment, but I couldn't. Something got me hooked to the seat. He also did not move an inch. He stood still watching me.

Then, Geoffrey broke the silence and said, "Sister Monica, I am very sorry to interrupt your moment with the Lord. I just want to thank you very much for taking care of me. That was really nice of you."

"With all pleasure," I said.

"Please, but there is something very important I want to ask you, if you wouldn't mind."

I nodded.

"I shouldn't ask you such silly questions, but I have to do this for a purpose, for my own good." "It's alright," I told him.

"To start with, did the Lord tell you something about me?"

"Why are you asking me such question?"

"You know I asked you permission before I posed this question."

"Okay, go ahead."

"Please, do not be bashful. Just tell me what the Lord revealed to you concerning me."

There was no room for lying. I nodded, but counter questioned him, "Please, what are you saying the Lord told you regarding me?"

Without wasting time, Geoffrey said, "As for me, the Lord told me you are His best for me."

"Me?" I asked, hypocritically.

"Yes! He told me He had already spoken to you about me, and that you are waiting for me to make a move," Geoffrey said confidently.

With that little information, tears filled my eyes. *Oh my Lord! You are extremely amazing.* I mumbled in my heart. Geoffrey questioned my reason for the tears. I couldn't explain everything to him at that point but I did later on.

Geoffrey then said to me, "I don't want to flatter you, but the Lord spoke to me the very day you entered the school premises. I already knew you were going to be my bride, but I also had someone else in mind. I did not want to give up on my own choice either. I have battled with the Lord and He has prevailed."

"You rejected me, because I wasn't good enough for you?"

"No, no. Please, don't judge me wrong. It was hard for me to obey the Lord to come to you when He spoke to me, because I know you are a Fanti, and I've learned that Fantis do not marry from other tribes easily."

"You know about Fantis? Then, why did you give me the book?"

"I decided I was going to be a little stubborn and leave the school premises even though I gave you the book in the first place.

I didn't have the courage to tell you face to face despite the fact that I knew the Lord's intentions for both of us."

With my head still bowed, I asked, "And what happened?"

"Actually, the Lord got my attention when I became seriously sick that night. He'd asked me earlier to talk to you before leaving, but I refused completely, and now here I am."

"Okay, thank you very much. I'm still praying. I am not quite sure things will really go through easily."

"Again? Pray for what again?" Geoffrey laughed out so loud.

"Why are you laughing?" I thought he didn't understand what I was saying, but he did. *He thinks I am stubborn, but I am not. I am only cautious.*

"Do you remember your first day at the school for the interview?" Geoffrey asked.

"Oh yeah, I remember very well. Were you the one who came out to greet me?"

"You have good memory. I was the one. You see, when Rev. Appekey's car stopped behind the chapel and you came out of the car, the Lord spoke to me so clearly and said, *'Geoffrey, this is My best for you.'* I struggled to believe what I was hearing, because my girl-friend of many years dropped me to go with another pastor from her tribe."

"Now I understand your reaction. Your heart was broken," I said.

Geoffrey became quiet.

"Please, where do you come from? What is your tribe?" I asked just to distract him from his former grief. It sounded silly, but I meant it. That's part of the piece I needed to fix into the puzzle God had given me.

"I am actually from Togo, but was born in Ghana."

"You are from where?"

"It is true, I am from Togo."

"Togo?" I stuttered. The revelation of his nationality scared me so much, because it reminded me of the earlier conversation with the Lord concerning the call to Togo. *Oh my gracious, is it part of the puzzle, Lord?*

"Most people think I am from Accra, but I am not. I'm a Ghanaian by birth, but a Togolese by nationality. Why did you ask?"

"I asked because that is the last fleece I have placed before the Lord. But it doesn't matter anymore."

"Okay. Now, will you be my friend and marry me?"

"I don't know yet. I have a big hurdle to climb. But first, permit me to ask you another question."

"Go on."

"Why are you sick to your stomach all the time?"

Geoffrey was stunned. "Hmm, is that what is bothering you? Aren't you also sick all the time?"

"I know I am not all that strong, but would you kindly answer me first?"

"Okay. My stomach problem is a little bit complicated. But I'll give you the gist of it. Will that work?"

"No problem. That will help me to know what I will be dealing with."

"I am not really sick in my body. I have a stomach ulcer, and I got it through persecution, suffering, and lack of food after I gave my life to Jesus at the age of 13."

"Oh, I have a stomach ulcer too."

"Welcome to the club," Geoffrey said. "And how did you get yours?"

I smiled. "I got mine when I lived with my sister Flora in Accra for almost a year after graduating from high school. She was expecting her first child, and Mother asked me to go and help her for a while whilst I waited for the result of the exams. But Flora treated me like a little slave girl. I would go days without food. I drank so much water, I thought I was going to drown in my own fluid." Tears flooded my face. "She made me to eat the uneatable!"

"I am so sorry, Monica. But you know the Lord will take care of you."

"Yes, He really will. I have come a long way with Him, and He hasn't failed me once."

"Now, is my response okay with you?"

"Yeah, I think it is okay."

"I am not rich. I don't have much to give you, but I will love you as much as I can, and as Christ enables me to. I don't even have a bed of my own now. Will you really love me in spite of this?"

"Brother Geoffrey, true love is not about material gains. True love is what binds two lives together in Christ. My Dad was rich. He had everything—cars, trucks, rented buildings, numerous wives and countless children. Yet, he left everything when he died, and we returned to poverty in just a short time, because his family came and took everything he and Mother worked for. They left us struggling, but God did not fail us."

"My Dad is in Togo right now. I lost the two brothers my Mom left with us. I am alone here in Ghana. The only family I have are those the Lord gave me in Christ—Brother Welbeck, Japheth Togbui and Essilfie Turkson. Actually Japheth was the one who brought me to Christ.

"No problem. We just have to obey the Lord, and all will be well with us."

"Thanks so much. Do you know that I have friends who are Pastors, and who dissuaded me from coming to you?"

"Why?"

"They told me I would spend all my time in ministry praying for a sick wife. But they didn't know my story as well. God's best is what I wanted, and it is you, Monica."

That day, Geoffrey proposed to me to marry him, but not with a ring. The procedure in my culture was quite different. I accepted his heart, because I knew it was the Lord's doings. I was already in love with him. And I knew the first two fleeces had been answered. But now, how am I going to face my family, especially Grandma?

I decided to go home and visit and have a good time with Mother. I knew Mother would be very happy to see me. Geoffrey gave me the money he would have used to visit the church he was taking care of. I took it reluctantly, because we weren't married yet. But his plea to not block his blessings won over.

[14]

LOVE'S CHALLENGES & PROVISION

Knowing how difficult Grandma was, I ran for refuge in the Word of the Lord before I traveled. That night, the Lord spoke to me and confirmed what He told me with His Word *(Genesis 28:15)*. With this assurance, I took off the following morning to Takoradi with the little money I had.

How happy I was when I saw Mother! She was also very happy to see me. It had taken time to visit due to financial strain.

Since I was supposed to be at the campus by the weekend to work at the International Correspondence Institute office (ICI), I didn't waste time to tell Mother what the Lord was doing in my life. It was a solemn moment when Mother learned that her daughter's lover wasn't a Fanti.

Perplexed, she voiced out, "Maame, can't you pray the Lord to exchange Geoffrey with a man from our side? I know God hears your prayers, and He can do whatever you tell Him to."

"Please, Mother, you don't understand," I responded. "It is not about the Lord changing Geoffrey to give me another mate. It is about being obedient to the will of God for my life. I've struggled with the Lord over this issue for weeks, and I'm confident that Geoffrey is God's will for me, and I for Geoffrey."

Mother couldn't believe her ears. She frowned. *She has now the audacity to talk back to me?* I envisioned, just by looking at her face. I felt she wanted to ask me that question. Yet she knew I'd never spoken back disrespectfully to her before.

"Mother," I tried to explain myself. "You know how I've lived my life all these years. I have waited for the Lord, and I just want to be in the center of God's will."

Instead of being angry, Mother stared at me as if she'd heard the voice of God. The expression in her face indicated that to me. Her eyes lit and her jaw dropped. She did not reprimand me either, but turned around and walked away into the bedroom. I followed her, trying to explain myself. She wouldn't respond. She rather sat on the bed, buried her face in between her thighs for a while and wept.

Thinking I might have offended Mother with my decision to marry outside my tribe, I stood there in silence, praying for a way out of the whole situation. My heart was breaking too. *The last thing I would ever do is to offend the mother who sacrificed her life to care for ten young children after the death of her husband, our father.* Somehow, I was now tossed between God's will and my love for my mother. *Lord, have mercy and help me.* I prayed silently and sobbed as well.

After a while, Mother lifted up her head. Tears dripping down her cheeks, she said, "You know how hard this is. But if that is what you want, then pray. We'll pray and see what the Lord will do, but pray really hard. I will be going to see Grandma this afternoon."

Who wouldn't pray for a Grandma who has become a cultural addict? Although I fasted and prayed all day, waiting for Mother to come back from Grandma, I still didn't have the peace of mind that Grandma could yield to me easily.

Mother returned dissatisfied. You could tell by her countenance that all wasn't well. Her face sagged in grief and disappointment. She was really unhappy. She sat in silence by the door and moaned for a while without saying a word. I wasn't anxious, even though I could tell by Mother's reaction that something wasn't right. But what, I had no clue. Patience and prayer were my options. I sat and watched her.

Finally, she broke the silence and said, "Monica, Grandma instructed me to tell you that as long as she is alive, you will never marry Geoffrey, even if heaven comes down. She emphasized that her decision is final, and that no one can overturn or change it, not even God."

What can I do? Should I back down? I contemplated. *'Not even God?' What does Grandma mean by that? That is really dangerous!*

According to my culture, Grandma's decision was final, whether good or bad. It was really alarming, but I wasn't shaken. On the other hand, I needed to respect my family. What a predicament! I was tossed between Geoffrey and Grandma, the will of God and the desire of my family.

Two days after, Mother proposed that we go and see Grandma so I could explain my decision to her personally before leaving for the school. "Maybe she would understand," Mother encouraged me.

I regretted going into her home. Grandma didn't even receive me. It was so humiliating when she scolded me before the entire family. She just looked at me and said, "You. You are really problematic. And you are always challenging what we believe in. Who told you that you can choose your own husband?" Grandma point blankly told me to go to hell with whomever I had chosen to marry, and that our marriage would be over her dead body.

Over her dead body? I'd heard that up to my neck, but now I was tired of hearing it again. I would either drown or live in God's will for my life. I needed to make a decision, but how?

My family knew my stand with the Lord that I wasn't going to compromise with the will of God, and they were all waiting to see what my reaction was going to be. My dilemmas increased. *No matter where the direction may go, I have to obey the Lord, because obedience to the will of God is always costly.* I told myself.

I went back to school without the response to the third fleece. Somehow, I knew my Heavenly Father was going to make a way through these difficulties as well. As for Geoffrey, he wasn't moved an inch when I told him of my dilemma with Grandma. He said to me, "Sister Monica, don't worry about Grandma's threats. God has a way of setting her aside."

Setting her aside? But how? We prayed for the appropriate time so he could go and meet my family to begin the process for the engagement. The wedding would follow later.

In my tribe, getting married is a step-by-step process that entails a lot of preparation. First of all, you just can't run away with someone's daughter and marry in secret. If the lady accepts the young man's proposal to marry him, the groom's father or relatives make all the necessary arrangements for the first step named "knocking."

The knocking process is to inquire from the girl's parents if their daughter is free to be engaged to their son. And if she is declared free and not engaged to any other person, the family proceeds to the second step, the engagement itself. It goes with the payment of the dowry, a Bible, the engagement ring to seal their relationship, jewelries and special cloths, plus whatever the family requires for the daughter's engagement. (Check this out in Genesis 24).

This second step is actually a legally binding marriage in itself, because once the dowry is paid, the man has the legal right to the woman as his wife, and it is sealed with the engagement ring. If they are Christians, then a church wedding followed before they live together. Geoffrey and I desired to please the Lord in all things and wait until our wedding day.

Since Geoffrey's parents were in Togo, a delegation from the church including my Pastor, Rev. George Appekey, represented his family. They went to my family so that they could begin the knocking. However, since Grandma had vowed that she wasn't going to change her mind, she stood on her grounds and sing-sang her old slogan, *"Over my dead body."*

Rev. Appekey interjected that if Grandma was God, then it was okay with him. But since she wasn't God, God Himself, the Creator of the universe, would bypass her to allow her granddaughter to marry the man HE Himself had purposed for her.

Obstacle Removed

On the 1st of January 1977, I was on my knees in the chapel praying, and thanking the Lord for the New Year given to me, when I heard the voice of the Lord. It was as clear as I am typing this story. He said, *"Monica, the obstacle is gone. And My purpose will stand."*

Although I couldn't comprehend the depth of what He was talking about, I wasn't all that excited. I felt in my spirit something tragic might have happened. I continued to pray.

A few days later, I received a letter from Jemima, announcing the death of Grandma.

She said Grandma's death occurred on the 1st of January! What a mystery beyond human understanding!

My heart broke. I wept bitterly for her, and although she was buried before I received the news of her death, I attended the thanksgiving service, which was scheduled later.

Mother told me what happened later on. "Grandma called for a family meeting and told us that she was going to die, and that you are the cause of her death. She distributed the little wealth she had to the children, grandchildren, and great grandchildren and left you out. Grandma also brought out a broom, killed a chicken, poured the blood on it, and broke the broom, denouncing you as one of her grandchildren."

Wow, I was shocked. Instead of repenting and accepting God's will for her granddaughter, she resented me and died. The Word of the Lord had come to pass. The obstacle had been removed. I wasn't happy that my Grandma was gone. I regretted her death very much, but God is still God when it comes to His Word. He said, *"Touch not my anointed, and do My prophets no harm."* I believe Grandma put herself in harm's way when she stepped on God's toes to persecute His child. For her to say that her words were final and that God couldn't even interfere with her decision in itself was very dangerous.

Grandma's death caused a great tension between me and my maternal family; especially my two aunties. They plainly rose up against me. I bore all the accusations for killing Grandma. Although the family knew what the truth was, the aunties intentionally set the truth aside to persecute me. It was hard to swallow, but I prayed for them. Obedience is always expensive. `

"The aunties have vowed to kill you too," Jemima told me. "You better pray hard! You know them. They said you killed Grandma and so they would also destroy you."

"The Lord will take care of me," I told Jemima, because I had done nothing wrong. The Bible says, *"The wicked plots against the just, and gnashes at him with his teeth. The Lord laughs at him, for He sees that his day is coming" (Psalms 37:12-13).*

The Lord said to me, "Monica, the level of your obedience will determine the level of your commitment to Me. And the level of your commitment will determine the level of your love for Me." That is self-explanatory. My love for God would always determine the level of how much I will commit to His cause, and my commitment will definitely affect my life of obedience. Obedience, I say, is *"The art of saying 'Yes Master', without further questioning or complaining."*

Even in those difficult moments of Grandma's death, I had strong faith that my Heavenly Father was going to be with me to the very end. And thank God, against all odds, the door flung wide open for Geoffrey to go ahead with the dowry. This time, home going took on a different meaning for me.

According to the custom, I needed to be present to receive the Bible and the engagement ring, which came with the dowry. Thus, having asked permission from school to attend the ceremony, I left Saltpond on a Friday afternoon after classes to return on Sunday. However, the night before my departure, I was warned in a dream not to travel that weekend.

It's been such a privilege to know things before they happen. God spoke to me in dreams, visions, and audibly numerous times. Many Biblical characters were given dreams and visions of impending tragedies or warnings. This phenomenon happened to the Godly and even ungodly alike: Abimelech *(Genesis 20:1-10),* Jacob *(Genesis 28:10-22),* Joseph *(Genesis 37:1-11),* Pharaoh's Cupbearer and Baker *(Genesis 40),* Pharaoh himself *(Genesis 41),* Nebuchadnezzar *(Daniel 4),* Daniel *(Daniel*

7, 8, 10-12), Joseph, the husband of Mary *(Matthew 1:19-25; 2:1315; 19-23),* Cornelius *(Acts 10:1-7),* Peter *(Acts 10:9-21),* and Paul *(Acts 9:1-18; 16:1-10).*

I left home for the bus station at five o'clock on Monday morning. Strangely enough, there was no straight shot transportation from Takoradi to Saltpond. I boarded the bus going toward Cape Coast with the intention of catching the first or second bus from Cape Coast to Saltpond.

When the Takoradi bus arrived in Cape Coast, the early bus heading towards Saltpond was almost full. Hurriedly, I ran for the last seat behind the driver. Just as we were about to leave, an elderly guy appeared from nowhere and stood in front of the bus and yelled out, "Driver, stop. I say stop. I want my daughter out!"

The driver was angry, but the old man didn't even care. He walked to me, and looking straight into my eyes, he said, "Daughter, come out of the bus, and give your seat to this guy standing here behind me."

I don't even know him, how can I be his daughter? I reflected. I said to him, "Please, I'm really late for school."

"Yes, I know, but it doesn't matter. You'll get another bus soon," he said. "Just come out and give your seat to this young guy." He looked too serious to argue with.

Having learned from childhood not to argue with elderly persons, I obeyed. Yet, when the bus pulled off, the person to whom I gave my seat wasn't even in the bus, and the old man was nowhere to be found.

Hey, am I the only one experiencing this? I was terrified. I stood there wondering what might be going on. Time passed, and there was still no bus to Saltpond. A few minutes later, news came that the early bus that I missed had been involved in an accident and many were dead. The bus collided with an un-coming truck.

Unbelievable! I was sobbing and shaking for the loss of lives. But I was grateful to the Lord for His love and protection. I lifted up my eyes to the sky and whispered, "Thank you, Daddy, for sparing my life." Out of the blue, a hand touched my shoulder gently and someone whispered into my ears, "Hurry! The next bus is ready to leave."

I turned around and there was no one, but there was a bus loading for Saltpond. It scared my pants off! I ran to the bus, still looking around for any strange manifestation, and we left. A few miles away from town, the driver lost control of the vehicle, and bumped into the rear of a parked gas tanker. As smoke began to fill the air, everyone became paranoid, struggling and breaking windows for a way out—fearing the possibility of the bus bursting into flames.

I tried to push up the window on my side to no avail. My mind went blank. I sat and sobbed, head bowed. Although I wasn't afraid to die, I wondered why I was encountering all those things within a day.

While I was contemplating on what had just happened, I heard an unexpected bang on the side of my window. I lifted up my head. Standing there by the side of the window was a handsome middle-aged man, dressed in white African attire. He was beaming up at me with a smile that lit his entire being. My window was opened as well.

"This is strange. Who opened the window?"

Without answering my question, the man said to me, "Hurry, I'll help you out through the window." He looked cool and confident. There was something about him that gave me a sense of calmness and assurance.

I stepped on the seat, and with the help of the strange man, I got out without a scratch. Now, with the stranger's hand clasped in mine, and tears dripping down my cheeks, I bowed as a sign of respect and said to him, "Thank you, Sir! Thank you very much for helping me out."

His kind eyes pierced into my heart as if he whispered to me, *"You are too special and cherished to be neglected."* He was so sweet and loving, it cut through my soul. It seemed he understood my heart even though I wasn't talking. He took my hand and walked me to the curb where a blue and yellow taxicab was waiting. "Board this one," he said. "It's going straight to Saltpond. You are in safe hands."

How did he know I was heading toward Saltpond? I wondered, trembling.

Then the driver of the cab said to me, "Sis, your suitcase is already in the trunk. Hurry up and let's go. It's getting late. We have a lot of work to do today."

Oh my! How did he identify my suitcase among the many? That was frightening. Now, I turned to wave goodbye to my helper, but he was nowhere to be found. "Where did the other guy go?" I asked the driver.

He wouldn't talk. I sat at the back, because there was another passenger in the front seat. The driver turned on the engine and we took off. The moment we took off, a cool breeze blanketed my entire body. I fell asleep in no time, which is unusual with me. I don't sleep in buses while traveling. I don't know how long I slept, but it was so soothing.

Out of the blue, I heard, "Hello Sis, we're here."

I woke up abruptly, got down, and breathed a deep sigh of relief. *We're already in Saltpond at the Bible school?* I looked around and wondered, *how did he know I going to the School?*

I got out of the car, walked as if I was drunk to the back of the car to take my suitcase. The driver tapped me on the shoulder and said. "Your suitcase is sitting on the lawn."

"Oh, thank you very much. But wait for the fare!"

"No problem, thanks for riding with us. The man who brought you to the taxi paid for it." He gave me a big smile and waved goodbye.

I was still looking and waving my hand in amazement at what I had just experienced. Mysteriously, I felt as if someone splashed something on my face. I tried to wipe it out. By the time I opened my eyes, the cab was gone. This was like the flash of a lightning bolt.

Am I day-dreaming or becoming insane? It set me to think. I picked up my suitcase and stared at the road for a while and walked away praising the Lord for His deliverance.

On the way to my dorm, I contemplated all the events that had taken place since I met Geoffrey including the opposition from Grandma and her death and the powerful deliverances and interventions. *Could that be God's way of showing me how involved He is in the affairs of His people?* But *who was the old man who kept me from being killed in the first accident?* I don't know. *Who was the white-gowned man who lifted me up from the bus? Who was the driver of the cab who brought me to Saltpond and disappeared?* I had no clue. Only Heaven knew.

I couldn't figure it out. I broke down into tears, because I couldn't help it. They were grateful tears in praise of God's amazing love and grace for me. I felt so blessed and cherished. It was evident that the Lord had great plans for my life. King David wrote,

I will bless the LORD at all times; His praise shall continually be in my mouth. My soul shall make its boast in the LORD; the humble shall hear of it and be glad. Oh, magnify the LORD with me, and let us exalt His name together. I sought the LORD, and He heard me, and delivered me from all my fears. They looked to Him and were radiant, and their faces were not ashamed. This poor man cried out, and the LORD heard him, and saved him out of all his troubles. The angel of the LORD encamps all around those who fear Him, and delivers them (Psalms 34:1-7).

God's promise of protection to a child of His is not obsolete. It is an everyday reality. Someone wrote, "In daylight or in the darkness, I have no need to fear; I know that I'm protected by angels hovering near." When you honor God, He will preserve your life. God always intervenes and brings deliverances to those who are His. I definitely received a big dose of miraculous interventions and was touched by angels.

Later that evening, I went to show my engagement ring to the Principal and all the missionaries. They were so excited and praised the Lord with us. We began to pray for the appropriate date for the wedding.

Miraculously, the Lord met all the needs we presented to Him. He used Friends and missionaries to make our wedding such a beautiful success. On the 30th of July 1977, the Lord joined Geoffrey and me at Evangel Assemblies of God church, Accra, for His glory. The Lord proved to us He was the Programmer, the Organizer, and the Provider of our wedding. That was the main reason we sang and dedicated this song to Him on our wedding day.

Unto Him be glory in the Church,
For now and ever more
Unto Him be glory in the Church,
For now and ever more
Unto Him, Unto, Him, Unto Him, Unto Him,
Unto Him be glory in the Church
For now and ever more

We also sealed our solemn vows to each other with the second song of our choice found in the book of Ruth 1:16-17. *"Don't urge me to leave you or to turn back from you. Where you go I will go, and where you stay I will stay. Your people will be my people and your God my God. Where you die I will die, and there I will be buried. May the Lord deals with me, be it ever so severely, if anything but death separates you and me."*

Geoffrey and I bonded like twins. I'm told that we were fun to watch. We were really a-match made in Heaven and shipped to Earth. Our marital life was like a Cinderella story. And in no time, the Lord blessed us with four sons—Jim-Kessler Mawuto (God's property), Scott Mawugnigan (God is great), Samuel Mawuena (God's Gift), and Othniel Edem (He has delivered me).

My life's story continued to unfold when I met the sweetheart of my life, Geoffrey Kwame Tomtania, not knowing that he also had a story to tell the world. However, with both of us in the ministry, the battle had not become easier, because our number one enemy was still alive and well on earth. His agents began to terrorize us wherever we went, even the innocent children the Lord gave u

Monica Tomtania - Spiritual Terrorism

144

[15]

GEOFFREY'S STORY

As for Geoffrey, his paternal grandpa was a powerful witch doctor. Not a "small one" such as we normally defined the witch doctors in our African expression. He was a threat to all the other witch doctors and priests in Niamtougou, Togo. He could appear and disappear at will while others looked on. He also travelled in the realm of the spirit to do havoc, casting spells on his enemies. And he boasted about his powers all the time.

Geoffrey's grandpa desired that one of his grandchildren succeed him. He chose Geoffrey because he was the oldest son. And so at the age of 5, Geoffrey was refused education and sent to the village to learn the art of being a witch doctor. Geoffrey's grandpa began a step-by-step initiation of his grandson into the demonic, but Geoffrey wasn't very happy.

"I didn't like it. I just wanted to be with my parents in Ghana," said Geoffrey. He desired to attend school and become a medical doctor. But in the meantime, there was no possible way out. He had to become an apprentice fetish priest.

Geoffrey said to me one day, "Darling, to be a witch doctor was a risky spiritual journey for a child. It was really frightening as well as fascinating. I could hear demons talking to my grandfather. I would see piles of broom sticks stand up and walk as humans, speaking and prophesying the future of seekers. The display of the demonic was too scary to look at. I was scared all the time. But somehow, I felt there was someone Bigger with me. I guess God was protecting me from being possessed."

Geoffrey's parents were then in Ghana, but he was stuck with the Grandfather in Togo until he turned ten.

"I had been praying, 'Oh God, if you are really alive, let my dad come and visit. I want to go back to Ghana and go to school. I don't want to be a witch doctor,'" Geoffrey told me. "But not long after that, my father came to visit. I shouted with joy, 'Oh God, you are truly alive. Now, show me what to do in order to go with my father.'"

Geoffrey's father was supposed to leave the following day after his two-week stay. So Geoffrey formulated a plan. He hid in the bus his father had boarded back to Ghana. It was a surprise when Papa Thomas, Geoffrey's dad, saw his son at the other side of the Ghana border.

"Kwame (Geoffrey's middle name), what are you doing here? Are you crazy?" He fussed and scolded him for a while, because he couldn't send Geoffrey back on a 600-kilometer journey alone to Niamtougou. Papa Thomas had to resume work the next day. So he took Geoffrey to Accra, Ghana. Geoffrey was ten years at the time he went back to Ghana with the father. And here is the rest of Geoffrey's story in his own words.

"As long as I was with Grandpa, I was alright and never sick. But I began to encounter serious attacks when I revolted and followed my father to Ghana," said Geoffrey. "But my journey into spiritual terrorism actually began when I turned eleven. The night the first attack came, I was fast asleep. Suddenly, I felt as if someone was yanking my skin off my body. An evil hand pressed through my chest to literally pull my heart out. The evil presence in the room was terrifying. I began to scream for help, but no one could hear me. My own voice echoed back to me.

Then I heard an ugly voice echoing in the room. It sounded like that of my grandfather, but even deeper than his. 'You cannot run away from me, Kwame. You signed a contract with me. You are mine.'

I knew I was in trouble, and I could die any moment if no one came to my rescue. I knew who my grandpa was. He'd traveled in the spirit to kill me, because I deserted him. I gasped for breath, 'Oh God, help me,' I cried. At that moment, I heard the weirdest and frightening growl in the dark. 'Well, Kwame, I will come back again, and this time you will either serve me or die.'

I woke up feverish, sweating profusely, and shaking out of control. My dad came to me and said, 'Kwame, I know what is happening to you. It's my father who wants to kill you. I will also fight him if he does.'

I was scared to death. I became sick for days. That begun a series of spiritual terror attacks that almost took away my life until I gave my life to Jesus at the age of thirteen. And even then, the attacks came in bits and pieces, because the devil does not retire. But I really thank God for His protective care.

Now, the work the Lord called me to do after college was even much higher and nobler than being a witch doctor. I have become a representative of the Most High God, invading the kingdom of the enemy and snatching souls from the pit of darkness in Jesus Name.

After secondary school, I worked with the National Bureau of Statistic, working with the huge computers called IBM. I had received a full scholarship from the

Massachusetts State University, United States, to attend Medical School. I was working to save money for my flight. While I was traveling to Abidjan to visit with one of my uncles and leave from there to the U.S., the Lord spoke to me and said, 'Kwame, why are you running away from Me? You have a higher calling to proclaim My Word to the lost. I will make you a guiding light that will bring many souls into My kingdom if you obey Me?'

I turned around, came back to Accra and resigned from my job. Everyone thought I was going crazy. But soon after that, Brazilian Missionaries, Kemuel and Pedro, came to Ghana, and with my French background, I was able to work with them and assist them in interpretation, because there are a lot of similarities in Portuguese and French. By God's grace, we pioneered six churches in no time before I decided to attend Bible school. I should have gone to the Bible school earlier, but I think the Lord was preparing me to meet Monica, my better half, hence the delay." (End of Geoffrey's testimony).

[16]

ANKAMU—MY FIRST PASTORAL EXPERIENCE

We took off from Accra after our one-week "so-to-say honeymoon" at the Mission Guest House to Ankamu, a village where Geoffrey was assigned to. This new pastorate became the ministry training ground for me. The first impression I had of the place was about convenience. I had become used to having a toilet inside our compound and not having to go somewhere to take a shower or go to the bathroom. But our all-in-one bedroom in Ankamu had nothing like that, no luxury at all. Even the bed the church bought for Geoffrey before we got married caved in and fell underneath us. We giggled over it many times.

"Hey Darling, where is the bedroom stuff you said you left in Accra when you were pastoring the church in North Kaneshie?" I asked, just trying to make fun of Geoffrey.

"I gave them to Sam Owuba," Geoffrey responded. "He was my spiritual son, and he got married before I did. So I gave him all my stuff."

"And you've brought your sweet heart to sleep on this yoyo bed?"

"Don't worry. Our end will be better than our beginning."

"Amen, I receive it."

I had visited Geoffrey once at this Church after our engagement, and I had a little notion of what Ankamu was going to be at least. Geoffrey did tell me a little bit about the suffering he was enduring in that village before our wedding, but I took it lightly. It was worse!

Surprise, Surprise!

Surprisingly, the first week of October, I found out I was expecting. In our finite minds, we'd tried to take all the precautions and pieces of advice given to us by our spiritual counselors, the Kesslers. But to our surprise, yet not God's, none of the precautions actually worked. I was very excited, because a medical doctor in Cape Coast told Geoffrey and me before our wedding that I wasn't going to have children.

Through an unknown angel, the Lord had promised me four boys at the age of 16, when I was with my older sister Flora. This was nine years later. The Word of the Lord is always true and trustworthy. But none of His promises became a reality without great challenges and near-death experiences.

As said earlier, my joy was so full, because the Lord had proven the doctor in Cape Coast wrong. But the complication of my first pregnancy was beyond my strength.

The three months we stayed at the Bible school was like hell for me. I was horribly sick to my stomach. Nothing could stay in my stomach and no medicine gave me relief. I was left with only a skeleton. And though it was really hard for me, I was determined to finish the school year.

The month of November was the most critical month in which I needed a miracle from the Lord. But God in His providence brought the McCormicks to visit the school.

I had gone weeks without food or water. I was very much dehydrated and weak. I stayed in our room, sick and tired of being sick. As I watched Geoffrey leave the room that morning, I felt in my heart he wasn't going to come back to find his sweet darling alive. It was with much pain he left the room after prayer, hoping for a miracle to take place.

Soon after, something strange began to happen to me. I felt I was drifting away to eternity. All of a sudden, my feet became very cold, and it moved from my feet up to my waist, while my heartbeat became weaker and weaker.

Suddenly, a bright light shone through the room. I saw my spirit coming out of my body, following the light as it became bigger and bigger. I knew I was no longer on the earth. Then I heard a call coming from afar: "Monica, come out from the grave and live!" It sounded like a rumbling thunder. The light projected me back to where I was lying. I began to breathe again. I knew the Lord was touching me.

You have to understand that Rev. McCormick was blind. He was a World War II veteran, who was shot through his temples and had since been blind. Yet, the Holy Spirit revealed to him that I was dying and used him to come to our room and call me out of the dead. Rev. McCormick was the brother-in-law of Miss Peggy Scott from Green Cove, Florida.

This was the fourth time I was snatched from the dead. Thank God, His grace kept and sustained me till we left Saltpond.

A Hard Life

Here in Ankamu began the struggles and hard times we never dreamed of having to go through. Our first problem was with a landlady opposite us who allowed us to use her outdoor toilet. Geoffrey accepted her offer willingly because of me, knowing I came from a different background. But after two weeks, the lady went against us. She told us we couldn't use her place anymore.

That wasn't a problem. I had vowed to the Lord not to ever complain about whatever He gave us and wherever He might lead us. A little "luxury" had been taken away from us, but it wasn't going to be a problem. We found ways and means to provide ourselves with a little bit of comfort.

There was another bathhouse by us, which had no door. So, we invented ourselves a door with one of my African wrappers. We enjoyed it as we took turns to hold the wrapper for each other to take our baths. Then when the need arose for one of us to see "the old man" (toilets), we strolled with our cutlass into the farms by the roadside, and dug holes for our convenience and covered it up. Anyway it was Biblical to do that.

> *Also you shall have a place outside the camp, where you may go out; and you shall have an implement among your equipment, and when you sit down outside, you shall dig with it and turn and cover your refuse. For the LORD your God walks in the midst of your camp, to deliver you and give your enemies over to you; therefore your camp shall be holy, that He may see no unclean thing among you, and turn away from you (Deuteronomy 23:12-14).*

The only problem was when the call came at night. It was hard to answer because of snakes. Not only did we lack the necessary convenient facilities, we also began to fight every blessed day with demonic forces in the village. These battles came in different forms. Sometimes they came through contaminated food, such as ordinary bread, corn bread, corn meals, and charcoals. Although it was a great challenge to our faith, we stood strong. The Bible states,

> *Be alert and of sober mind. Your enemy the devil prowls around like a roaring lion looking for someone to devour. Resist him, standing firm in the faith, because you know that the family of believers throughout the world is undergoing the same kind of sufferings. And the God of all grace, who called you to His eternal glory in Christ, after you have suffered a little while, will Himself restore you and make you strong, firm and steadfast. To Him be the power forever and ever. Amen (1 Peter 5:8-11).*

One particular time, the enemy disguised his attack through a bag of charcoal brought to us as a gift, which almost killed me. We were really in need of it, because we used coal pots to cook. I got up the next morning stronger and healthier than ever to make fire to prepare oatmeal Auntie Esther had brought to us. The moment I lit the fire, I felt as if someone was pouring liquid fire over my head. I did not understand it at first. Geoffrey called me into the room and prayed over me, but it did not stop until I finished cooking and turned the fire off.

Whenever I poured kerosene on the charcoal and lit it, I would literally feel as if I was burning myself up. From the crown of my head to the tip of my toes, it felt as if I was turned into a living charcoal. I could be sitting in the room, yet I would feel the heat in my bones. Then it went to Geoffrey. Both of us began to feel the heat anytime I lit the fire.

At first, we did not know that it was the charcoal until the Lord spoke to me about it. We exercised faith, prayed over the charcoal to neutralize all demonic connection, poured the blood of Jesus over it, but it did not work until we got rid of it. The day we threw the bag of charcoal away, we all felt okay.

How could that happen to us? Up till today, I still do not understand why the Lord permitted certain things to happen to us in that village. We weren't living in sin. I was a virgin before we married, and we were on fire for the Lord. We may not have all the answers to all our questions in life, yet we must trust Him without wavering.

I remember the fresh baked hot corn breads (boodoo), which another lady brought to us one evening. We had no food and should have eaten it the same night, but we didn't feel led to eat it.

We decided to go to bed hungry at the prompting of the Holy Spirit than to eat something that could destroy us. We placed the two oven-fresh boodoo in a bowl, covered it up and left it under my small kitchen table. By the next morning, worms were popping out and dancing everywhere.

Imagine what would have happened had we eaten! We would have suffered from a disease no doctor would have been able to diagnose, and we may have died. Demonic worms would have eaten us alive. Who knew?

I can still remember the day we woke up one morning to find out that the two little chickens we brought from Accra, which weren't grown enough to lay eggs, had already two eggs under them that night, as if they had laid magical eggs. Supernatural, isn't it? We understood the deal. The witches and wizards were trying every means possible to destroy us.

Later on, we learned that the witches in the village had vowed that we would run away from the village or they would bury one of us. No church or their pastors, with the exception of the

Catholics, had been able to survive in that particular village. Yet none of these problems shook us, for we knew the Lord had promised never to leave us nor forsake us. The Bible says,

> *All who rage against you will surely be ashamed and disgraced; those who oppose you will be as nothing and perish. Though you search for your enemies, you will not find them. Those who wage war against you will be as nothing at all. For I am the Lord, your God, who takes hold of your right hand and says to you, 'Do not fear; I will help' (Isaiah 41:11-13).*

The Dirtiest Attack

Another funny attack happened one Friday morning. We were supposed to attend the Friday early morning-prayer meeting at five. We woke up at four to pray. Geoffrey wanted to go out and urinate. I felt led to give him the chamber pot I had been using every night since we were denied access to the in-premise toilet.

Afterwards, Geoffrey said, "Darling, I have an uneasy feeling in my spirit. I want us to stay in and pray instead of going to the church. I believe Mr. Arhin, one of the deacons, will lead the prayer."

That's unusual with Geoffrey. He was a faithful and a passionate leader. We stayed indoors and prayed for the church. At about seven, we heard the screaming of people behind our door. Then a knock, bang, bang on our window!

"Who is it?" Geoffrey asked.

"Pastor, it is me."

We recognized the voice of Mr. Arhin. He had come with a few of the members who came to the prayer meeting to check on us. Geoffrey was about to open the door when Mr. Arhin shouted, "Pastor, please don't come out. There is something strange in front of your door."

"What is that?"

"Something really strange, and you don't want to know it. I will explain it to you later. Permit us to clean it up first. Then I will tell you what that thing was."

Mr. Arhin and the members prayed so loud that the neighbors surrounded the house. They were praying in the Spirit and cleaning at the same time. We had no clue as to what the strange thing was. However, when they began to clean up, we got the message. The unpleasant smell that was seeping through the door into our room was very bad. Anyway, we kept our noses covered with the sheets until they were done. Finally, when we opened the door, we understood Mr. Arhin's message. We had to leave the house for a while.

According to those who were cleaning up, witches had come in the middle of the night and eased themselves in front of the house, placed eggs, needles, and little pieces of their juju stuff in the feces and left. Their intentions were to kill us, especially the first person who would step into the feces. They were agents of the devil. But God was with us. We weren't scared. Rather, we prayed unceasingly for mighty breakthroughs, for discernment and protection, and He was with us.

The most interesting part of this journey was that the Holy Spirit began to reveal all their demonic plots to us. The same mighty hand that had guided us earlier and performed miracle after miracle before He joined us together was unwavering. The Lord was faithful, so we depended on Him for protection, for provision, and strength to continue in the ministry. We also knew He'd never failed us and He didn't.

Not only were we battling spiritual forces we were at war with bad economy and food shortage. There was famine season in Ghana, and staple foods were rationed. It was very difficult to lay hands on food, and for a pregnant woman, it was unbearable. I tried to drink much water just to satisfy my hunger. And sometimes, it felt as if I was going to pass out.

The 35cedis (Maybe $10) salary could not take us up to two weeks since we had to buy everything. Thus, the Lord in His providence gave us a piece of farmland on the road to Gomoa Assin. We planted cassava (manioc), corn, and vegetables, and peppers.

Unfortunately, we weren't the only ones who were hungry. Nature was too. I remember the times when Geoffrey would get up early morning after prayer to check on the farm, hoping to find some cassava, or corn and was disappointed, because the squirrels and grass-cutters had already made their trips. We made fun of it and laughed, but it wasn't easy at all.

The fate of Geoffrey was also weighing heavily on me when I would watch him wrench in pain because of the ulcers in his stomach. Hunger left him tired and weak. It became as if both of us were dying gradually with stomach ulcers. Even though it was very hard for us, the Lord always used other means to meet our needs. Many times the Lord would speak to friends like Brother Essilfie Turkson and his wife Deborah of Accra to come to our aid.

Often times, we became overwhelmed by all the malicious acts of witchdoctors and our own lack of necessities. In all these insurmountable problems, we were never discouraged. We continued to go about our Father's business.

The hard life and the great sacrifice in the ministry, coupled with the pregnancy and the spiritual warfare were taking a toll on me. I still recall the day when I had a horrifying dream in which I was fighting with terrible fearful beasts. In the fight, the Lord showed me the face of one of the ladies we knew in Saltpond. She had transformed herself into one of the beasts, trying to remove the baby out from my womb.

Still in the dream, a small voice told me to be careful when that particular woman paid us a visit, or else the baby could be aborted. *She is not part of our family, and we haven't invited her. Why will she come and visit us?* I asked myself when I woke up.

With my health already going downhill, Geoffrey didn't take the dream seriously, thinking I was hallucinating or maybe having nightmares because of my constant fever. My dreams usually came true if care was not taken, no matter what I was battling with.

It was a Friday morning, when someone knocked at our door. When I opened the door, I saw the most incredible thing. Standing there, was the very woman the Lord had spoken to me about. She had brought us the very items I saw in my dream—cassava, plantain, different kinds of vegetables, and smoked fish.

The moment I took the bag of food, my heart began to pound. I thanked her and gently dropped the bag on our kitchen floor. Then I went in to the room to pray. There and then, the Lord spoke to me clearly, *"Monica, do not to eat any of the food she brought. That is a demonic provision to destroy you."*

The temptation to fix some of the food was too strong to resist. I couldn't refuse to go along with Geoffrey when he said we could pray over it in Jesus' name, and consume it. Of course, we didn't even have a cup of rice at home. We were so hungry that we forgot about the past miracles and breakthroughs we'd seen. We followed our desires blindly thinking the Lord was going to protect us. We prayed fervently and poured all the blood of Jesus on it for protection and sanctification and cooked some of the foodstuff.

A few minutes after lunch, we began to experience fever chills. By 4 p.m., I was sicker than Geoffrey, having contractions. Geoffrey advised me to take one painkiller, but nothing seemed to work. The whole night was a nightmare to Geoffrey, because there was no way he could take me to the hospital at Apam.

We had no car and no money. We prayed and cried all night for forgiveness, and by morning I was healed. We threw the rest of the food away that morning, and the peace of God came back to us.

Our disobedience reminded me of the prophet who was sent to Samaria. The Lord gave him specific instructions—not to eat anything in that city, and to return by a different route. When he disobeyed, he suffered the consequences, death. (Please, read I Kings 13). Unbelievably, the dream almost happened exactly as I had seen it, had it not been for the mercies of God. Obedience is really better than sacrifice in all ways!

God being so merciful and good, Auntie Esther visited us from Accra the same week we threw the demonic provisions away. She brought more than a month's supply of food, even more than what the lady brought to us.

Isn't God faithful? Yes, He is! But satan will always counterfeit God's provision to destroy God's children. He did it with Pharaoh's magicians. He did it with the old prophet who brought in the man of God who spoke against King Jeroboam in Samaria. Satan tried to distract the Lord Jesus in the desert at His weakest moment, and he is more than willing to use the same tactic again and again on any desperate soul.

God will always warn His servants of on-coming dangers. We will avoid many troubles if we'll pay serious attention to His voice, the dreams and revelations He gives us. Many times, we Christians always forget that when God warns us about something and we disobey, we remove ourselves from His protective care. To me, it was the mercy and the power of God that kept me and my baby safe that day.

Divine Provision

One spectacular miraculous provision the Lord brought to us left us talking about it for years. We weren't able to eat a regular meal the night before, because we had only a small loaf of bread and one small can of Peak evaporated milk left. We used the little Ovaltine left and made us hot chocolate and went to bed, praying the Lord for the next provision to come.

We got up at four as usual to pray and went to join the saints at church for the normal morning-prayer at five. Coming back from church, I told Geoffrey how hungry I was and reminded him of not having any food at home.

"Sorry, Darling," Geoffrey said. "I wish there was something I could do to help."

"I know," I said. "We haven't had Mama Sarah's roasted cassava and peanuts for a while."

"I think she is very tired."

Mama Sarah was the 85-year-old lady in the church. She was like Anna in the Bible and the only generous giver among the congregants, but she was really poor. Now she was getting really tired. Her husband was about 88, and they lived just behind the church.

We could have asked some members, whom we knew could help us, but the Holy Spirit restrained us. He had, many times spoken to us to depend on Him wholly for provision, because He is our Source, and that we should never ever beg for bread.

We went home, knowing that the whole day was going to be one of those days we fasted by force. I thought the Lord must show up or else I could faint. We drank water from morning to about 12:30 in the afternoon. I was okay but weak for being pregnant without food for two days. And above all, we did not even have the money to go for a maternity check-up. We prayed believing the Lord would perform another miracle again and again that day.

Suddenly, we heard a car honking. When it honked the first time, we did not think it was for us, but when it honked for a while, I felt it might be for us. Geoffrey was still on his knees, so I walked outside to check on the honker.

Oh my goodness, the honker was a brother we knew from Cape Coast Assembly, Mr. Nzole. He knew where we lived, but He'd never been to our house before.

"Darling, it is Brother Nzole. Please, come out," I called out to Geoffrey.

Brother Nzole beckoned me to hurry. As I walked to welcome the brother, Geoffrey came out. When the brother opened his trunk, I almost fainted with joy. It was filled with what we'd asked the Lord that day—canned salmon, mackerel, sardines, milk, Ovaltine, sugar, rice, bread and etc.

"Wow, a surprise from God," we all screamed. "How did you know we were praying for a miracle?" Geoffrey asked him.

"I got up this morning with you on my mind," he said. "I prayed for you and went to work, but the Holy Spirit wouldn't take you off my mind. I prayed and asked Him what He wanted me to do. He spoke to my heart to bring you food. So I went and got few things, and I want to give you some money so that you can buy whatever you need later on."

"Oh Lord, thank you very much," we all exclaimed. "It is not enough, but I hope to be a blessing to you as long as the Lord gives me grace. May God bless you in the work you are doing for His glory," Brother Nzole said.

"Not enough? You don't know what that means to us."

We prayed a blessing over him, and our angel friend and Brother in Christ drove back on more than a thirty-five-mile journey to work that same day. Before leaving, he left us with a sum of money, which kept us for at least three more weeks. *Oh, how much He cares!*

Brother Nzole came all the way from Cape Coast to Gomoa Ankamu in obedience to the Holy Spirit to bring us provision. The wonder of this miracle came from the Lord through a willing vessel, who desired to listen and to obey. That is what true dedication to the Lord is.

We hauled the miraculous provision into the room and sat down to thank God for His extraordinary provision. We worshipped the Lord and jumped on it right away, like hungry bears to munch on the bread.

Through it all, our ministry in Ankamu became successful and we opened three annexes within the same year. Geoffrey preached in English and I interpreted, because the dialect of the people Ankamu was similar to mine. We walked miles to minister in neighboring villages and won souls for Christ. We labored faithfully with the Lord until the Lord asked us to move to Togo.

[17]

A MIRACLE CHILD

We arrived at Ankamu very much depleted, and so I became sick again. Now being in Ankamu with all its challenges had left me weak and pale. I was already in my 6th month with lots of challenges. My stomach wasn't protruding much at this time, but I became weaker and weaker as the days went by.

I thought I wasn't going to live to see my baby born. I prayed earnestly, asking the Lord to make my life a miracle for others to know Him. It was within that week of asking Him to spare my life that the Lord spoke to me in a dream. He said, "Monica, I am renewing My call to you and Geoffrey to move to Togo, but Geoffrey doesn't want to go. I have been dealing with him since. If he doesn't obey Me, I will take you home to be with Me, and Geoffrey will have to go to Togo alone. "

"What? Please, Lord, that can't be possible. I am willing to obey You no matter what."

"Yes, I know. But I will take you home with me if Geoffrey doesn't obey the call. The plan I have for both of you is bigger than what he is seeing right now."

I woke up terrified. I wept and prayed for a while before I told Geoffrey. When I narrated the dream to him, he became even more frightened than I was. He assured me he will give it a second thought, because he loved me very much and was not willing to sacrifice me. Even then, he continued to argue with the Lord like Moses, until my condition worsened.

All of a sudden, I began to experience contractions one morning. I felt I was going to lose the baby. We prayed and rushed to the hospital in Apam, but they did not know what to do for me. The doctor told Geoffrey point blank that I would lose that baby within few days. The only option he gave to us was to admit me at the hospital, but the hospital had neither ultra-sound nor any other necessary equipment to check to know what the problem was. So I refused to stay.

Interestingly, the Lord had already spoken to Geoffrey not to allow the hospital to admit me. "He said that if I did, you would die," Geoffrey told me.

This was a Wednesday. In the back of my mind, I confessed our sins of disobedience, standing upon His promises for a complete miracle. I knew this was happening because of Geoffrey's unwillingness to accept the call to Togo.

My condition worsened moment after moment. I was in much pain and agony. Geoffrey could not go anywhere. He stayed by my side, fasting and praying for a miracle.

On Saturday night, March 24th, 1978, I became unconscious. This fatal night, Geoffrey was kneeling by the bed. He did not know I was out of my body watching him. The entire room was filled with a bright light. I stood there looking at him as he wept before the Lord. He got up and tried to talk to me, but I was gone. He began to cry, asking the Lord to forgive him for refusing to obey the call.

I did not know what happened next. The only thing I can still recall was when I sneezed and came back to myself. This miracle happened at about two o'clock that Sunday afternoon. Geoffrey told me what happened with tears.

"Darling, at about 7 p.m. on Saturday, I felt something had gone wrong. Koffi Abban, our newest convert, came and joined us to pray. (Koffi Abban is now one of the pastors of the Assemblies of God in Ghana). We prayed till midnight, and he left for his house. When he left, I examined you, and felt no life in you. You were not breathing. I rolled you over and began to clean you up. Still there was no sign of life in my Darling. You were gone.

"I knew I was in big trouble, but I refused to be defeated. That was the time I began to repent of my doubt. I cried and begged the Lord to spare your life and bring you back to life. I told the Lord I was going to obey Him and go to Togo if He brought you back. Peace began to flood my soul. I knew the Lord answered my prayers, yet you were still the same by daybreak.

"I needed to preach that morning. So I cleaned you up, locked the door, and left for church. No one knew what was really happening. When I came back, you were still unconscious with no sign of life. You were cold. I knew you were dead, but I continued my plea before the Lord.

Suddenly, at about 1 p.m., I felt a deep calm and peace in the room. The presence of the Lord became so tangible. I began to praise the Lord for answering my prayers. At 2.10 prompt, I sensed life coming back in you, because you became warm. As I continued to praise the Lord, you began to breathe, and then sneezed three times. Praise God! I got my miracle back. Now, I am going to Togo."

The Lord spared my life but not without complication. I felt as if my stomach had been divided into two, upper and lower cases. I could still feel the movement of the baby on the upper part, but it was too close to my heart, and different from the usual all over movement. Then I could feel a terrible heaviness on my pelvic area. It felt as if I had two babies in my tummy, one moving close to my heart, and the other as dead and heavy as a rock, but there was no way I or the doctors could know what was happening. It was painful and pathetic.

No more wasting of time, and no more false sacrifice. We were ready to answer the call. The following week, we gave our resignation to the church, and began the preparation to leave Ghana for the mission field in Togo.

Our resignation was a big shock to the congregation, especially the new converts, and the elderly folks. Many of them came to us after the service to convince us not to leave, having thought we resigned because of hardships. We made it clear to them that it wasn't hardship, but the Lord was leading us to the country of Togo. In order to retain us now by all means, the church board met and surprisingly opted to give us a raise of salary from 50 cedis to 150 cedis overnight. A hundred and fifty percent increase in just a week?

Within that same week, three other churches: Cape Coast Assembly, Evangel Assembly and Dansoman Assembly, gave us a call to become their pastors. Not only that, mails and calls began to flood in from many of our dear friends. And even some of the missionaries who knew Geoffrey very well, tried to persuade us from going down to Togo.

Some of our minister friends even fasted and prayed for the Lord to discourage us from going to Togo. Late pastors, Alex Nortey, Franklin Nti, and Isaac Sam of Saltpond, and many others, fasted and prayed diligently for us to stay in Ghana. I guess they did not know the mind of God. Even, Papa Klottey, one of the deacons from Evangel Assembly, sent us a letter, promising us of his full financial support in the ministry and for us to become their pastor at the Evangel Assembly of God, Accra. He also promised us full scholarship at the West African Advanced School of Theology, if we would reject the idea of going to Togo.

When all the notes and letters were coming in, the Lord reminded us of Pharaoh's compromise when He commanded Moses to let His people leave Egypt. I knew in my heart that all these friends meant well. Their appeals and offers were from their hearts, but they were the baits of the enemy to keep us out of God's will, and I believe Geoffrey knew better.

We did not have the money, or necessary support we needed in the ministry from any church or individuals. Yet we determined, like Moses of old, to suffer doing the will of God rather than living in wealth outside His will. We have put our hands on the plough, and weren't going to look back.

A month before we moved finally to Togo, we traveled to Accra where Geoffrey left me with Auntie Esther. Geoffrey went ahead and traveled to Togo to meet with the General Superintendent, Rev. Pasgo Bila, who assured us of a church at Tabligbo. I was so excited about Tabligbo since I could not speak French or the native dialects of Togo.

After negotiating with Mr. Koffi Nkum, one of the church members, who owned lots of mini-buses, he offered us a cheaper ride to Togo. In the middle of May 1978, we finally made our way there with all our belongings, nothing left behind. We were about 20 miles to the border when the driver told us he didn't possess international driver's license for neither himself nor the mini-bus. It is not easy to cross African borders without international driver's license. One must be prepared to either give a bribe, and we weren't willing to do any of that.

We stopped the bus for a moment and prayed. At that moment, the Holy Spirit whispered to my heart and said, "Monica, watch and see if I will not give you this miracle also. You will cross this border with no problem to prove that I am the One sending you to Togo."

I told Geoffrey and the driver what the Lord said. They were encouraged. Then I remembered the story of the Apostle Paul on his journey to Rome. Though there were storms and difficulties along his path, the angel of the Lord appeared to Paul and encouraged him to go on.

> *For there stood by me this night an angel of the God to whom I belong and whom I serve, saying, 'Do not be afraid, Paul; you must be brought before Caesar; and indeed God has granted you all those who sail with you.' Therefore take heart, men, for I believe God that it will be just as it was told me (Acts 27:23-25).*

I wasn't surprised when we drove through the border without a problem. The presence of the Lord was so tangible. I felt as if He came to sit on the driver's seat and drove us in to the land of Togo Himself. No one asked us about any immigration papers. It was a free ride with Jesus. Praise God, He did it again!

Upon arrival in Lome, we were given the old guesthouse in Calvary Temple to unload our belongings, until we were sure of where we were going. Geoffrey took the driver back through the borders. And God's favor led him back to Ankamu.

We lodged at the guesthouse for three days, waiting to know where we were supposed to go but nothing was decided yet. Knowing I had no knowledge of the French language, we made a deal with the General Superintendent to allow me to go back to Tema to have the baby.

With this assurance, we decided to leave for Tema to have the baby before returning for our final move to wherever the Lord had in mind for us. A friend of ours had already opened his home for the period of stay with no charge in Tema. The baby was due in June, so with the little money friends gave us, we were able to purchase a few baby items and left for Tema.

During our stay in Tema, Geoffrey would leave sometimes for Togo to visit the church. Geoffrey returned from Togo on the 1st of June, 1978, which was a Thursday. Being tired from all the traveling, he retired that night and slept deeply as usual. The next day, we had a good conversation on all the good and bad days we'd seen in the ministry in Ankamu and giggled about it.

It was about eight at night. I was relaxing on the bed beside Geoffrey talking about the revelations the Lord had given me in his absence. I described a fight I'd had in a dream with my witch aunt and the warning I'd received not to go to the General Hospital to have the baby. We prayed against any attack of the enemy.

I said, "Darling, here we are resting in the beautiful home of Brother *Jay (name changed) and his wife!"

"That is really amazing. It is Heaven-sent," Geoffrey replied.

Just contemplating on the Lord's goodness, I asked, "What happened to Ankamu?" Anyway, we knew Tema was transitory.

"It's behind us," we said in unison. We laughed so loud, Brother Jay knocked on our door, wanting to know why we were so joyful.

Scary Moments

I wasn't having any contractions that day, but I began to feel some uneasiness and pressure under my lower abdomen. The pressure under my pelvis was so uncomfortable I decided to sit up. The moment I lifted my head up above the pillow, I felt as if something exploded out of me. It was like the blast of a dynamite, and very hot. It tore my underwear apart. I tried to gain posture, but it wasn't possible. The force of whatever exploded out of me threw me back on the bed on my back.

Geoffrey jumped out of the bed. I leaned over to see what was happening. We were really shocked. The whole room was baptized and stained with blood. The worst part of this was the humongous blood clots and flesh that had smeared everything, tainting the walls and the shelves in the room of our friends. It was very frightening.

Geoffrey tried to help me out of the bed, but I was bleeding profusely. He ran out to get help from the family. By the time they arrived, my stomach was almost flattened, as if there was no baby in my womb anymore. I became scared and felt like crying.

"Oh God, what is happening to me now?" I muttered.

"Darling, nothing bad will happen to either of you, okay?" Geoffrey said.

"I know, but look at my stomach."

Geoffrey played the man! He prayed and encouraged me. He then wrapped me with the bed sheet and helped me to the bathroom. Out of the blue, an excruciating pain took hold of me. It seized me so hard I felt like pushing. The moment I did, flesh and clots gushed out. The lady of the house told me the baby had already come out.

Meaning I had miscarried a dead baby? No! That is not possible. God hasn't brought me this far to do that to me. We rushed out to the nearest midwife. She examined me for a while, and told us she was incapable of helping me, because the problem was very serious.

"Serious?" Geoffrey asked.

"Yes, I cannot help her," she said emphatically. "Go to the General Hospital."

I knew better. We drove to all the clinics nearby, but they all turned us out without any help. By that time, I was in severe pain, exhausted, and bleeding profusely. And although I was in that serious condition, my heart was still at peace.

While we were driving away from the last clinic, I asked brother and his wife to wait for a while and pray again. The moment we began to pray, the Lord said to me, "Monica, *Go to VALCO hospital. There I will take care of you.*"

I whispered to Geoffrey, "The Lord says we should go to VALCO hospital, and He will take good care of me."

Geoffrey transmitted the message to the family, "Let's go to VALCO hospital."

"To VALCO for what?" they both argued. "Do you know anyone who works there, Pastor?"

"No. The Lord told Monica to go there, and I support her." "Don't make a fool of yourself. VALCO doesn't take strangers," the brother's wife said in frustration.

"I will not make a fool of myself," replied Geoffrey. "I know the Lord speaks to Monica. I've proven it over and over and know it is true."

"Just because you are a man of God, that's why I have to follow you to that place," Brother Jay also expressed. "And I've known Sister Monica very well, even more than you. She is a woman of God. But VALCO hospital, how?"

The couple thought I was losing my mind, knowing VALCO hospital is for the workers of the Volta River Aluminum Company and never for the public. I insisted on what the Lord told me. Finally, they all agreed, and we drove to VALCO hospital following the voice of the Lord.

As soon as we arrived, two nurses came to my side, asking whether I had ever visited the hospital prior to that day. They made it clear to us that the hospital wouldn't take care of anyone who did not have a record with them. I told the nurses that I had a record with them, but I had nothing to prove it. They turned us away.

We went back and sat at the parking lot contemplating on what I'd said the Lord told me. They really concluded I had lost it completely.

"Lord, You told us to come here, and I know You are going to glorify Your name," I mumbled a prayer to Him. "Please, show us what to do."

I was frustrated myself, but as we pondered on what to do next, the Lord spoke to me, "Monica, check in your purse. There is a VALCO card inside."

Geoffrey was holding my purse at that time. So I asked him for my purse.

"Darling, what do you want from the purse?" he asked. "Please, take it easy and I will help you with it."

"Please, the Lord just told me that I have a VALCO card in my purse," I told Geoffrey.

"True? A VALCO card in your purse? Darling, don't make a mockery of yourself again," Geoffrey whispered to me. "Brother Jay and his wife maybe thinking you are losing your mind as a result of all the things you've been through."

"Don't worry about them. I heard Him say that to me right now, please," I assured Geoffrey.

"Okay. You know I believe you, because you a woman of God, and God speaks to you."

I was more than desperate to see my baby born. I was in shock and pain. I took the purse from him and slid my hand to the side of the purse. What a surprise! I found my miracle, a VALCO maternity card. What a mighty God we serve!

We began to praise the Lord while Geoffrey ran to give the card to the nurses. As soon as they saw the card, I was rushed immediately into the intensive care unit of the maternity ward. As I lay there on the bed, I wondered if I'd ever gone to VALCO hospital. Then I remembered the precise time.

We had visited a sick brother of Auntie Esther at the VALCO hospital at the beginning of the year. And knowing I was pregnant and sick all the time, Auntie Esther had asked her cousin, who was a medical doctor at VALCO to examine me. God, who in His infinite wisdom knows the end from the beginning, programmed all those events in advance to save my life. I was amazed at how wonderful the Lord was to me.

After examining me for a while, the doctor concluded, the baby might have died earlier and been miscarried. *Miscarried a nine month-old baby? No, it is unbelievable.* I was feeling the movement of the baby that night before we retired on the bed. That's not possible. I knew my Lord hadn't brought me that far to leave me. In my heart I believed I would leave the hospital with my baby, no matter what. Although I was still bleeding and in much pain, I could still feel the butterfly movements of the baby inside me.

"Ma'am, I can feel the movement of the baby inside me," I told the midwife.

"I am not sure what it is, but we'll monitor you for a while until the doctor decides what to do with your case," she replied, without checking to confirm what I told her.

I was taken to the intensive care and given a bed to monitor my condition. Unfortunately, from that Friday night, we did not see our friends again. What happened? I don't know. We were left to ourselves. We had no car and there was no one to help us, no family member around to care for me. Geoffrey tried to bring me food at least once a day at the hospital, and he had to buy the food from vendors.

Meanwhile, Geoffrey began his normal routine of fasting and praying for God's intervention. The doctor came for his usual rounds on Monday morning. When he saw the severe pain I was in, he instructed the nurse to prepare me the next morning at 6 a.m. for surgery and then left.

That same night, at about 10 p.m., the presence of the Lord came upon me like liquid fire and enveloped me. I began to worship Him even in my pain, tears running down my face. I fell into a deep sleep for four solid hours. I had not slept for four days because of the pain. In a dream, the Lord was speaking to me about the baby in my womb. He told me I was going to have a baby boy with no problem, and that the baby was for Him.

The Lord said to me, "*Monica, every male that opens the womb is Mine. Mawuto is consecrated to My service. He is a Levite, My servant. He shall be My instrument of praise and worship for My glory. My Word will never depart from his lips. Your generation shall be blessed, because I am your inheritance.*"

There was no ultrasound then to tell the sex of the baby, but I knew he was going to be a boy because of the prophetic word I received at age 16. And now the Lord was confirming His word to me again in a dream. I woke up abruptly with severe contraction and this song on my lips.

My God is able, He's able. I know He's able
I know my God is able to carry me through
For He healed the broken hearted

And set the captives free
He healed the sick, and raised the dead
And walked upon the sea
My God is able, He's able. I know He's able I
know my God is able to carry me through

I was in labor, but I did not know how to go about it. I got up and began to walk around, but it was unbearable. The pain was so intense, I was shaken. I could neither sit nor walk. I felt the time was up, but the nurses were nowhere near me, although they were supposed to monitor me.

An older patient in the same ward with me signaled my problem to the midwives, "The young lady in my ward is going to have a baby."

"No, she is not going to have a baby. She is having another problem," they told her. "She'll go through surgery at 6 a.m."

"I say she is going to have a baby," the lady argued with the nurses. "She is in labor and you are saying what? She cannot wait for the doctor at 6."

The nurses maintained that they weren't going to come and see me, because I was going in for surgery in the morning. I believe the midwives were tired and relaxing. They didn't bother to come at once. They thought it was the same old problem, miscarried baby-syndrome. But the other patient kept on begging them to take a look at me.

"I say, take a look at her first before you decide on what to do next," the Good Samaritan insisted.

Finally, one of them came and took me to the delivery room at about 5:00. I didn't have my watch with me, because it did not take ten minutes when the baby's head began to pop out.

Their eyes were that big, I felt they did not believe I was going to have a real baby.

At about 5:15 a.m. on the 6th of June, my miracle baby boy was born. He did not cry, so I thought he wasn't alive. And the midwife stood there, astonished, mouth wide opened, watching something underneath me in amazement. I thought something was wrong with me or with my baby.

She then screamed and called out to the other nurse who was washing and sterilizing something, "Hey, look at this!" The other nurse rushed to the scene. Both of them began to shout, "Wow, the pastor's child is praying. The pastor's child is praying."

I propped my head forward to see what was happening. I was amazed myself at God's miracle. Our son was born with both hands clasped together in a prayerful mood. *Oh, how I wished Geoffrey was here to take his picture!* Anyway, God knows and bears witness of this fact! I prayed and prayed until the child in my womb also responded to its Creator in prayer. It's beyond human understanding, but it is a fact. It is the truth between my God and me. He is the Almighty One, before whom we'll all stand one day.

Geoffrey was at the beach praying at that particular time. But when he came back, he told me that he heard the voice of the Lord precisely at 2 a.m. the same time the contraction intensified telling him, "Geoffrey, it is done, begin to praise Me."

At about 5.45 a.m., I heard the voice of the doctor, yelling at the nurses to hurry up and take me to the operating theater. "Doc, she had a baby," one of the nurse said. But he wasn't listening to what they were telling him, until he entered the labor room where I was.

"What, how did it happen?" he asked the midwife.

"We don't know, Doctor," both of them said, just shaking their heads. "And the baby was born praying. I guess the Mama prayed until the baby also joined her. " They all giggled.

The doctor stood there in awe and exclaimed, "Indeed, God is wonderful!" Yes indeed, he witnessed the miracle of a faithful God.

Isn't it so wonderful to pray until the baby in your womb begins to pray too? My heart began to sing to the praise of the One who delivered both of us from death for His goodness towards us. Men could not figure out what my problem was, and for five days, I stood at the brink of death in agony, but God had it all together for His glory! They might have thought of taking me to the operation room at six, but God had a different plan. Praise to His Name!

Reminiscing about the pain I underwent for three good months, I can now understand how glorious and miraculous my God is. The Lord preserved the baby and me against all odds. Only God Almighty, YAHWEH can do that.

We named our miracle baby, Jim-Kessler Ebo-Kobina Mawuto Tomtania (*his African names, Ebo-Kobina a Tuesday born; and Mawuto meaning: God's property or one who belongs to God*), because of the word the Lord gave me concerning him.

I knew this firstborn son was going to be a Levite, who will usher men and women into the presence of Yahweh, just as the Lord told me. I laid my hands on him and prophesied over him saying, "*Jim-Kessler Ebo-Kobina Mawuto, at the sound of your voice of praises and worship, intercession and music, let men revere Lord, the God of Abraham, of Isaac and of Jacob. At the sound of your music, let the heavens open; and let His glorious anointing fall in a mighty way to liberate captives. May you be an instrument of blessings all the days of your life, because you are*

His inheritance, set aside forever for His glory, in Jesus's Name, Amen."

[18]

A JOURNEY TO THE UNKNOWN

I regained my health back very rapidly. Exactly 18 days later, June 24th, we packed up again and were on the road to Togo. We left Tema that morning at 9. We were like Abraham, following the leadings of the Lord. It was a real journey to the unknown. We did not know where the Lord was taking us.

A soon as we arrived in Lome, we were asked to reload our belongings and to continue the journey. We were not permitted to take any rest, not even a day of rest. Had we known that was going to be the case, we would have stayed in Tema till the end of the month to rest. We reloaded our belongings on the General Superintendent's Peugeot caravan and took off toward the north, not knowing where we were going. There were six of us in the car with our belongings tied to the top, and a few packed in the boot. By this time it was about 4 p.m.

We arrived at Notse at about 10 p.m and rested for a few minutes. We took off from Notse, heading toward the unknown pastorate on a non-paved road. The road was terribly bad. Tossed through stagnant water, potholes, rocks and mud for more than an hour, we arrived on a bridge that almost knocked my heart out.

The river was halfway flooded. The potholes on the bridge were much larger and dangerous than the ones on the road itself. There was no support at the edge of the bridge to protect someone from falling off into the river. Moreover, it was a one-way route across the bridge. Drivers coming from all directions have to begin to honk about a mile away to avoid crashes on the bridge.

Crossing over to the other side of the bridge was like a dream to me. But Rev. Wagbe, the driver of the car, was very confident in himself. I figured out he knew what he was supposed to do in those potholes.

Since it became impossible for the van to go through the bridge with all the weights, the other passengers got off to ease the load off the car for a safe crossing. I sat there terrified with my 18day-old baby. Soon we were on the other side. The rest joined us.

I thought the trip was over. But that was just the tip of the iceberg. Then we began another adventure in and out of the forest trying to find the best hole or pathway to traverse. The road was completely inaccessible. Our belongings on top of the car were ripping apart. I could hear the rattle of breakages and the squeaking sounds of our furniture.

At one point, I thought we were going to crash into the ravine. I prayed and prayed. I was scared. The route became more treacherous as we approached another village named Assrama. And so to make the burden a little lighter for the Toyota caravan, the four men got down again. I stayed in the van with the driver. The guys cut branches and logs here and there to cover up deep water-filled potholes on the slickly, muddy road.

My heart pounded as the holes and slime tossed us up and down in the car like a paper boat on a wild rough ocean, with the baby on my lap! My lips quivered with the chilly climate. We hadn't thought to bring a blanket with us. The baby was warm enough but not me. My legs shook wildly. I was aching all over, hungry and a little bit overwhelmed. I felt we had been betrayed, but I kept on singing and worshipping in my heart.

Suddenly, I heard the Lord whisper to me, "Monica, fear not. I called you, and I will be with you. I have summoned you by name; you are Mine. I will protect and preserve your lives, nothing shall ever harm you even in the village I am taking you to. My Name shall be exalted in this village. Do not be afraid."

"Hmmm, thank you very much, Lord," I mumbled in my heart. "That is really assuring and comforting, Abba. Yes, no one called us, but You."

To travel on that kind of road 18 days after delivery with all the complications I had was agonizing. Yet through this, my baby, "God's Property," was literally sound asleep. This type of travel was normal to most of our Togolese pastors, but to me, a city girl, who had never experienced such hard travel on an impassable scary road, it was a nightmare.

At this point Geoffrey whispered to me, "Hi Darling, how is the journey?"

"What? Why are you asking me?"

"Do you know that you need a special PhD to drive on these roads?"

"PhD, what is that, a doctorate degree?"

"A Pothole Dodger degree," Geoffrey laughed. Geoffrey was a comedian.

"Oh, my goodness," we giggled.

The other pastors didn't grasp our reason for laughing on that terrible road. Maybe they thought we were crazy. A few miles later, the General Superintendent, Rev. Bila Pasgo, announced to Geoffrey in Hausa, "Na go de, Allah! Nous sommes arrivés à votre nouvelle station (Thank you, Lord. We've arrived at your new station)."

Geoffrey responded, "Na go de, Yesu." (Meaning: Thank You, Jesus).

"Mais il ne faut pas descendre encore jusqu'à ce que nous sommes sûrs que les gens sont prêts à vous recevoir ici (But do not get down yet until we are sure the people are ready to receive you here)."

"What did he say?" I asked Geoffrey. I had no knowledge of the French language, with the exception of these few words, "bonjour, bonsoir, and merci".

He translated the message to me and said, "Darling, I don't think the villagers were informed of us coming here."

"What? They were not informed of our arrival?" "I guess so. But let's pray and see what will happen," Geoffrey responded.

Finally, after more than 6 hours on 130 kilometers of road, we arrived at our destination at 2 a.m.—Kame, our first Mission field in Togo. There was darkness everywhere. The rainy weather was very chilly. The whole village was practically quiet. Not a human sound could be heard, only the hooting of owls. The villagers were sound asleep.

With their flashlights, the General Superintendent and the others got down to knock at some doors. They assembled a few guys and talked at length. I didn't understand what they were saying, but I guessed it was about us. And the way it was going, it seemed the elders of the church didn't have a clue regarding us, let alone being their new pastors. As a result, no official preparation of accommodation was planned for us. They had to come up with something.

Within a few minutes, some of the women were already up, removing basketfuls of millet from a nearby mud house. As the women went in and out of the house, carrying millet into a nearby kitchen, I dozed off in the car alone with my baby. I did not know where Geoffrey went.

Somewhere around 4 a.m., someone opened the rear door of the car and heaved a deep groan. I woke up abruptly, gasping for breath. I was scared to death, thinking a wild beast was coming after my baby and me.

"Jesus, Jesus," I shouted.

"Oh, Darling, I am so sorry." Geoffrey held me tight and apologized. "I was just trying to vent out my frustration." He didn't seem to be happy at all.

"You really scared me. It's chilly."

"I know, but I don't have control over it. Wear my sweater."

"But what's going on?"

"I don't know where the 'Big Guys' went. They left and went somewhere in the village to rest, but here we are."

"Darling, why are you frustrated?"

"I don't know, Darling," Geoffrey replied soberly. "I was only thinking about you."

"About me? Why? The Lord had already assured me of His presence."

"I don't think it's fair for them to have traveled with us to this point, and then leave you and the baby in the cold without helping us to a place of rest," Geoffrey said, trying to hide his feelings of disappointment about the place and the house. He turned his face away from me.

I knew Geoffrey wasn't concerned about himself, but about us—the baby and me. But at that moment, none of us had a clue of what was happening. It wasn't his fault. We were in this together for His glory. We had journeyed through the mud and the rain, the rocks and everything. We were still in the crevice of the unknown, but God would definitely be with us. I encouraged myself.

Helping me out of the car, Geoffrey walked us to our new parsonage. Our bed frame with the mosquito net was set up, without a mattress. We had left our yoyo mattress in Ghana, thinking we would have time to buy another one in Lome before leaving, since that was the original plan. But plans had changed without our notice, and we had no mattress to sleep on. We placed blankets and sheets on the bamboo mat they placed on the bed frames. The bamboo mat was really very strong to support the two and half of us, and off we went to sleep.

Tired from traveling that far with all the tumult, I slept like a baby until about seven o'clock, when I was awakened by two women from the church. They were ready with hot water for our showers.

As soon as I stepped outside, the peace of God enveloped me from the crown of my head to the bottom of my feet. Even though it was a typical third world village, I knew immediately that this mission was the will of God for us for the time being. Having not given it a thought, I breathed in deeply and said, "Thank You, Lord."

At that instance, Geoffrey echoed behind me, "Thank you, Darling. Thank you for accepting to do this with me."

"Oh, don't worry. The Lord will take care of us." I began to sing, "I'll go where You want me to go, dear Lord Over mountains or plain or sea I'll do what You want me to do dear Lord I'll be where You want me to be."

[19]

MINISTRY IN KAME AND THE WITCH DOCTORS

Ministering in Kame was not as easy as we thought. In fact, the spiritual aspect of this village was harder than Ankamu. From the entrance of this village to the end, idols and their altars were lined up like poinsettias in someone's garden.

We knew our success in the ministry would depend on the power of God and prayer, because Kame and Athens in the book of Acts had many things in common. There was a god for everything. Each family had its own altar, and every child had a kind of fetish. And so prayer for the village was very crucial.

Moreover, in this part of the world, unbelievers, especially fetish priests, priestesses, and witches, prided themselves of belonging to and serving Satan. They boldly confessed their dedication to the devil by the sacrifices they made.

Sacrifices were made to these idols with anything their fetish required, and they did this almost every day unceasingly. These sacrifices were horrifying, and the stench of dead animals filled the whole atmosphere of the village.

Coupled with the unhealthy stench, there was also a heavy spiritual blanket that weighed heavily on the village. Thus the

Word of God is true when it affirms that the sacrifices pagans make are to demons.

> *Therefore, my beloved, flee from idolatry. ...What am I saying then? That an idol is anything, or what is offered to idols is anything? Rather, that the things which the Gentiles sacrifice, they sacrifice to demons and not to God, and I do not want you to have fellowship with demons. You cannot drink the cup of the Lord and the cup of demons; you cannot partake of the Lord's Table and of the table of demons. Or do we provoke the Lord to jealousy? Are we stronger than He? (I Corinthians 10:14, 19-22).*

Each night ushered us into heavy sounds of tam-tams and demonic incantations as witch doctors sang and chanted. Just the sounds of the voodoo songs sent chills into our spines. These priests and their shrines surrounded our little house, and there was no way we could close our eyes to sleep at night. As a result, we also took the nights as our opportunity to pray and intercede on behalf of the village and the believers. We rested during the day when the villagers went to farm.

We decided that something needed to be done to break down the demonic strongholds that have bound the people. The first initiative the Holy Spirit gave us, as we prayed, was to organize prayer and fasting every Friday for the entire congregation, from morning until He stopped us. As the Lord began to move, miracles and conversions became daily events in the local assembly.

Seeing the effect of the Friday prayer and fasting, we extended the same to the last Sunday of the month as well. Then, the morning service went on from 8 a.m. till 2 p.m. Then from 6 p.m. to 9 p.m. that same Sunday, we organized what we called zonal prayer meetings or cell groups in the entire village. We prayed at the same time with no interruptions for two solid hours. It was an awesome experience.

I remember one incident that hasn't left me since. On one such Sunday, as we were praying, the power of God descended and enveloped the entire village. Witches screamed. Forces of evil trembled. The entire village was charged with the power of God.

We had two visiting friends from Ghana, Professor Ankwanda of Apam Secondary School, and a friend of his. We were praying intensely, but I really needed to use the bathroom, so Geoffrey came out with me. Professor Ankwanda and his friends also briefly stepped out of the room, still praying in tongues. It was a beautiful bright African night.

As soon as I entered into the outhouse, we heard a squealing sound. When we looked up, we saw a huge eagle-like bird descending right upon us. It was really demonic. Another one was shrieking on the other side of the village. In unison, we all screamed at the top of our lungs at the one that was coming directly at us, *"The blood of Jesus rebukes you. In the name of Jesus, we send the fire of Holy Spirit against you. We cast you out of this village in Jesus name ---."*

The demonic bird turned around and flew past us. It fled to the backside of the village where other believers were also praying. As the voices of believers rose to Heaven, the Holy Spirit came down like a strong wave over the village and a gunshot was heard. We didn't know who shot the gun. Screams and shouts of praises and Halleluiahs were heard all over the village for several minutes. Then perfect silence. We went back inside the house praising the Lord.

That night, the tam-tam drums and incantations we usually heard every night didn't make a sound. By morning, the heavy blanket of darkness hanging over the village was gone. Everyone felt it, even the chief of the village who wasn't a Christian said to us, *"Pastors, God has visited our village. Thank you for coming to Kame."*

By the end of the same day, two of the witches in the village died. Wow! The Word of God is true and trustworthy! Jesus said, *"And these signs shall follow them that believe. In my name they shall cast out devils ---" (Mk 16:15).* From that day onward, Kame became a different village altogether. Church growth began.

As the Lord began to move, miracles became a day-to-day event in the local assembly. Conversion to Christ from idol worship happened on daily basis. And as the power of God descended and enveloped the whole village, witches screamed. The forces of evil trembled. Incredible miracles of powerful deliverances from demonic oppressions and healings happened in the village and in the church as well. Deliverances from poisonous snakebites and demonic spells became a normal lifestyle. Souls ran to either our home or the church to accept Christ as Lord and Savior. Revival had begun.

As for the revival in the church, public confessions told of hidden sins, from manipulations of demonic powers among Christians, to anything you can imagine. The Lord was really at work. The thick demonic atmosphere that hovered over the village began to melt.

Suddenly, the sleeping giant that had held the villagers captive woke up. And oh, my, demonic displays became wild and rampant. The priests and witches cast spells on us constantly. One of the brothers of the village's chief, Koko (name changed), a witch doctor, turned on us because of the massive conversion of his adepts to Christ.

It was really rewarding to see the conversion of souls to Christ, but it wasn't an easy road for Geoffrey and me. Since the Master promised that His ever-present presence would carry us through difficult moments, we leaned on His promises. We knew that the One in God's people is still greater than the enemy.

One afternoon, soon after we finished praying and asking the Lord to bring us provision, we heard a knock on our door. It was the son of Koko.

"Good afternoon, Pastor," the young man greeted. "My father sent me with this agouti he just caught in his farm."

"Oh, thank you very much," we said and took the meat. (Agouti is a tropical animal about the size of a rabbit. It is very delicious and a delicacy in Africa). However, before this happened, the Lord gave Geoffrey a dream concerning a gift he was warned us not to eat it. We understood the power behind that so-called gift.

Although we did not have any meat at home that week, we discarded it. Why? We'd learned our lesson with what we suffered in Ankamu.

Koko became very unhappy with us, because he saw it in the spirit of witchcraft that we didn't eat the meat. So he tried other means to no avail. He brought cooked delicious foods, special drinks, and different kinds of veal meat, which we knew had been consecrated to demons. We didn't touch any of his gifts. Koko's last resort was to cast a spell on us through some potion. That didn't work either. But rather, the Lord began to work in his own family, and his own children converted to Christianity.

Amega Fafa

One midnight, Fafa (name changed), another wicked fetish priest, sneaked into our house and sprinkled a demonic potion inside the compound. He knew we would be at the church's early morning prayer meetings.

As usual, we normally left the house at five in the morning. Having the perception that it was farming season and no one could possibly be around, we decided to stay in and pray till seven. But as the Holy Spirit would, we prayed and interceded past nine.

Just as we were about to come out, we heard a knock at our door. When I peeped through the window to check on the knocker, I was really astonished. It was Fafa.

"What does he want?" I whispered to Geoffrey.

"Don't worry, I'll open the door and see what he wants," Geoffrey said. Both of us greeted him with a handshake according to tradition, but he wouldn't take our hands or respond. He just stared at us.

"Hello, Amega Fafa" Geoffrey addressed him again. "How are you?"

"Ah, ah, ah, there is no problem," Fafa stuttered. "I just came to check on you."

"Oh, thanks so much for coming to check on us," I told him.

"Didn't you go to church today?" he asked.

"No, we stayed in and prayed for everyone, including you. Why are you asking?"

Amega Fafa heaved out a deep sigh of regret, shook his head. He rushed away abruptly. As Geoffrey was following him to the gate, he saw the unbelievable. There, in front of the main gate, was spread a demonic black powder. That was when we understood that Amega Fafa didn't come to check on us as friends would, but he was doing so to see the effect of his potion.

Amega Fafa was a very wicked man, and was bent on destroying lives. But oh la, la! Unfortunately for him, he had walked in his own curse unknowingly. By the time he arrived home, his feet were swollen. He had been caught in his own trap. His own fetish had turned against him, and since he couldn't reverse his own curse, he was taken to another high profile witch in Benin. He was there for months before he returned to Kame, but he was still sick when the Lord took us out of Kame.

Soon after that, some of Amega Fafa's children gave their lives to Jesus when they had seen the power of God. Other priests, who knew their juju business was no longer prospering, planned to cross Geoffrey in the middle of the road and kill him.

The first time this kind of plot came to our attention, the Lord warned Geoffrey not to travel as planned that day. He postponed his travel to Lome till the following week without informing anyone. So their plans were foiled.

The last attempt to kill Geoffrey was reported to Fo Jean, one of the deacons of the church, by the son of another witch doctor who, in turn informed us. These kinds of plots went on for a while without success, because God always warned us. We knew our lives were in danger, but the Lord always took care of us.

Amega Titi

Geoffrey traveled one morning to Lome. Knowing the spiritual warfare and terrorism we were engaged in in this village, I waited upon the Lord the whole day with prayer and fasting. I was alone with our two children. I prayed passionately and covered the children with the blood of Jesus before going to bed.

I woke up abruptly at midnight with a terrible dream of an attack on two of the village children. The Lord showed me the face of a short, weird man I had never met before. The guy had transformed himself into a whirlwind (a tornado) and snatched away the two children I was seeing. In the dream, I was screaming and chasing after this person, until I snatched the children from him. I was telling the parents to protect their children with the Blood of Jesus.

The Bible says that we have overcome the enemy by the Blood of Lamb of God, who is Christ our Lord *(Revelation 12:11)*. Then I woke up. I knelt to pray for the children. As soon as I finished praying, I saw a literal fire burning behind our bedroom window. It looked like a pillar of bonfire. Suddenly, a horrifying male voice called out of the flames, "Paitor shi. Paitor shi," (meaning: "Pastor's wife, Pastor's wife." The villagers did not know my real name).

I did not respond. Then I felt as if the enemy was crawling into the room through the window where the flame was. It was really visible.

Oh my God, what is this? I jumped out of the bed and shouted, "I rebuke you in the name of Jesus Christ. I put out your fire in Jesus' Name. I pour out the fire of the Holy Spirit on you. Get out of here right now in Jesus' Name or else you will die in minutes..."

In seconds, the presence vanished from the window. The fire died down, and I heard the weirdest scream and groaning! It sounded like an animal in a terrible agony. Then the voice of a man followed, moaning and saying, "Please, don't kill me. Please, don't kill me."

I re-sent the blood of Jesus and the fire of His presence against the witch behind my window. The fire died down, but the moaning persisted for a while.

Gradually, everywhere became calm. Although I was terrified at first, the fear melted away when I saw what had just happened, and I sang and praised the Lord. After that, I communed with the Lord and asked, "Papa, who is that?"

"The village witch," He said. "He came to kill you, but My blood almost destroyed him. I have given him a chance to repent and to do right. If he does, he will live. If he refuses to repent, he will die, because I am a consuming fire."

At the same moment, I could hear screams throughout the village: "Jesus had defeated you. You are a liar. The blood of Jesus rebukes you. The fire of the Holy Ghost is against you."

I praised the Lord, singing, *"There is power, power, wonder-working power in the blood"* on top of my voice worshipping the Lord at that time of the day. It was about 2:30 in the morning. Then the Lord told me that the man would come back the next day to confess Him as Lord because of the power in the blood.

Geoffrey came back home the next day at 4 p.m. I narrated the incident to him. He became so excited and said, "Darling, I really thank the Lord for you. You wait and see. The witch will come and accept Jesus. If he doesn't, he will surely die."

At about six in the evening, I heard a knock on the gate while washing dishes by the kitchen. I saw an unbelievable figure standing there, with its head covered. It was the guy I had seen earlier in my dream.

Quickly, I rushed into the room to call Geoffrey. I guess the witch saw Pastor Geoffrey coming home on his motorbike and decided to come before it was too late. Geoffrey came out and beckoned the man to enter. He opened the palm branched gate and entered, his head bowed and trembling.

We greeted and welcomed him politely into our compound. We gave him a seat, and went in to pray for a few minutes. Then Geoffrey said, "Amega Titi (that was the real name of the witch), is there anything we can do for you?"

"Pastor, I want to accept Jesus as my Savior," he said.

"What prompted you with that decision?"

"Nothing."

"You said 'nothing'. If you tell me the truth I will help you."

"I, I, I cannot continue in this satanic worship or else I would die," he stammered, shaking badly.

"Okay, let me help you here. What did you come to do in my house last night?' Geoffrey asked.

"Ah, ah, I don't know?"

"Do you really want to give your life to Jesus? If you do, you will no longer have to sacrifice and incant to the devils you have been worshipping before. Do you agree?"

"Yes, yes, I know, I don't want to die," he stuttered. "I want to accept your Jesus."

By this time, the whole village had surrounded us. We didn't know who signaled them that Amega Titi was in our house. Many were afraid, yet others were skeptical. However, some believed that he had encountered God somewhere. I knew it, but I said nothing to no one.

"Are you willing to repent for all the atrocious things you committed and all the people you've killed with your juju?" Geoffrey asked him.

"Yes, Paitor (Pastor)."

"Okay, kneel down and raise your two hands; then say this after me." Geoffrey instructed him to pray and confess Christ as Lord.

Amega Titi knelt down and with his two hands up, he confessed Christ as Lord, repeating every word Geoffrey ask him to. "Heavenly Father, I come to you in Jesus' name. I know I am a sinner. I confess all sins and I denounce all satanic and idol worship. I ask the Lord to forgive me of all my sin and wash me in the blood of His only Son, Jesus Christ. From this day forward, I accept Jesus Christ as my Lord and Savior. I believe He is the Son of God. I believe He died on the cross for my sins. I no longer belong to the devil. I belong to Jesus. I sever all other relationship with the devil. And I ask You, Lord, to help me serve you all the days of my life. In Jesus's Name I pray, A-men."

We saw the genuineness of his confession and the fear of God that had seized him. Then Geoffrey asked him to put his hands down. But the moment Geoffrey tried to lay hands on him and pray, the man trembled and screamed, "Aye, aye, please, please, do not kill me."

"What's wrong, Amega Titi?" Geoffrey asked

"There is fire in your hands. I was burning up. Please, don't kill me," he confessed.

Geoffrey didn't mind him. He prayed over Amega Titi and rebuked the spirit of witchcraft and demons to come out of him. Amega Titi screamed for a while and then stopped. Amega Titi got up with smiles on his face but still shaking.

Before he left, he said, "Paitor, would you kindly send people to my house to burn down all my idols and fetishes. I don't want to serve the devil again."

"Don't worry. We are coming in full force in Jesus's Name to destroy everything," we assured him.

As he walked outside the house, we all felt Christ has won a great victory for His church, and Kame would never be the same. There was joy and dancing all around the village as the news went into all the quarters, but not without some doubts from some of the Christians. Some feared he had pretended to accept Christ in order to find a way to destroy them. But we made the congregation to understand the authority and the privileges we have in Christ over the powers of the enemy. We read *Mark 16:17-18* and *Luke 10:1819* over and over to them to affirm their faith. That evening the church service was turned into prayer, praise, and the pulling down of fetish thrones and altars.

My father-in-law had come to visit that day. He, being the son of a witch doctor and still not converted to Christ, was overwhelmed with fear to see what we were doing. I could hear him screaming, *"Hey, Kwame (Geoffrey), don't do that. You will die for breaking the devil's altar."* Anyway, we had a powerful service that night and burned down a whole hut full of idols.

Now, you may wonder who this Amega Titi was. Amega Titi was the head of all the witches in that sub region. He was a notorious witch who never spared anyone who crossed his path. He had no mercy for anyone, not even children. But when it came to the power of Christ, he had to bow his knees and declare that Jesus is Lord. And when he gave his life to Jesus, the enemy lost a battalion. Some of his wives and children also gave their lives to the Lord. At the present, one of his sons is a pastor in Togo.

After Amega Titi's conversion, many other voodoo priests came to Christ and testified of the power true Christians have in Christ, and the privileges every Christian has under the power of the blood.

"It is pathetic that many Christians don't know of the great power and privileges they have in Christ," one confessed. "We really feared true Christians. That was reason we tried all the time to attack them. They are a real threat to us."

Even Amega Titi himself gave a testimony of how he had attempted numerous times to snatch away Christians in the spirit, just to find out they were either covered with blood or fire. He said that other Christians were covered with swords or angelic beings all around them. He confessed that every true believer in Christ Jesus has a kind of protection around him or her, depending on the kind of prayer they prayed for protection.

Do you know what time witches go on full time duty to plan their actions against Christians during the day? They are on a 24hour schedule with no shifts. But they operate heavily between 12 midnight and 4 in the morning. This doesn't mean that they do not operate during the day. Witches and demons operate anytime. But darkness favors them a lot, because humans sleep at night. Wicked spirits love darkness.

Do you remember the fetish priest I talked about earlier who was related to my family? He came at night. The other witch doctor in Kame also came at night. So, don't play with the times the Lord wakes you up in the middle of the night. Pray, spend time in prayer, because satan and his cohorts never sleep.

The Transition

Six months into our ministry in Kame, Geoffrey and I were invited to attend a conference in Ghana, which was organized by Evangelist Morris Cerullo. Soon after the conference, Geoffrey was chosen to attend the first Morris Cerullo's School of Ministry, which was being inaugurated in San Diego, California.

Geoffrey left for the United States on January, leaving Mawuto and me in the hands of the Lord, and with the remaining money he had, 2500 CFA. We lived with Geoffrey's friends before the baby and I became seriously sick.

Oh, my! How frustrated I was when I was told I was pregnant. I had no clue. Not even Geoffrey. Mawuto was only six months old and was still being breastfed. There was nothing I could use to supplement for my baby's breast milk when the doctor told me point-blank, "Don't give him the breast milk again or you will lose the baby."

That was awkward, but I had to obey. *What can I do?* Mawuto refused to drink the baby formula. And anytime I forced the formula, he threw up and became sick.

"Oh God, please help me," I cried out. "Here I am, so sick and confused as to what I should do for my baby. And Geoffrey doesn't even know I am pregnant! My God, am I going to die? I am so sick. The baby is sick. I have no money, and no food. What do I do now?" There was only one thing I could do—go back home to Mother at Takoradi.

That was a difficult decision I made, because I couldn't understand the dialect of the people we were ministering to in Kame. That was where I entered into the enemy's territory again, because the auntie who vowed to kill me now wanted to seize the opportunity to kill my son.

A few months into our stay in Takoradi, I woke up in the middle of the night really terrified of a dream I had about Mawuto. I saw my witch aunt in our house, conspiring with one of my nieces to bring Mawuto to her for a special sacrifice. I prayed and informed Mother soon after I woke up.

Mother became so upset and screamed, "What again? After all these years, she is still following you and your offspring? I will not sit here to see my grandson killed."

At this time, Mother had become a true dedicated child of God. Geoffrey led her to Christ soon after our wedding. After all, marrying Geoffrey wasn't a bad investment. We prayed together over Mawuto and I went ahead with my chores. And although I was pregnant, I fasted that day for the protection of my son.

Mawuto had just started walking, wobbling, and falling down like all other kids. He was ten months old. So I sat on the porch watching him as he took one step after the other, and felt so proud of him.

Suddenly, an internal voice spoke to me, "Keep an eye on Mawuto." The voice came twice. I brought him inside, but he wanted to play outside. There was nothing I could do other than to keep my eyes on him and pray in the Spirit. The angels of the Lord will protect him.

Unexpectedly and without warning, a feminine figure swooped my son from the floor like a hawk preying on its victim. "Jesus, Jesus, leave my son alone. You can't have him, in Jesus's Name," I yelled on top of my voice. "Whoever you are, stop there right now in Jesus's Name."

At that point, the figure dropped my son, and ran out. Mawuto fell on the cement floor so hard, I wanted to cry. We came out, screaming at the witch, clapping and yelling at the top of our voices. "Leave the boy alone. You cannot have him."

What we saw sent chills all over me. The moment it stopped, it turned to be one of my nieces, the one I saw in the dream. Mother walked to her and slapped her. "Who sent you? Tell me right now."

Head bowed, she said, "Please, forgive me, Ma, the auntie sent me to bring the boy to her for a sacrifice." "Where is she?" I asked.

My niece looked around and then said, "She was standing here right now. I guess she disappeared. She asked me to bring Auntie Monica's son to her."

Oh my goodness, what a dilemma. That was it. I left and went to Accra to wait for the return of Geoffrey. And right at the airport, when Geoffrey was signing the papers of arrival, the immigration officer stole Geoffrey's Bible and the carry-on in which he had all the monetary blessings he received from friends he met in the U.S. We returned to square one with no money, and had to borrow money from a friend to return to Togo. It was hard to swallow, but we still had Jesus!

[20]

A TODDLER'S PRAYER

When we returned to Kame, termites had invaded our house, and destroyed almost everything we owned. But the Lord was with us. He also helped me to deliver our second child, Scott Mawugnigan (God is Great), safely on the floor of our small mud building's living room, because the small clinic that served the surrounding villages was three kilometers away. I couldn't walk that much. Geoffrey and another elderly woman in the village assisted me. What an adventure!

There is a saying that "Experience is the best teacher." That is really true, especially when it has to do with one's health. Geoffrey had strong metabolism but not I. His only problem was the stomach ulcer he was battling with. Other than that he was the strongest one in the family. But I was experiencing increased stomach problems.

We had been drinking the water from the tap, but the water for the babies was boiled. After a stool test in Lomé, it became clear that we were all infested with worms. That was when Geoffrey approached a missionary to buy his used filter before starting the needed treatment to eradicate those worms. And now that we were four, we had four mouths to feed and water.

Good pipe borne water was considered an essential commodity. On many occasions the water turned red because of rusted iron rods. The villagers depended on rainwater, or deep bored-hole water, which wasn't very reliable. The other alternative was river water, but it was filled with worms.

So Geoffrey left for Notse to buy more Alum and a bigger plastic container for the handy filter. We used the alum to purify our water before filtering it. It was normal for Geoffrey to travel outside the village with his motorbike. As he always did, he traveled to Notse once a week to buy household essentials. The motorbike we were using was actually a blessing from the Lord.

Before Geoffrey left, I told him of a dream I had two days prior and asked him to really be careful and sensitive to the Holy Spirit. Left to me alone, I wouldn't have allowed him to travel that day. But men are quite different. Geoffrey said the Lord would take care of him if He gave me the dream, so he took off to Notse that morning in order to be home by noon.

When he wasn't home at the scheduled time, I became a little bit concerned. I prayed and interceded for his safety. *I guess he did not find what we needed in Notse, so he might have gone to Lomé.* That was my intuition.

I was in the kitchen preparing food for the babies and our evening dinner at the same time. A sense of urgency bumped into my spirit around one o'clock in the afternoon. I knew something was wrong. But what could that be? I couldn't stop cooking, so I continued to cook while praying in the Spirit and interceding for Geoffrey at the same time.

Meanwhile Mawuto (Jim), who had become very popular in the village, was playing with some of the children around the corner of Petro's house. I could hear the children clapping and chanting "Mawuto, Mawuto." *That boy is something else*, I said to myself. I continued to pray and do my chores as usual.

A few minutes later, I felt a tug behind me. I turned around, and standing behind me was Mawuto. He was pulling my wrapper and saying, *"Mama, pray Daddy. Mama, pray Daddy"* in a toddler's accent. He was only 26 months old.

"Yeah, I have been praying," I told him softly, but he wasn't satisfied with my answer. He continued to pull on my clothes, trying to drag me to follow him into the room to pray with him. The other children were standing at the entrance of our little kitchen hut watching us. I shut the kitchen door and left with him to the living room. He literally dragged me there. He knelt down before the couch to pray, while I sat at the edge of the other couch where the baby was sleeping. He prayed more fervently than I was.

I could hear our little son saying, "Jesus, Daddy, shoukou shoukou shoukou, Jesus, Daddy, shoukou shoukou shoukou," tear drops on his eyes.

What is he saying? I had no clue. Only God knew what he was saying to Him. I guess he was speaking in unknown, heavenly tongues. I prayed in the Spirit, but my mind was still listening to what he was saying to God.

After some time, he said with a strong affirmation, "Amen, Amen, tant you, Tesus (Thank You, Jesus)" and breathed in a deep sigh of relief. Then he got up and said to me, "I yove (love) you Mama" and vamoosed.

Oh my, I saw an incredible picture of the glory of God mingled with tears on his little face. Wow! A toddler crying and praying to God for his Daddy! I felt at peace that whatever danger Geoffrey would have been involved in, the Lord has heard our prayers and he would be safe.

As Mawuto left with the friends who were playing around the house, I said in my heart, *Lord, this was the very child who was born praying. You have a serious mission waiting for him.* I cherished him very much and prayed for him always. I continued to pray in the Spirit.

Geoffrey arrived home about 4 p.m. He wasn't as excited as he normally was. He looked very quiet and pensive. He first gave me a kiss and went straight inside the room searching for his boys. I was trailing behind him. He picked up Mawuto, who was at that time napping besides his brother, then the baby. He came out the door and gave me a big hug and went and sat on the couch. He sat for a while, still holding on to the children and breathing hard, hmm, hmm.

"Darling, what is wrong?" I asked.

He breathed out a deep sigh of gratefulness to the Lord and said, "Let's pray. Thank You Lord Jesus. Thank You for bringing me home. Thank You for my dear wife and my two little children. Thank You for the life You've given us. Thank You for Your protection and Your provision. I will always be grateful...." he went on and on for a while, repeating the same phrase.

Finally, I responded with a big Amen when he was done praying.

Then Geoffrey asked, "Darling, what were you doing between 1 and 2 p.m. today?"

"We were praying for you," I replied. "What went wrong?"

"You can't believe this. The Lord delivered me from a terrible, fatal accident," Geoffrey said, tears flowing down his cheeks.

"Oh my goodness! Isn't God wonderful?" I exclaimed. "I had a check in my spirit to pray and was already praying in the Spirit when Mawuto came to pull me in to the room."

"Darling, when I saw the miracle, I knew immediately that you were praying for me."

"Oh no, I don't want to take all the credit. I prayed, but the one who really touched the heart of God for you was Mawuto," I confessed. I briefed him on how Mawuto had come to strengthen me to pray more, the manner in which he interceded, and how God in His Sovereignty used our son to touch His heart for his deliverance.

"Thank you so much, Darling, for being sensitive to the Holy Spirit. I thought about the dream and prayed for His protection as well."

"No. The glory goes to the Lord and the credit to Mawuto," I emphasized.

Geoffrey then told me why he left Notse for Lome and this incredibly story of deliverance:

"Darling, I didn't get what we needed in Notse, and felt the need to continue on to Lome. After the normal shopping, I visited some of my Nigerian friends, who really blessed us financially. (He showed me all the gifts he received).

It was getting to one o'clock in the afternoon, and so I made my way back home. About halfway to Notse, an oncoming truck derailed from its route and swayed toward my side of the road. The truck had already tossed the first car into the curb and was heading toward me. I didn't know where to turn, because there were deep rifts on each side of the road, and I didn't know which way the truck would actually turn to before crashing. It was coming right on me. I knew I would be dead in seconds if the Lord did not intervene. I was praying fervently for protection.

Suddenly, a few yards away from where I was, something strange happened. The truck changed route, turned toward the opposite direction and crashed into the hole. It was as if a mighty hand came down and pushed the truck away from me. I really saw the hand of God today."

Halleluiah! Praise the Lord! I shouted. That was a miracle indeed! The children woke up and we sang and worshipped the Lord together for the great deliverance He gave to our family. But it happened when a toddler heard the voice of God to join the Mama to pray. Had we not prayed, the enemy would have won and killed Geoffrey as the dream indicated.

Miracles, you may ask? Yes, miracles, and we saw them every day. The Bible admonishes us to train up our children in the way they should go. We began our day every morning with prayer and the reading of the Lord. We brought our children into the living room during prayer time; even a week old baby to join us. We wanted them to learn to commune with God at an early age by our own example. We laid hands and prayed over them every day. And the Holy Spirit empowered them at a young age and enabled them to pray.

[21]

SCOTT'S (Mawugnigan) INNER STRENGTH

Two years later, the Lord brought us to Calvary Temple, Lome. Praying over the children every day, especially every night before going to bed, was like drinking water to us. The children always received a blessing before and after everything. That was part of the training and lifestyle.

This evening, the children went to bed as usual while we lingered in the room talking and praying about some issues. We had just gone into our bedroom when I heard someone's scream. It was Mawugnigan.

Geoffrey was sleeping deeply. (He falls asleep faster than me. He didn't hear a thing. I am a very light sleeper. I hear almost everything that goes on around me when I go to bed). I jumped right up from the bed and rushed to their room. Both of them were wide-awake. I guess Mawuto heard his brother and got up also, but he went back to sleep the moment he saw me. As soon as Mawugnigan saw me, he said sobbing and trembling terribly, "Mama, I saw the woman. I saw the woman."

"Which woman?" I had no clue of who he was talking about.

"That woman. She came through the window like a big, big lion dog. She had long fingernails. She is a big, big dog. She wanted to bite me. She was doing like this, grrrr, grrrr like a lion."

I held him close and prayed that the Holy Spirit would calm him down. When he became calm, he said, "Mama, let's go. I want to sleep in your room."

But I wasn't going to encourage that, so I prayed over him again and said gently, "Listen, your name is Mawugnigan. It means God is great. God is in you, and you are stronger than that woman. You are stronger than the dog, okay. You have power in Jesus's Name, and you are powerful. Jesus is sleeping here in the room with you. That woman can't do you anything." He was listening very attentively and nodding. "Now, go back to bed, and if she comes back again, say this, 'I rebuke you in Jesus's Name. Okay?' And knock her down."

"Yes Mama. I'll knock her down in Jesus's Name." I knew he was gaining confidence.

"With the power you have," I made a fist, "send the witch to hell with the blood of Jesus. Send the fire of the Holy Ghost on her, you hear?"

"Yes Mama, I have power in Jesus's Name," he said, showing off his little "guns." His face brightened up.

At this time, Geoffrey was up standing behind me. We both prayed over them and went back to our room to sleep, believing that the Lord would protect them.

A few hours later, I heard a yell, "JE—SUS, JE—SUS, FIRE!"

Oh, oh, I rushed to the room. To my surprise, they were all fast asleep. *Wow! This is amazing.* I retreated back to our room and went to sleep.

We met in the living room in the morning for our usual morning devotions. None of us talked about what Mawugnigan experienced that night until after the prayer.

Immediately after the prayer, Mawugnigan said, "Daddy, you know what?"

"What's wrong, son?" Geoffrey said.

"Daddy, the woman came back again."

"Which woman?" Geoffrey asked, because he had no knowledge of our conversation.

Mawugnigan began to demonstrate the way the woman looked. "That woman. She was a lion dog. She was doing grrrr, grrrr. She wanted to bite me. But I said the Name of Jesus. Then Jesus came and chased the woman away."

"Wow, praise the Lord!" we all shouted. "Mawugnigan, you are a warrior."

"Mommy, there was fire with Jesus. Jesus had fire," he said it with such excitement.

We became very proud of him. I understood what he was talking about, because I heard JESUS, JESUS, and FIRE!

We were praising the Lord for the victory when we heard a knock on the door. Claude, Geoffrey's younger brother, who was living with us then and attending high school, stood up to open the door. He found out it wasn't any of our church members but a neighbor. The lady apologized for coming to the house so early, and made her way into the room.

Mawugnigan was sitting close to me at that time playing with Samuel, his younger brother. The moment he lifted up his head and saw the face of the woman, he yelled out, "Daddy, Daddy, this was the woman who came to kill me."

The lady stepped back, wanting to defend herself before the boy. But Mawugnigan wasn't giving in to her lies. He wouldn't allow her to talk. "No, I saw you, you were the one. Jesus punched you, isn't it? I said, in the Name of Jesus, and His fire burned you, and you ran away."

Wow! By this time she was on her way out through the door, running away for her life. Somehow we were a little bit embarrassed, but we knew the boy was saying the truth. As for us, we continued to pray for her. We didn't see the lady for a while. A few months later, we heard she had died, confessing that she came to attack our children and the fire of the Lord burned her.

What an encounter! But through this testimony some of her relatives gave their lives to the Lord. But that wasn't the end. The battles continued.

[22]

JIM'S (Mawuto) COMBAT

Things were going on as usual with the church. The Lord was moving, and the church was growing rapidly. But new battles in Lome had just begun, because each territory has its own prince, combat and strategy.

As veterans in spiritual warfare, we taught our children at an early age the basics in spiritual warfare to help them resist the enemy. Ignorance is one of the devil's arsenals in the Christian camp. As we moved from one place to the other, the challenges increased.

All our children had their share of demonic attacks. We could hear the children many times in their sleep saying, "The Blood of Jesus rebukes you," or sometimes, just a simple rumble of the Name of Jesus on their lips. However, this day it was quite different.

One morning, Mawuto, who was now 5 years old, woke up abruptly, crying in the middle of the night. "Mama, my head, oh, Mama, it hurts."

I ran to the room and prayed over him. He looked scared and bewildered. "What is wrong, Mawuto?"

"Mama, the teacher hit me on the head. It hurts," he said, tears running down his cheeks.

"Which teacher?"

"The one who came here yesterday. She hit me on the head with an iron."

"Calm down. It was just a dream. You will be fine."

"No Mama, she said she will kill me."

"No one can do anything to you, okay. The Lord will protect you."

"Okay, but I am not going to school today."

"We will think about it in the morning."

Although there was no bump, bruises, or any other visible sign on his head, I took his dream seriously and prayed over him. Early that morning, Jim protested that he wasn't going to go to school. I resisted the temptation of keeping him home. I didn't want to encourage him to miss school. He left grudgingly, and I prayed for him.

Geoffrey was studying at the West African Advanced School of Theology in Lome. I had the other two children to work with, which was manageable. Mawugnigan (Scott) was outgoing and brave. He did not fear anything. Food and sleep were his priority. As long as he was satisfied and had taken a good nap, he gave me no problem. Mawuena (Samuel) was the sweetest among the three at the time. He wasn't a crier either. He slept well or stayed up playing in his crib. That gave me time that morning to pray for Jim.

We had planned our annual harvest sale that evening at the church. I finished my house chores early before the church members arrived. I sat on the couch and meditated on the Word of God.

At that point, I heard a whisper again in my ear, "Monica, why did you not protect Mawuto, and you allowed him to go to school today?"

"Oh Lord, I am so sorry." I didn't want to encourage him to school on trivial issues.

"Pray for him, the enemy wants to destroy him. They've given a price over his head, but I have kept him safe. He will live to declare My Name."

They've given a price over his head? Oh no. Was that what he experienced the night before? I became so sad, that I wasn't able to listen to the heart of my son. I asked the Lord to forgive me and protect him. I felt I needed to do something about it. So, I ran downstairs and brought Mawugnigan up to the living room.

I knelt and prayed for Mawuto, pleading the blood of Jesus over him, and destroying the work of the enemy. I prayed and cried my heart out until I had peace that the Lord had answered our prayers.

About an hour later, the phone rang. "Hello, this is Pastor Tomtania's house," I responded.

"Pasteur, je suis la secrétaire de l'école primaire Catholique à Assivito (Pastor, I am the secretary of the Catholic Primary School at Assivito)."

My heart began to race. Something had gone wrong!

"S'il te plait Madame, (Please, Madam), votre fils est blessé (Your son is hurt)." In short, she said that Mawuto had been involved in a terrible accident. He had fallen from a great height while playing with the other kids, and he was hurt.

I had learned some French, and asked, "Où est-il? Devrais-je venir pour lui prendre maintenant? (Where is he? Should I come for him right now?)"

""Non, ne venez pas à l'école. Il est déjà sous anesthésie à l'hôpital. La blessure est vraiment sérieuse. (No, don't come to the school. He's already under anesthesia at the hospital. The injury is really serious)."

In the normal circumstance, I would have panicked and gone crazy like a wild mother bear, crying for my boy. Somehow, I wasn't shocked. I had peace, because the Lord had already intervened. And it was exactly the same time the Lord spoke to me concerning the price on his head.

I sat on the couch and contemplated the dream Jim himself had earlier, and the mistress involved. The lady he dreamed about was the head of the school. *But what has the boy done for her to attack him? Why does she want to kill him? Maybe there must be a clue somewhere that would help us to connect the dots.*

An hour later, one of the teachers brought Jim home. I couldn't believe what I was seeing. His head was bandaged. And as explained to me, he had a big cut on his head and had gone through surgery. His white school uniform given to me was soaked with blood. He was trembling in shock, and his temperature was so high, I wondered why no medication was given to him.

I held him in my hands and prayed. He sobbed and sobbed for a while, and said, "Mama, God is good. Jesus saved me."

"Yes indeed, He did."

"Mama, I saw Him. Jesus was there with me."

I sobbed. I knew the Lord was there, hence the reason he did not die. He preserved him from death. I decided there was no need to fuss. The Lord was and still is his Defender and Protector. We thank the Lord for preserving his life.

Until this time, the boy who they said pushed Mawuto was nowhere to be found. Maybe he didn't even exist. So what was that? Another mystery again? But two years after, the lady Mawuto saw in the dream, confessed to another pastor when she went to him for deliverance. She confessed that she wanted kill our son, but the Lord came to the rescue of the boy. That incident reminded me four years earlier when my witch aunt wanted to sacrifice my son

[23]

THE DEMONIC FRUIT

With the pregnancy of this third child, Samuel Mawuena, I had great appetite and a craving for coffee. Knowing I couldn't drink coffee because of previous allergic reactions, I compromised and mixed a quarter of a teaspoon of Nescafe with my Cocoa drink, inventing my own mocha. And can you believe this? Samuel is the only mocha son I have. He loves every bit of it.

I also craved every good and healthy food, especially vegetables and fruits. It wasn't so with the other two. With Jim Mawuto, I had no choice than to eat anything that came my way. With Scott Mawugnigan, I had a great appetite and craved everything a pregnant woman would love to eat, but I didn't get any. There was no money to buy them, and Geoffrey wasn't there to share the experience with me. He was in the United States, and I delivered three weeks after he arrived.

Somehow, I had been craving mangoes for three days. It wasn't the season for mangoes, but Geoffrey promised to find some of the grafted mangoes at the supermarkets. The night after Geoffrey promised, I had a dream that one lady came into our home to visit. She handed me two beautiful fruits. They looked like the crossed-breed huge mangoes we have in Togo. So excited about the fruit, I cut a slice and ate. But as soon as I finished a piece, I began to vomit and have diarrhea. I felt I was about to miscarry the baby, and I was rushed to the hospital.

A man came and stood by the hospital bed and said to me, "If you will obey the word of the Lord and not eat of everything people bring you, you will keep this baby to its full term. But if you do not obey, you will lose him. Remember, the hand of the Lord is on this child. He is a prophet to the nations, and the enemy will do whatever it takes to eliminate him."

I was really terrified when I woke up. Geoffrey and I prayed seriously about it that morning before he left home. It was a warning from the Lord. I even warned the boys not to accept any food from friends at the nursery and anywhere.

About nine o'clock the following morning, I heard a knock on the door. It was a certain lady I had seen at the church. She handed me two of the very same mangoes I was craving.

"Wow. This is an answer to prayer," I said, because I had forgotten about the dream. "Thank you very much, Mama Lucy* (name changed)," I told her. "I have been craving these mangoes for three days now."

"Thank you also. See you on Sunday," she replied and left immediately.

After lunch, I washed the mangoes and was about to cut a piece, when I felt a check in my spirit. It was then I remembered my dream. The Holy Spirit was warning me not to eat. I decided to wait until Geoffrey arrived home.

What was wrong with the fruit? You may ask. Yes, it was only a fruit, but when you've learned to be sensitive to the Holy Spirit, obedience to His command is better than satisfying your cravings. I kept the mangoes on top of the counter.

Geoffrey arrived from school an hour later without my mangoes. He had searched everywhere without finding them. I was a little bit disappointed. I told him of the beautiful mangoes and the check I had in my Spirit. So I replaced my appetite for a mango with an orange. It wasn't that bad, but it wasn't what I was craving.

After resting for a while, Geoffrey brought out the mangoes. He laid hands on the mangoes and prayed. He cast out all the demons and "whatnots", cleansing the fruit with the blood of Jesus. Then he sat on the couch with confidence, giggled, and grimaced, and gave me one of his romantic looks.

I laughed and left to the kitchen. Immediately, I remembered the totality of the dream. It was like I was watching a film. I shouted, "Darling, please do not eat those mangoes. Have you forgotten the dream?"

"Oh no, I did not," he replied. And to make fun of me, he said, "You are not to eat of this mango. It was a warning to you but not to the three of us (he and the boys). The fewer, the merrier, we are stronger than Goliath." He smiled. Jim and Scott laughed as well.

"Please don't eat it. If it was bad for me in the dream, it may affect you too," I argued.

"I've prayed over it," he said. "The Bible says if we even drink deadly stuff, it will not harm us. Isn't it? Why are you afraid?" He was making a joke out of it.

"No Darling, the Bible didn't say that you should drink poison when you've been warned in a dream not to. If you didn't know it, the Lord will protect you. But if you know there is poison in the cup and you stubbornly drink it, you will die."

"Preach on, Madam Pasteur."

He did not listen to me. His love for mangoes had blinded him. That was scary to me. I wasn't going to eat any. I knew better after all that I'd been through. Geoffrey sliced one of the mangoes. He gave small slices to the boys. He also took a piece, and then wrapped up the other half.

"Why didn't you eat the whole fruit?" I asked.

"I didn't want to. You think you scared me?"

"Yes, I know I really scared you."

"Of course not."

I guess he was a little cautious too, but he played it tough. We prayed together as our custom was and went to bed. I woke up abruptly in the middle of the night to find Geoffrey very sick. He was in and out of the bathroom many times and was restless all night. It was unusual for him, because Geoffrey was a deep sleeper. When he hit the bed, no amount of noise could wake him up. But this night, it was quite different.

The boys were also calling out for him, "Daddy, Daddy." They were having fever and diarrhea, and throwing up pieces of a "demonic" mango. I prayed and prayed for him and the children the rest of the night till morning. God spared their lives.

What would have happened had they eaten up the whole fruit? Death? Maybe. Think about what would have happened to me had I disobeyed. God is so good to those who fear His word. That actually taught us another great lesson about food. And then I thought about the intentions of the giver, the odds and probabilities that she would hurt us, when I didn't even know her yet. But why did she come with the demonic fruit to kill me and my baby? I had no clue.

Soon after that, Geoffrey called me and said to me, "Darling, I am so blessed to have you as my wife. Although I am the head of the home, the Lord has made you the ears, the eyes, and the heart of our family. You hear, you see, and you understand a lot of spiritual things. Rarely do I dream about stuff like this. So pray for me, so I won't doubt any word the Lord would give you concerning the spiritual and physical well-being of our family."

I was really flattered. And thank God, the Lord saved us. My third child was breached. It was a miracle I survived. He's the "sweet one, who didn't cry much."

[24]

SAMUEL'S STRUGGLES

Geoffrey was still furthering his education at the West African Advanced School of Theology, Lomé. The two older boys were also in nursery. That gave me a little break to do my normal chores and relax.

Two days prior to that time, I was so tired from running around with the Mawuto and Mawugnigan before they left for school. So I gave myself a small nap on the couch beside the baby. It was maybe a thirty-minute nap, but I had a dream that really disturbed me. And since my dreams always had a deeper meaning, I became scared.

In the dream, I saw myself fighting with someone, who had come to the house to snatch my baby away from me with force. I fought very hard, calling out the Name of Jesus. And since she felt I was overcoming her, she called out for re-enforcement. Two others came in to fight me very hard. And when they almost took the baby away, I shouted, 'In Jesus's Name. You will not have my baby.' Suddenly, a hand came out of heaven, snatched the baby away from them, and gave my son back to me."

I woke up abruptly, sweating profusely, and screaming with the same words coming out of my mouth, "In Jesus's Name, leave my son alone. You cannot have him." God gave me the victory in the dream, but it felt so real that I shuddered in fear. I sat up and prayed passionately against the fulfillment of that dream, pleading the blood of Jesus over my son. He was only nine months old.

I told Geoffrey about the dream when he came home with the boys. He suggested we fast and pray seriously over the dread, knowing my dreams are prophetic. And we did.

The next day, it was getting to eleven o'clock in the morning. I realized we had shortage of a few groceries for the preparation of the evening meal. I decided to carry the baby on my back to the market. Since we didn't have a car and walking to the market was inexpensive, I gave it a try. That wasn't the first time I had walked to the market with the baby on my back. It was only about ten to fifteen minute walk. Geoffrey would have given me a ride on his Vespa had he been home.

As I was bargaining with a vendor at the fish market, I felt someone touching the baby. When I turned around, one lady said to me, "Oh, what a nice baby? It is so cute. Is it a boy or a girl?

"A boy," I said politely.

I thought she was only a little curious woman, but there was something unusual about her that made me wonder who she was and what kind of spirit was animating her. I whispered a prayer over my son and left. I decided to take a taxi back home with the few things I bought.

Someone tapped me on my shoulder and said, "Hey Maman, ton enfant est entrain de mourir (Hey Mama, look, your child is dying)."

"What? My son?" I panicked. *Jesus, help me,* I mumbled while looking at the bystanders who had surrounded me. Immediately, I pulled off the cloth I had used to tie my son on my back.

What a shock! My son, Samuel, was foaming, eyes turned in and unconscious. "My goodness, what is happening?" I cried.

224

Is that for real? I was baffled.

"Allez, allez à l'hôpital avec lui. (Go, go and take him to the hospital with him). Vite, vite, (Hurry, hurry)," everyone screamed.

Having forgotten what I had bought at the market, I ran, yelling out for a taxi. *Oh God, where do I go? What should I do?* I moaned.

"Go home and seek My face. I am with you," I suddenly heard a voice. It sounded really sweet and beautiful.

"Thank You Lord, I will." Within a few minutes, I was at the house, running up the stairs with my baby praying, "Jesus, please, save him."

Hurriedly, I laid him on the bed, removed his clothes and called upon the Lord for a miracle. A few minutes into prayer, Samuel's foaming stopped, and his eyes rolled back to normal. Then he opened his eyes and smiled. I sang and praised the Lord, thinking it was over. But little did I know that this was just the beginning of a long spiritual battle with witches that would terrorize our son.

Meanwhile, I contemplated on how I would go back to the market to pick up my groceries. Would they still be there? Or more so, someone might have already taken the ill advantage to steal or make use of the items. A few minutes later, I heard a knock at the door.

"Who is that?"

"It's me, Mama Pastor, a friend of your family."

I opened the door. There in front of me, was standing a young man, holding the bag of groceries I had left at the market. *Oh my goodness*, I shouted. I was thrown into an extra shock to witness this miracle.

"Thank you very much, sir. God bless you."

"No problem. God bless you too," he said, and he was gone.

That was unusual, because I did not even know the guy who brought the groceries home to me. And for the fact that he came to our home made me shiver. I had no clue as to who he was. All I could put finger on is that there was an unusual power that was at work in our lives. "Thank you, Jesus."

As for Sam, he went to sleep right away after I changed his diaper and fed him. Hurriedly, I went to the kitchen to prepare supper before the family arrived. I thought all was well, because Samuel was sleeping soundly. And because the kitchen was just a few steps away from the where he was, I sneaked in to check on him from time to time.

Rethinking on what I had seen earlier at the market, I felt I needed to intensify my prayers. I began to pray. By the time Geoffrey arrived home with the other children, Samuel was playing on the floor. Suddenly, he began to have diarrhea. We prayed and gave him all the prescribed medications to no avail. Then he began to throw up. I thought he was teething.

We prayed and decided to take him to the clinic behind Fleau Jardin. Dr. D'Almeida examined him thoroughly and found nothing wrong. He gave him three shots and medication to stop the diarrhea and told us to go home. But he remained the same. Within a few minutes of the shots, I thought my baby was going to die.

Although I was scared, I wasn't going to give up. We continued to pray. About five o'clock in the evening, someone knocked at the door. When Claude opened the door, it was Evangelist Joshua Adelabu from our church. He walked to me and said, "Praise the Lord, Mama. I came purposely to tell you of a revelation that Lord gave me two days ago concerning Samuel. I saw you fighting with some people over Sam. It was a tough battle."

"Oh, my goodness," I interrupted him. "I had a similar dream. It was really awful."

"Yes, it was. What I saw was really scary. It will take a miracle to overcome them. They will follow you everywhere to kill the boy. But please, pray! Pray very hard and don't give up on your son. And the Lord will give you the victory."

"Thanks so much, brother. I know the Lord reveals to save," I told him. That confirmed the dream the Lord gave me. I have been there, and I knew that my Heavenly Father reveals to deliver.

We prayed together. And before Evangelist Joshua left, he added, "Please, the Lord sent me to tell you to take what He showed you seriously. Do not give up on that child until victory is won."

Like Mary, the mother of Jesus, I kept every word seriously in my heart and prayed passionately for a miracle. The all-night prayer meeting we had with him seemed like God was far beyond our reach. Our son was between life and death. Very early in the morning of the third day, we went back to the pediatrician again. He gave that poor little thing three shots again without explaining what he was doing. And nothing changed. My son was dying.

Finally, we decided to try another doctor. We boarded a taxi straight to Dr. Trenou's clinic. This doctor knew us very well, because a few of his relatives attended our church. The moment Dr. Trenou saw Geoffrey, he left whatever he was doing and came to us. After checking the boy, he said bluntly, "Pastor, that boy is almost gone. There is nothing we can do in this clinic for him. I don't think he will survive! This is very serious."

"Yes, we know, Doc. But our child will not die! God will heal him," we all said in unison. "Do something about it, Doctor. God will use you to help us."

He looked at us in astonishment. His eyebrows furrowed. I think he was saying in his mind, '*They think they know better than me. I've practiced for over forty years, and I know this is the only way to say it. This child is not going to make it, whether they believe it or not. He is already dead.*'

He sat down on his couch, placed his right hand under his chin, and scratched his head, while our baby was dying. I felt the old man was really doing some thinking. I could read it on his face. But I was desperate for God's intervention, because according to the dream I had and what the Evangelist came to tell us, the witches were in to win. We continued to pray.

Then Dr. Trenou got up and paced back and forth, in and out of his office. While he was guessing and thinking on what to do, our baby was also jerking, foaming in his mouth and convulsive. "Oh Lord, help us! Papa, I am counting on You," I prayed and prayed.

"Darling," Geoffrey said, "Don't be afraid. The Lord will take care of him. He reveals to deliver." We clasped our hands together and prayed, not knowing what Dr. Trenou was doing.

Finally, the old Dr. Trenou said, "Okay, you are going to take the boy to the General Hospital right now. I will give you a note to give to Dr. Tatagan. He is my friend and also the Chief Pediatrician at the hospital. He will take good care of him. Run, it is very, very crucial. There is no time to waste."

"Thanks, Doc." We ran out. With the note, we hurriedly boarded another taxi straight to the General Hospital at Tokoin, Lomé, praying for divine favor and a miracle. Upon our arrival, we saw that Dr. Tatagan was meeting with other doctors on another patient. But the moment the nurse gave him the note, he excused himself and came to see our son.

Dr. Tatagan also knew Geoffrey very well because of his frequent visit with patients at the hospital. But our son, who was already in a convulsive state, was now jerking violently. It was really frightening and faith breaking. I was determined not to quit praying. The Lord had spoken and I would not give up.

Samuel was admitted immediately at the pediatric intensive care unit. The doctor gave us no hope whatsoever. He was placed under oxygen. More medication was administered, but no improvement. We continued to pray. After praying with us, Geoffrey left for the house to take care of the children, who had been left with the church janitor. I stayed close to my baby, praying and calling him out of the dead, snatching him from the hands of the forces of evil.

I had not eaten anything that day. I guess I was fasting indirectly. Around 11 p. m., the convulsions reduced and he went straight into a coma. Then all his vital organs began to shut down. Two unknown nurses walked to me and encouraged me to stand strong and pray. They were so caring and sweet. I didn't even know them. *Maybe they are Christians or angels in disguise.* I felt at peace. God was watching over us.

Soon after they left, another nurse came in out of nowhere and removed the oxygen. She left the I.V. on him and said to me, "You, you better stop that prayer and go home. That baby is dead already. He is not going to make it through the night. He is gone. I say that he is already dead!"

There was something evil about her. I lifted up my head and looked straight into her eyes. It was scary. She looked exactly like one of the ladies I fought with over my son in the dreams. I gathered courage and starred harder into her eyes.

She stared at me angrily. Suddenly, her face changed. I thought I was dreaming. And without a second thought, I said with confidence, "Miss, that baby will live. God gave him to me, and He will heal him for His glory. You demons and witches, you can't have my baby. He is a child of God. His name is Samuel, God's gift. I dedicated him to God. God has His seal on him."

"Okay, we will see if that God you are talking about will really do His job right," she replied angrily. She went into the office and returned with another nurse who looked even more devilish. Both stood there ridiculing me.

Then I remembered the story of Elijah and the prophets of Baal in I Kings 18. This wasn't my battle. It was the Lord's, and the Lord God Almighty that I serve never loses a battle. He's fought worse ones than this for me, and He was going to give me victory over this one too. If He raised me from the dead at the age of ten, and He did the same for Lazarus, He would do it again (John 11:1-44).

That night, without exaggeration, more than ten children died in that ward. The enemy and his cohorts had come to ravage innocent lives, but they would not have mine. I stood firm. The only thing I had besides the boy and the diaper bag was a small stool I was sitting on and my Bible.

Although I was somehow scared, I clung to the Lord. I didn't move away from him, not even to go to the restroom. The fact that I had fasted eased my bodily movements. I didn't want to give the enemy another chance to touch Samuel again. I sat beside him, praying and reading the Word of God over him.

> *The right hand of the LORD is exalted; the right hand of the LORD does valiantly. I (Samuel) shall not die, but live, and declare the works of the LORD. The LORD has chastened me severely, but He has not given me (Samuel) over to death (Psalms 118:16-18). With long life He will satisfy you (Samuel) and show you (Samuel) His salvation (Psalms 91:15 - All emphasis are mine).*

Even though there was no change in his condition, I clung on to the promises of the Lord. Although he was lifeless, I trusted in the One I served who is Life Himself. Without a doubt, this was a battle between the Lord and the powers of darkness, because their mockery continued on until about 4 a.m.

I also kept on travailing in prayer, although I felt Samuel was gone. But nothing would stop me. I intensified my prayer in the Spirit. Suddenly, I felt something break in the spirit realm. The presence of the Lord overshadowed me. I sobbed. His peace flooded my soul, and I sang this chorus softly,

You are the Mighty Man in battle, El-Shaddai
You are the Mighty Man in battle, Jehovah-Nissi
You are the Mighty Man in battle, El-
Shaddai You are the Mighty Man in battle
Glory to Your Name!

In obedience to the promptings of the Holy Spirit, I placed my hands on my son and prophesied over him. I said, *"Samuel Mawuena, you are God's gift to me. You will live and not die. You are a mighty man of valor, God's battle-axe. You will bring in sons and daughters into the kingdom of God. Your future is bright and glorious. The devil and his witches cannot kill you, because your blood is mixed with the blood of Jesus Christ. Live, Samuel, live to give Him glory."*

I spoke God's prophetic destiny upon his life. I placed my hands on his feet, praying from that point up to his head, rebuking the spirit of death to release my son out of its grip. At that instant, I felt a release of fire in my hands. My hands were burning up. Immediately, my hands generated heat into his body, starting from his feet up to the head. Glory! I was into this battle alongside the Lord. It was such a good feeling. The fear in my heart dissipated.

All of a sudden, I felt a rumbling in Samuel's stomach. God had answered our prayers, and a miracle was in the making. A few minutes later, a release of gas and runny hot feces came out of my baby. I turned him aside to clean him up. The feces were so hot his bottom was burned and peeling off. His skin was raw red.

"Oh Jesus," I cried. My heart broke, and I sobbed.

I called out to the nurse to help me with something to clean him up, but she wouldn't mind me. Thank God I had two more cloth diapers left. One of the mothers offered me a few pieces of her old African cloth, which she was using. Oh, what a treat!

I continued to pray while cleaning him up. I was still wiping him when he sneezed the first time, then a second time. At the third sneeze, I felt him breathing very well. I praised the Lord, singing out loud. At this point, the two nurses and a few of the mothers stuck their heads around and stared.

From there, the boy opened his mouth. His little tongue was rolling in his mouth as if he was telling me he was thirsty. I placed a teaspoon of water on his tongue. He swallowed it. I was very excited. I repeated it for a while. Then he went to sleep.

I knew one victory would lead to another. Samuel was not dead, but God had brought him back to stay. After a while, he opened his eyes. I gave him more water, changed his diaper and left him to sleep on my lap.

This was the fourth day. And I had not slept at all. My body was aching and very tired, but my spirit was very strong. The Bible says that those who wait upon the Lord will surely renew their strength *(Isaiah 40:31)*.

At about six o'clock, the "mocking bird" nurse, came back to do her usual rounds to finish up her time and leave. When she saw the baby cleaned and breathing on my lap, she shouted, "Hey you, you are a witch! What did you do to that boy?"

"It is Jesus Christ, and not me," I said.

She grew very angry, and walked out of the ward. Dr. Tatagan was also at the door, coming in for his early visits. He walked over with two other nurses. But when he saw Samuel on my lap, he also exclaimed, "Is this the Pastor's son? My goodness, this is a miracle indeed! I have never seen this before."

Geoffrey arrived at that same moment. Dr. Tatagan shouted in French, ""Bonjour Pasteur, ton fils est vivant. En effet, il s'agit d'un miracle. Je savais que vous étiez à la maison en priant à Dieu pour votre fils. Je suis vraiment impressionné par cela. (Hello Pastor, your son is alive. This is a miracle indeed. I knew you were going to the house and call on God for your son. I am really awed by this)."

Geoffrey nodded. He rushed over. We celebrated the Lord's victory. Soon after, upon the doctor's orders, we were transferred into another ward where we stayed for two more days and were discharged.

And although this episode wasn't the last war I had over Samuel, the Lord saw us through them all. I will never cease to praise His wonderful name! Even after years of living this incredible miracle, anytime we met Dr. Tatagan, he asked us of our miracle son.

Unusual Hot Water Burns

After the Lord's great victory for Sam, we enjoyed great health for eleven more months. Then another tragic thing happened. My older brother, Ernest, had come to visit us from Port Gentille, Gabon, on his way to Ghana. I had not seen him for years so I was very happy to see him that day. It was a quick visit.

The third day of his stay, I had another dream. I saw this particular lady, of which the Lord had already warned us of, wanting to snatch Samuel from me again. When she could not do so, she poured hot water on him and said, "This time, you will not survive."

I woke up terrified and said to Geoffrey, "Darling, I don't understand all these revelations and dreams. What have we or our children done to always fight for our lives?"

"Darling, we are really fortunate to see things before they happen so we can pray against them. It's a blessing."

"I know, but I am tired of fighting all the time. It's wearisome."

"Don't you know that you are a warrior? The Lord has equipped you to fight such battles. And our testimonies are going to help others in their fight against evil."

"Thanks, but pray for me. I am really exhausted physically."

Geoffrey and I fasted and prayed for Samuel. The same week, I caught a terrible flu and was unable to do much in the kitchen. Geoffrey took care of the kids.

One morning, Geoffrey prepared a vaporizer for me to inhale in a small yogurt cup. He asked me to come out and use the concoction. He was still preparing breakfast for the boys. Whilst I was dragging myself from the bed to go to the living room, I heard the most agonizing scream that tore my heart.

Geoffrey ran to Samuel, but it was too late. The hot water in the small yogurt cup was over his face, on his stomach, his arms and part of his right leg. Not knowing the extent of the burns, Geoffrey picked up the boy.

"Ouch Daddy!" He screamed. His skin peeled off from his arms, and got stuck in Geoffrey's hand.

"What is happening?" I rushed out of bed. Although my head was spinning and my body was aching badly, a mother's instinct for her babies doesn't know pain sometimes. What I saw drove me crazy. I couldn't believe my eyes. "What happened? Please, tell me," I asked trembling.

Geoffrey was dumfounded. He just stared at me and said, "The enemy will not win this battle."

Mawuto and Mawugnigan began to tell me what actually happened. A conspiracy orchestrated by the enemy had turned a little yogurt cup into a bucket of hot water. And Samuel was burned so badly—stomach, one arm, and half of his face and neck—exactly like what I had when I was nine months old. Only that mine was deeper than his.

We rushed him to the general hospital. That became our two-week stay at the hospital again. It was a nightmare, but God allowed this for a purpose. Our faith was shaken again!

In most of the hospitals in Africa, a relative or a friend of the sick had to stay with the patient to facilitate the care. This bipartisan effort for patients also helped the nurses and doctors from doing everything for the patient.

As for me, the fever and cold reduced drastically. And when you are nurturing two young kids, between the ages five and four, and burned-up Sam at the same time, it becomes wearisome. I had no family member close to me to help take care of the children. I was in and over my head.

A day after the incident, the Lord warned us not to allow anyone to visit him, and so we left a message at the hospital. And "A NO VISIT" sign was placed at the very ward the children with such critical conditions were. But the enemy had a way of violating even the law.

I was informed that anytime I left, a particular lady would come to the gate and introduce herself as the auntie of my son. But the hospital officials refused to allow her to enter. She tried numerous times and disguised herself as a family member. Miraculously, the Lord warded her off our son and protected him.

Geoffrey and the children were still in school, and so during the day, I would go home after the doctor's visit, take my shower, go to the market, and prepare food for my family. Then as soon as I was done with all my different obligations, I would leave for the hospital and stay overnight.

Before leaving the hospital each morning, I would tie one of Samuel's hands and one foot to the cot to prevent him from scratching the wounds. The other two were already affected so he couldn't move them. I would leave his food with either the mother of a patient sharing the same ward with us, or with one of the nurses. I prayed and pleaded the blood over him before I left the hospital. And although we stayed at the hospital for three weeks, God gave us favor with all the nurses and doctors, and they were really kind to us.

Samuel, being a very good boy, and who didn't cry very much, helped to facilitate this effort. He could sleep for hours. But anytime he was awake, he would begin to sing his favorite two songs. Most of the doctors or nurses who heard him sing always stopped by his ward to listen to him.

Although he sang in French, they couldn't figure out the real meaning of the song until I told them. He was 22 months old. The Bible says, "Out of the mouth of babes will God's praise be perfected." His favorite choruses were these:

Son Nom est Jésus, Son Nom est Jésus,

Son Nom est Jésus le Roi
(His name is Jesus, His name is Jesus,
His name is Jesus the King)

———

Il est mon Ami à tous les temps
Jésus est mon Ami à tous les temps
Je rire, je chante, je suis comme un roi
Il est mon Ami à tous les temps

(He is my Friend at all times.
Jesus is my Friend at all times.
I laugh, I sing, I'm just like a King,
Because He is my Friend at all times)

Although he was suffering, Samuel would sing and sing until he fell asleep. Good report about him always came to me when I returned. That really brought glory and honor to the Name of the Lord in the hospital. Even at the hospital, without saying a word, the songs he sang impacted many lives.

Truly, what the enemy meant for evil, the Lord turned it around for His glory. The result was phenomenal. Some of the nurses gave their lives to Jesus. We were also able to witness to some of the patients as well. In all, God received the glory. Day to day as Sam began to heal and bloom, I literally saw the greatness of God being demonstrated in his life.

You see, God has already planned the destiny of every child that would come into this world. Psalms 139 emphasizes this point. Therefore, caution should be taken by parents and those around these precious little one, and know how to help guide them into the fulfillment of their purposes in life. The enemy may try to shorten their lives, but God has the last word.

Today, Sam is a graduate with his B.Sc. degree in Medical Lab Technology from the University of Southern Mississippi. I know that one day he will become a missionary medical doctor, because God has prepared him to use his pain to gently heal others. Today, he leads worship, and preaches at his local church, working with his pastor in missions and outreach.

[25]

OTHNIEL'S (Edem) CHALLENGES

I was very much exhausted with all the hospitalizations, spiritual warfare, and family responsibilities, coupled with taking care of visitors who came through the parsonage. I also could not deprive my husband of his marital rights, though I was tired and fighting the evil one constantly. My lack of time to sleep and care for myself wreaked disaster to my physical life.

A month after we were discharged, I found out I was pregnant again. Oh, my gracious, what was I going to do? My confession was coming back to haunt me.

From the first month to the last month, everything went wrong. It was like living in hell to me. And many times I wondered whether the baby would survive. We didn't have a car. Geoffrey was still in school. And shepherding a church and attending school wasn't giving him enough time to finish the course as he had planned, in two years.

On my side, I needed to see the doctor often because of complications. Taking a taxi was the only option, and the price I paid was enormous. Right at the beginning of the fourth child's pregnancy, I knew in my spirit it wasn't going to be easy. The Spirit of the Lord whispered to my spirit that the battle for the life of both of us had already begun. Sooner than I expected, both of our lives hung in the balance, as I struggled to survive in between life and death to reach the ninth month of delivery.

Tripping and falling became the norm for me. Imbalance, dizziness, heart-racing problems, and all the complications, threw me on the waves of life's tempestuous sea. The waves of death and life flooded violently over me each day. It was a fight for survival. No amounts of vitamins, no amount of folic acid, or natural organic food we have in Africa, were able to stop my health problems.

Although we were aware of the presence of the fetish house by the parsonage, we didn't take the demon worshippers seriously. And although we were aware of their incantations and demonic activities, we had no clue they were fighting feverishly against us.

I was preparing one morning to go to the clinic for a checkup. It was nine o'clock, and the children were already in the chapel playing church as usual. Out of the blue, I heard, "Mama, Mama." Since I knew my children were downstairs playing, I didn't respond, because the voice sounded deep and really evil. A few minutes after, I heard it again, "Mama, Mama." This time, it sounded like Scott's voice. Still, I didn't respond. I picked up my handbag and headed toward the door. As I was closing the door, I heard the same voice again for the third time, "Mama, Mama." Chills went all over me.

I felt that the call was coming from the fetish house. To my astonishment, in the lane, I saw the fetish priest, holding a bowl full of blood, facing our door, and calling me. (They did not know my real name. Everyone called me Mama).

The moment I saw him, I yelled out, "The blood of Jesus rebukes you. The blood of Jesus rebukes you." He dropped the bowl and ran into the house. I made it safely to my appointment. Within the week that followed, the fetish guy died.

Wow, the Lord struck quickly. But the man's death led to the conversion of two of his nephews—*Koffi and Kodjo (names changed for privacy).

A month after this incident, I was in the chapel praying with the ladies when I felt led to go back home. I whispered to Mama Rhoda Ndukwe, the women's ministry president, to intercede for me. As I climbed the stairs, I heard people talking behind the wall. I waited silently, praying for God's protection on my family and myself.

At that time, I saw Geoffrey coming. I signed and told him to be quiet. We stood there, listening to what they were saying. One woman called out the name of their idol and said, "As we are burying this pregnant goat alive, so should she die with the baby she is carrying ---." Another one said, "Let her suffer before she dies, for placing a curse on our brother." Then they buried the pregnant goat's body alive, and left the head up.

I placed my hand on my lips, not wanting to let them know we had heard and seen their schemes. Geoffrey and I intensified our prayers by destroying their evil schemes and reversing their word curses on me.

Oh my goodness! I began to sob, not for myself, but for the pregnant goat. How frightening and pathetic it was to hear the groaning of the goat until it died!

Still, I experienced all kinds of abnormalities in my physical body. One day I fell in front of the porch of the church the moment I came out of the taxi after a check-up. I lay there for some time, because I lost consciousness. But God kept me from harm. By His grace, the Church janitor, Papa Remi, watched over me till I came back to myself. He was afraid to pick me up because of the baby.

Another day I was climbing the stairs to the house when I fell, hitting my right side on the rails. The pain was so excruciating. I cried my heart out. But God sustained me. I gradually crawled upstairs and lay on the couch till Geoffrey arrived with the boys. Still another day I fell behind the church office while walking to the church to pray. There was no one around to help me, but God was there. I got up with no wound or scar, but I limped home due to a pain in my foot.

During those times, the Lord sent a faithful son of His, brother George Mensah, from Aflao church, and who is now a missionary living in Texas, to live with us. He was a humble young man of God, whose servant heart impacted all of us, especially our children. Brother George had received the call to fulltime ministry, but he wanted to sit at the feet of Geoffrey to be coached. He also helped me with the children. These two men, Brother George Mensah and Papa Remi helped me climb the stairs time after time when I fell and couldn't pick myself up.

Geoffrey also helped me do the laundry every weekend. We didn't have a washing machine, but Brother George gave himself and even washed our clothes for us as well. All these and many others I cannot thank on paper because of their volume. An unseen hand guided and protected both of us from severe injuries. But this next particular episode needs to be told.

The battles I was fighting during the pregnancy made me feel in my spirit that this child had a wonderful prophetic destiny, a mission to accomplish. Although I had lots of complications during this pregnancy, the delivery was fast, so much easier than all the others. At 12:05 a.m. on the 5th of September 1984, our fourth son Othniel Edem was born. Othniel means, God is Strength, Force, or Warrior. The name Edem we gave him meant *'He has delivered me.'*

Somehow, I felt in my spirit that Edem wasn't going to have an easy life because of what the Lord spoke to me concerning him. He said, "Monica, the enemy will fight him; he will be swayed in the storm from left to right. But just like Joseph, he has a mission to accomplish in preserving lives for the kingdom. And like Othniel in the Bible, he will bring deliverance to many by the power of the Living God, and by the word of his own testimony in Christ Jesus."

The very day Edem was born, the prophecy I received at the age of 16 was re-enacted. Indeed the prophecy had been fulfilled to the letter. The Lord has given me a wonderful husband and four sons. I was living in a country other than Ghana. And now what else? When will the remaining prophecies of greatness and material blessings be fulfilled?

While still at the clinic contemplating on His Greatness, I heard the Lord speak to me in a dream: "Monica, you and the children I have given to you are for signs and wonders to the nations of the world. You will be instruments of My glory and the manifestation of My power. Watch, the children will rise in power and glory. They will usher many into glory. They will turn many to righteousness. My Word shall never depart from their mouths. And because of My hand and favor upon them, many shall stumble with jealousy. Their choices will affect others positively or negatively. But I will perform every word I've spoken concerning you, and every word spoken concerning them shall be fulfilled. I AM the Lord, that's My Name. I have said it, and it shall come to pass at My appointed time."

Wow! I wept and praised Him for loving me that much. Thank God that prayer has been and is still an integral part of my life. I live on prayer. I cannot do without it.

The League of Witches

Soon after Edem's birth, the league of witches who vowed to destroy our family by killing all our children, gained access into our home by introducing a daughter of theirs, who was related to us. I would call her Shay. Geoffrey knew Shay had serious spiritual problems, but not to the extent in which the Lord began to reveal to us. The revelations we received were really scary, and I would have preferred a different route with it. We would come to some.

Maybe you want to ask, "Why were you people attacked all the time?"

I don't know the answer myself. I have been wondering about it all my life. But looking at the vessels the Lord used to bring deliverances and blessings to others in the Bible, one can see that, in one way or the other, they all went through unbearable trials and difficulties, which were orchestrated by the enemy. Left to the devil alone, Joseph should have been killed, but God made a way through a different route—slavery, in order to lead him to the palace. But the good news is that the Lord was with him. That's all he needed, and that was exactly what we needed as well. The grace and mercies of God sustained me from day one to the day of delivery.

Passion & Consequences

Geoffrey always had passion for deliverance, but even the Lord Jesus didn't force Himself on others. In the time of Jesus, either the sick had to make a move or friends brought them for healing by faith. They came, they believed, and they went home saved and delivered. Even demon-possessed individuals were brought to Him at the faith of others who were interested in their deliverance, with the exception of the man at Gadara.

None of the mind bogging revelations the Lord was showing me frightened Geoffrey. He wanted to see the little girl, Shay delivered, by hook or crook. Meanwhile, the children began to experience numerous satanic attacks – screams at night, fevers during the day. The children would literally see Shay trying to rip their throats. And sometimes, the attack left visible marks on them. It was really scary to live with a witch under your roof.

I was in the kitchen cooking one day when the Lord asked me, "Monica, where is Edem?"

"Lord, he is sleeping on the couch."

"Check it out right now or he would be dead in a minute."

I ran out of the kitchen. In a flash, I saw someone carrying my baby on her side running out through the door. "Shay, where are you going with my child?" I shouted. The moment I called out her name, she turned around, and smashed the door against the head of my six-month-old son, dropped him, and took off.

What a pathetic cry I heard! The boy screamed so hard. My heart sank in. I wanted to run after her and give her one dirty slap, but I couldn't. The Lord restrained me. I grabbed my son and prayed. Blood was coming out of his nostrils. A large lump was forming on the side of the head. I put iced on the lump, but it didn't help. It continued to grow bigger. We prayed and rushed him to the hospital, but nothing was actually done. The doctor said there was nothing wrong with him, and that he was going to be fine.

We came home disappointed with the doctor. We encouraged ourselves with the fact that we have The Great Physician on our side. We intensified the prayer covering over the children. But that wasn't the end of Shay's demonic caprices.

A week later, the children were playing downstairs where there was enough sea sand. We normally had wedding receptions at that particular spot. I watched the children closely for a while. I left Edem (Othniel) with Mawuto (Jim) and Scott, and decided to run upstairs for a minute to check on the food I left on the stove. I had not even reached the kitchen when I heard a cry, which ripped my heart open. I rushed back downstairs, and oh my! I saw the unbelievable. My son was lying face down in the sand and jerking, almost unconscious. On top of him was one of the church's long heavy benches!

Papa Remy had been watering the flowers when this thing happened. He couldn't run fast to pick up the child because he had a handicap. I ran and grabbed my son, crying for God's intervention.

"Who did that?" I said hysterically. The other children were crying, "Mama, she did it. Shay did it."

The 13-year-old witch, who denied any involvement with the devil, was the one who lifted up the bench length-wise, and pushed it on my son to kill him. But the Lord miraculously preserved his life.

I informed Geoffrey what had happened when he came home. Being very furious with what she had done again to our son, he decided to interrogate her one more time. This time, she became bold in her response, "My mother asked me to kill your children. I have been given an assignment to destroy all the Tomtania family, starting from yours."

"What?" Geoffrey yelled and turned pale. He threw a fit of rage, took hold of her clothes, and said, "You don't know who you are fiddling with. Be careful, or else you will be consumed by the fire of His presence." He would have disciplined her severely had I not intervened.

We sent for the father to come down and hear what was happening. When the old man came, he testified to the fact of her being involved in witchcraft. But he begged us to keep her for a while just in case she changed her mind and sought to be delivered.

The old man said to us, "I was a witness at Kame with what happened to the witch when I visited. And I know your Jesus has the power to deliver her. He can deliver her as well. Please help me with her."

Although this guy was a Muslim at the time, he testified to the fact that Jesus is the answer to all problems, whether spiritual, physical or moral. But the problem was that when the dad was there, Shay affirmed her desire to be delivered. But as soon as Grandpa left, she refused categorically, and said that her mother would kill her if she accepted the deliverance.

A month after this incident, a dreadful fever attacked Edem. He was going in and out of coma. We knew nothing else other than to pray and take him to the clinic. Following a thorough check-up with his doctor, we found out that he had a huge boil on his head. That was impossible, because I bathed him every day. It seemed it popped out just in one day. What a mystery!

The astonishing part was that the boil grew very fast within the week to the size of a golf ball. He slipped in and out of coma. His doctor, Josephine, wasn't ready to cut it open. She was afraid the baby would die in her hands.

I was confused: Edem must survive this demonic boil or die? What had I done to merit all these attacks? I prayed and sobbed with no answer from anywhere. My faith in God as Jehovah Rapha was being shaken,

After prayer and fasting, we went back to Sister Josephine and begged her to cut the boil open. She was unwilling to do so.

And as for Edem, he was convulsive with 103° temperatures. My son was dying. *Oh God help him,* I cried.

Still fearing for the life of the baby, she finally accepted our offer, with the exception that we sign a release paper. We prayed. And she sedated Edem. As she cut through the boil, Sister Josephine shouted, "My goodness, Pastor! There is something unusual in this thing."

We encouraged her to do her job while we prayed for the Lord to guide her hands. She cut through it and removed the demonic implant. It looked like a bird claws intertwined in a human tooth and wrapped in human hair. What a mystery! It left a big hole the size of a Ping-Pong ball in his head.

Immediately after she removed the strange cyst, Edem's temperature began to drop. He gradually came out of the coma and survived. My late Pastor and Father in Christ, Rev. George Appekey, witnessed this miracle. He was with us that week conducting spiritual renewal meetings at our church. He interrogated Shay, and she affirmed that her mom placed the bird claws in Edem's head. And had it not been our prayers, the claws would have slowly dug deep holes into his brain to paralyze and kill him.

What is it like to be a woman of faith, and still live in constant fear of something unusual and unexpected happening to you or your children? The story of Job was mine as well, but God was the Conqueror who fought for us! The plot to destroy little Edem was so vivid and unexplainable, but the Victorious One was with us. Yes, the One who is Strong and Mighty in battle delivered our son from all the assaults of the enemy.

[26]

I WILL KILL YOU!

Before this time, Geoffrey was supposed to travel to Yamoussoukro, Ivory Coast, to attend a conference. Knowing the fourth baby could come any time before he returned, we prayed for someone to assist me with household chores and the boys.

At first I rejected the idea of having a housemaid. I argued with Geoffrey that Mother was able to manage with ten children after Dad passed, but I had to understand that the nature of our work was quite different from Mother's activities. I was then serving as the Women Ministries Rep for the Golfe Prefecture, the National Financial Secretary-Treasurer, Missionettes Coordinator, a mother, and a pastor's wife, and a minister, et cetera.

I love to minister to people. I love to work with the Lord to help those who need spiritual and emotional aid. But at times, life's demands makes one sick and exhausted in the ministry. You go to bed tired. You get up out of bed exhausted, especially in Africa, where the pastor becomes "the head" of all the families in the church.

The most challenging part is when all the visitors who were traveling from all points of Africa from Ghana to Benin, Nigeria or Burkina Faso, and vice versa via Lomé, stop between midnight and two in the morning, hungry. Yet, most of them are not willing to eat just a snack and go to bed till morning. They always want a real meal, and we couldn't reject their request.

Lomé was the central point for travelers at that time. But there were no MacDonald's or Kentucky Fried chicken anywhere for us to make a quick drive-through to get them some food. We didn't have big refrigeration at the time. Sometimes, I had to start from the scratch to cook in the middle of the night.

These were times when a good loving mother and wife became grumpy, and a jovial Spirit-filled pastor became irritable. These were the times you would want to take whatever help that comes to your door without even seeking the face of the Lord. This was where we were. I wasn't mean, but I was sick and tired of being sick. I couldn't function very well. My heart was racing all the time.

Geoffrey was also tired, because of school, the ministry, and family responsibilities. He was desperate to find someone who could assist me, at least in taking care of the children in his absence. And at the same time, we were afraid of what we could bring into our home. We prayed.

In the heart of our search, a girl who was part of the Missionettes showed up in Geoffrey's office. She told Geoffrey she wanted a place to stay in order to serve her God better. She narrated the kind of persecution she was receiving at the hand of her aunt.

At first I thought it was great. But when I met the girl myself, I felt immediately in my spirit that she was an agent of the devil sent to destroy our lives. Geoffrey took my intuition seriously, yet the intention of helping *Patty (name changed) find deliverance if she so desired.

Thank God that prayer has been and is still an integral part of my life. I live on prayer. I cannot do without it. With much prayer, the Lord crippled and prevented Patty from operating in the family till after the fourth baby was born.

Two months after delivery, something strange happened which altered my life forever. On November 10th 1984, at 1:25 in the morning, I woke up suddenly, because I heard someone open our bedroom door. The dining hall light shone through and the door was shut.

Thinking it was Geoffrey who was coming to bed, I sat up and called out, "Darling," but that wasn't the case. He didn't respond, and I didn't feel his movement.

That is weird. I knew Geoffrey was in his office praying and preparing for Sunday morning service. *But who came into the room?* I couldn't tell. The baby began to cry, so I sat up to feed him. Then I felt a strange and bizarre dark presence walking in the room. I put the baby down, got up to call out to Geoffrey again, but helas! The fight had already begun!

Suddenly, an evil hand held my throat, choking me. "In Jesus's Name," I said. "In Jesus's Name, leave me alone," I mumbled again, trying to free myself from the demonic grip. We fought for a while, while my spirit whispered unceasingly, *"The Name of Jesus! In the Name of Jesus!"*

Each time I mentioned the Name of Jesus, I gained an extraordinary strength to fight. I couldn't tell how long we fought. All I could recollect was when the Lord injected an extraordinary power in me that brought the demonic one down to the floor. I was screaming, "The blood of Jesus rebukes you. The blood of Jesus rebukes you."

The moment the demonic force hit the floor, a huge mask came off, and I saw her face. It was Patty, the maid who had just come to live with us. "In Jesus's Name, Patty, what do you want?

What do you want from me?" I shouted, petrified.

She was boiling up with rage. Her face changed from a human face to all kinds of scary demonic faces. Suddenly, she kicked a sharp blow to my lower abdomen, and said in an awful, fearful male tone, "I'll kill you and take your husband." Then she disappeared!

"Jesus, please help me!" In pain, I yelled at the top of my voice.

Geoffrey heard, and rushed straight to get me. He staggered over the force of evil that was coming out of the room and yelled out, "In Jesus's Name, I rebuke you," and stumbled over me. It was the force of the spirit that was leaving the room that hit him. It was like a strong whirlwind that shook him up, he told me later.

I was bent over in pain, kneeling on the floor. Carefully, he helped me back into the bed and prayed over me. It was hard to sleep after such a terrible experience. I was stupefied. But the Lord was fighting my battles, because Jesus was in me, and is greater than the devil and his allies.

I couldn't understand why the Lord allowed such things to happen to me. I wasn't a prayer-less Christian. I wasn't living in sin. I was doing the right thing, living the Word daily by His grace. *"But why? Oh Lord, why? Why me again?"*

Geoffrey wrapped his arms around me, laid hands on me and prayed. As it would go, I woke up that morning bleeding. We knew it wasn't physical but spiritual, and so we didn't go to the hospital right away.

When daylight shone through, we confronted Patty in the parlor, after our morning devotion. But she denied any involvement with witchcraft. We intensified our prayers with many days of fasting. Finally we went to see one Dr. D'Almeida. He ran some tests and found nothing wrong, yet the bleeding persisted. We knew the cure couldn't be a human doctor's, but that of the Great Physician.

Months passed by. The pain and bleeding continued. Still they couldn't find anything wrong with me. Through fervent prayers and persistent calls to the doctor's office, an ultra sound was administered. His final diagnosis was that my womb was swollen, and it could be that I had fibroids. Needless to say, we knew the swelling was the result of the demonic assault on my lower abdomen.

Life wasn't normal again; I couldn't enjoy my family, not even my new baby. I pitied Geoffrey very much and cried a lot, asking the Lord to take me home with Him. But He wouldn't answer my prayer.

From the General Hospital to the University Hospital and from there to other clinics and doctors' officially became the norm. Yet my condition worsened. I felt like the woman with the issue of blood in the Bible (Luke 8:43-48; Matthew 9:20-22), because Geoffrey was spending his salary on medication and physicians. We had no insurance, and the church wasn't paying for our medical bills, not even our children's school fees. We fasted and prayed. We stood on the Word of God, and professed the promises of God for healing to no avail. All I wanted was to touch the hem of His garment and live.

Suddenly, one morning, the bleeding stopped. Then a strange anemia settled in. Doctors tried to draw blood for certain tests but could not get clear blood. Dr. Agbodadze, a member of our church, had tried desperately to help me recuperate, but became very much disappointed. He had done everything within his means to detect the cause of the anemia and the pain with no result. Finally, he demanded one more blood test in his office at the Tokoin Hospital.

Geoffrey took me there that morning. The lab technician came to draw blood. He poked me numerous times in different places, but he couldn't get enough blood out. His eyes sank in as if he had seen a ghost, me. He was disappointed, and frustrated. About an hour of pinching me here and there, he retrieved a few drops of blood from the hardest and most painful spot, my wrist. But the little blood sample he took was mixed with water. With tears in his eyes, he said to Geoffrey, "I can't believe this, Pastor, Mama is a living dead."

And true it was. I was like a living-dead surviving only by the power of the Holy Spirit and the grace of God. It became necessary for me to receive a blood transfusion once every month because of the anemia, coupled with the normal menstrual cycle. By this time we had changed doctors, because Dr. Agbodadze was transferred to another town. Dr. Fiadjoe of Clinic Biasa had become our doctor now.

I was wasting away little by little, but my faith was still strong. In times like this, the enemy intensifies his attacks through negative thoughts, fearful dreams and even through loved ones. Not only was he attacking my body, but he was also attacking my mind, by using dreams and other people to send condemning words to me. I had numerous dreams of seeing myself in a coffin and people wailing over my death. At one point, we received numerous calls from other brethren concerning dreams of my death.

What on earth was happening? I thought. "Is it evident that I was going to die for a witch to bewitch my husband and destroy my children? Never! Prayer and the Word were my only weapon. Geoffrey would often bring the children into the room to pray for me. My heart broke when I heard Jim and Scott pray, "Jesus, don't take our Mama away. We love her, please, don't take her away."

A Taste of Job's Story

Two weeks passed after the heart wrenching prayer of the children and still no improvement, two Christian brothers, *James and Jason (names changed), paid me a visit at the clinic where I was receiving blood transfusions. After thanking the Lord, one of them said to me, "Mama, we know that Jesus paid the price of our healing in full. And a child of God is not supposed to be sick. Many churches have fasted and prayed, and still you are sick. That means there is un-confessed sin in your life and you need to repent. Any un-confessed sin can prevent you from receiving your healing. But if you confess right now, we will pray for you and the Lord will heal you right away."

I was shocked, but I said, "Please, brothers, I know I am not perfect. I have confessed all my sins, and I do it daily. The Lord knows that I am neither living in sin nor hiding any sin in my heart. I knew no man before I got married, and have lived in purity of thought, heart, and life. I have never cheated or stolen anything from anyone. I am not harboring hatred, jealousy or any other sins. Tell me, if you know something I do not know. Maybe the Lord has revealed something to you, please."

"You see, you are full of pride. You are praising yourself. Mama, don't allow pride to come between you and your healing. You know that your heart is not clean, you know that." They sat and condemned me like Job's friends.

I was crying my heart out. "Brothers, I know I am a sinner saved by His grace alone, and the Lord knows my heart. I am not trying to pride myself. Only God is good. So pray for me."

They stood up and left without any word of encouragement or prayers, because they thought I was living in sin. They felt I needed to be crucified alive for sins I had never committed. I sat on the bed sobbing and asking the Lord to search my heart and forgive me of any hidden sin, sins of omission and of commission, and heal me of this terrible demonic orchestrated disease.

After they left, the battle intensified. The enemy bombarded my mind with all kinds of accusations. He said to me, "You see, you are suffering because of your sins. Even all the members of the church of Jesus Christ know that. You are living in sin, hence the reason you were attacked, and God has also abandoned you. "

I was like Job, trying to find clues to this terrible attack and its aftermath. And instead of receiving encouragement from friends and family in Christ, I was being condemned for sins I had not committed, and the enemy knew it too. And though I fasted and prayed, it seemed God was nowhere to be found. Like Job, I lodged my complaint to the Lord and held on to His Word. I hung on to this particular passage of Scripture.

> *"Look, I go forward, but He is not there, And backward, but I cannot perceive Him; [9] When He works on the left hand, I cannot behold Him; when He turns to the right hand, I cannot see Him. [10] But He knows the way that I take; when He has tested me, I shall come forth as gold" (Job 23:8-10).*

This particular day, I had just come home from the hospital after a blood transfusion. My heart was racing. I could not stand on my two feet. My arms were swollen. Geoffrey was running around panic-stricken. I was walking on a thin thread between life and death, and could go down in seconds. He was afraid of losing me. He helped me slowly into the bed and knelt by my side, crying and pleading with the Lord to heal me.

Here, the truth hit me very hard that I was really dying, while the enemy played on my mind telling me, "Monica, you have to accept that you are dying. Just tell the Lord to take you home. It's not hard to die, and even God wants to take you away, anyway. Don't you see what you are going through? Even God wants you dead."

It was hard to accept, but I believed it and began to cry to God to take me home. Here I was, now counteracting the prayer of my children and my dear husband! But I couldn't help it. Rapidly, in answer to my prayer, I saw chariots of gold coming toward me. Their appearance was so beautiful. The horses were pure white and clear as crystal. The voice behind the chariots said, "Monica, we've come to take you home. But why do you want to do that?"

"Lord, I am tired. I am always in pain, and I can't take it anymore."

"What about the children that I gave you? What about Geoffrey? And what about the ministry I have called you to?"

"Lord, I am willing to stay if you will heal me."

"I am willing. And My grace will sustain you."

At that instance, His presence covered my entire body with His peace and grace. The chariots also retreated slowly into the heavens. Then I fell into a deep sleep, which I hadn't had for months. I woke up at the touch of a hand on my chest. It was Geoffrey who was still kneeling by the bed, crying his heart out to God. He had heard my conversation with the Lord. He thought I was probably dead. He placed his hand on my heart to see whether I was breathing or not. That was when I got up.

He breathed a deep sigh of relief and said, "Thank you, Jesus." But the first thing he did when I opened my eyes was to scold me for asking the Lord to take me home. "Darling, do you want to kill me? How can I survive without you? How am I going to take care of these children? And who will help me in this ministry?" He kept on talking, tears flooding down his cheeks.

Yeah, Geoffrey was right. I was selfish, but anyone would have done what I did in that condition. Though I wasn't healed on the spot, I felt a great relief in my spirit, and knew the Lord took control and His grace would sustain me no matter what.

After this heavenly encounter, I began to regain my strength, but the pain in my lower abdomen continued. It was going to be a gradual healing. The Lord answered Geoffrey and the children's prayers, because I am still alive!

We shouldn't have brought Patty into our home in the first place. But we did, and we faced the consequences. Even then, I give glory to the Lord that my life was altered for His glory. Because it gave me another view of how spiritual terrorists work, and it equipped me on how to relate more to those who are going difficult moments in life.

On the surface, it seemed the enemy was winning this particular battle, but I knew the Lord would one day break through with a mighty victory for His glory. And that He had a purpose in allowing me to go through what I was going through.

[27]

A STRANGE VISIT & ITS AFTERMATH

Soon after this, I had another vision: I was standing in our living room when someone knocked at our door. I opened the door to an extraordinary individual I'd never met before. He was unimaginably tall and exceptionally handsome. Yet, he was surrounded with the very presence of evil. He stood at the door gazing at me, and asked permission to enter.

"Who are you? And what do you want from us?" I asked him.

He introduced himself to me as Lucifer.

"No, Lucifer, you cannot enter this house. In the Name of Jesus, leave right now!" I commanded him.

He staggered, at the mention of His Name as if he was drunk.

I said again, "This house belongs to Jesus. My family belongs to Jesus, and I am a child of the living God, bought and washed in the blood of Jesus Christ, my Lord."

"I know who you are," he said, staggering as if he had been electrocuted. "And I know who your family is. But I have access to this house, because I have my properties here."

Very confused and furious, I asked, "What do you mean? You have something here in my house?"

"I wouldn't have come here if I didn't have anyone or anything that belonged to me."

"Okay, what do you have in my house? Show me, and I will get them out at once."

At that instant, he walked past me to the first room by the living room where Shay and Patty were sleeping. He pointed to both of them and said to me, "These are mine, and for that reason, I have free access to this home. I connect with them and they do likewise. If you don't want me to come here again, kindly give my properties back to me."

"Okay, get out right now in Jesus's Name, and we will make sure you don't come to this house again." He disappeared immediately. Then I woke up.

Wow! What is this? Imagine living with Lucifer's agents. Although we knew we had under our roof two witches ready to work with satan against us, we underestimated the extent of their connections and operations. It was time for them to leave, and this time we weren't going to play around it again. We prayed and confronted both of them.

The younger one, Shay, wouldn't even talk. Her heart was as hard as stone, and we knew it. As for Patty, she said to us, "Pastor, my problem is too complicated. When I was about eight years old, my grandmother took me to the riverside in our village. They performed intensive demonic rites over me, and placed certain demonic marks on my body. And when my grandmother began to incant, there came out of the river a big serpent. I was then sitting down naked by the banks. The serpent entered into my body via my vagina. Then Lucifer appeared. He was very handsome. I was then given to him in marriage. And this was the ring that sealed our union (the ring was on her middle finger). I feel the movement of the serpent in my belly all the time. Lucifer also comes very often to have sex with me. As for me, my soul has been consecrated to Lucifer. Everywhere I go, I have to do whatever he bids me. I don't think there is hope for me."

"Definitely, there is hope," Geoffrey said. "That's why we allowed you to stay with us. And far more, Jesus came to set the captives free, and you can be free even today if you are willing. Do you want us to pray for you right now?"

She gave us flimsy excuses, and begged us to wait until she went home to Ghana to remedy the situation. I felt she wasn't willing to be delivered, because, if Amega Tata, and all the witch doctors we encountered had their deliverances, why not Patty?

I was really frustrated. I wanted Geoffrey to send them away that very day. But there was not much argument on my part that could convince him to let them leave. Geoffrey's argument was that the Lord had brought them to us for deliverance and freedom. That was actually true, but were they really willing to be free?

"If we send them away, the devil will destroy them," Geoffrey said. "The Deliverance Team is there for that purpose. I've already talked with them, and they are fasting and preparing for this week. We will, by His grace, get them delivered in Jesus's Name."

"I agree, but is it for real that they want to be delivered? Or are they like Elymas in the book of Acts who want to destroy the work of the Lord?" I argued this with Geoffrey. (Please, read Acts 13). "They've stayed too long. They don't want to be delivered, and I suffer with the kids all the time."

It was hard to get the truth out in such matters when it seemed we were playing with the enemy. We knew that the two girls were sent to destroy us, and it was being proven to be true. I knew they didn't want to be delivered. Why should we sleep with timed-bombs? I don't know. How foolish I felt.

The Astral Projection

A few nights after this, after our normal evening prayer, Geoffrey and I stayed late to watch "Indiana Jones and the lost Ark." Geoffrey wanted the two of us to relax after all the combats and confrontations. We didn't have Christian television back then, and someone had just given us a small television set as a gift. The Togolese TV was airing the movie, and we took the opportunity to watch it. That was a onetime deal that we could enjoy time alone with without being distracted.

The children were fast asleep on the floor. It was around 10 o'clock, when we decided to put the children in their respective beds. But when we came to Shay, we decided to leave her there for a while till we were ready to go to bed. I still don't understand why we were prompted to do that.

When the film was over about midnight, I decided to wake her up so we could also go to bed. I felt she wasn't breathing. She was lifeless.

"Darling, come and see this. What is happening here?" I called Geoffrey.

"Wait, let me check and see again." He turned her around, trying to wake her up to no avail. "I think she is out of her body," Geoffrey said. "You know that she is a witch. This is what they call astral projection."

"Oh my God, what are we going to do?"

"We are going to sit here and pray until she comes back.

Then we will take this opportunity to pray for her deliverance."

"What if she refuses?"

"Then we will send her back to her parents," Geoffrey emphasized.

"Remove her from here and put her in her bed," I said. "If you remove her from where she is to another place, she will die. Because when her spirit comes back and it doesn't find her where she left, it wouldn't enter her body again, thinking it is a strange body. We don't want trouble."

"What? How do you know that?"

"From my Grandpa, and it happened numerous times when I was with him." Then Geoffrey said something, which really opened my spirit to another spiritual truth about witches. "Darling, if I were cruel," he said, "I would just grind hot peppers and smear it all over her body."

"No, that's not good. I know you wouldn't do it."

"She deserves it. Witches deserve that."

"And what will happen if you do that?"

"When she comes back into her body, she will begin to scream and confess all her evil deeds and then die!"

"No, I don't want her dead," I said. "I want her to know Jesus and be delivered. But how did you get to know all these secrets?"

"You remember I told you that my grandfather was a witch doctor? This is what he said he did to destroy other witches."

"Do witches destroy one another? I don't believe it."

"Yes, they do. Doesn't Satan destroy his adepts? Demons can't destroy themselves, because they are spirit beings. Only God can destroy them. The Bible says, "Every kingdom divided against itself is brought to desolation, and every city or house divided against itself will not stand. If Satan casts out Satan, he is divided against himself. How then will his kingdom stand?" (Matthew12: 25-26).

"Yeah, Jesus said that the devil has come to steal, to kill, and to destroy (John 10:10). Anyway, I agree with you. We were not called to destroy lives but to bring them to the saving knowledge of our Lord. And we will do whatever it takes to help them find deliverance if they want."

We sat and waited and prayed for Shay to come back to her body. Suddenly, at five minutes after four, we felt the flash of a light coming through the window, and oh la, la! Shay was back into her body. She rubbed her eyes when the brightness of the light hit. And when she saw us staring at her, she trembled. We were very calm. We didn't threaten her. What we wanted to know was where she went and whether she wanted to be delivered or not. And her response stunned us.

"No! My mother would kill me if I do. She comes in the spirit every day to take me to their meetings."

"Where did you go this night?" Geoffrey interrogated her.

"My mother came in the spirit and took me to Kpalime and Niamtougou."

"To do what?" I asked.

"To celebrate a feast in Papa's farm in Kpalime, and --"

"Papa's farm? Geoffrey interrupted. "Now I know why the old man has been having all the problems he's been talking to me about."

That day, Shay confessed a lot of things her mother's group had done against Geoffrey's father and the family, and what they intended to do in the future. This time we gave her the choice to either leave or be converted. She chose to leave, but Patty begged us to give her time. Above all, we got the necessary information we needed to defeat their purposes.

Thank God, that this time we had the boldness to make the right decision with the intention to seek deliverance for her. We did not leave Shay alone. We spoke of her to one of our minister friends, who visited Grandpa from time to time to pray with him. He began to talk to Shay about Christ. (You see, a prophet has no honor among his own). About a year and a half later, Shay's mother died, confessing all the evils she had done, what she had planned against us, and how the Lord smacked her good.

Soon after, Shay also said she gave her heart to the Lord and was attending one of the churches. But was it true? And I did not know why we allowed Patty to stay. Maybe time would tell.

[28]

THE POISON

In 1986, the Lord opened the door for Geoffrey to travel to Singapore to attend Haggai Institute for six weeks. It was necessary for him to go, but I released him reluctantly. I was afraid something evil would happen to me in his absence.

This was the same year in which the nation of Togo experienced its first terrorist attacks. From that day on, Lomé, the capital of Togo, went through lots of political upheavals. And so it was also hard for me to release Geoffrey to go to Singapore when I wasn't sure of what might happen to me in his absence.

Geoffrey's younger brother, Richard and his family were living with us at that time. We had a house full, and about 15 mouths to feed each day. Life wasn't all that easy during those moments, when all we could feel was the enemy throwing darts in all forms—ingratitude, rebellion, insults, sicknesses, and all forms of demonic attacks. I was sometimes gripped with the fear of not living long. It seemed as if my life was hanging in the balance.

Geoffrey departed on Friday evening. We got up sound and strong the following day with no incident. That evening, we cooked rice and chicken. I shared the dinner, and everyone had their share. I set my food on the dining table, covered it up with a napkin and went to take my bath before eating. "No bath, no eating," was my own policy.

I was under the shower singing when the Lord spoke to me audibly. "Don't eat the food when you get out. It has been poisoned."

What? Is this true? What have I done to be poisoned? After all the services and love shown to these people? Does someone want to kill me in Geoffrey's absence? Who is that person who wants to kill me now? Is it with real or spiritual poison? I interrogated myself and continued to sing.

"The food you left on the table has been poisoned. Don't touch it," I heard it again.

Does God speak in the bathroom? You may ask. Oh yes, He speaks anywhere. It was so simple and so clear. But when I heard Him speak to me the third time, I froze. My heart was beating fast. I thought I was going crazy.

My food has been poisoned? I quickly ran out of the bathroom into the bedroom and spoke to the Lord. I went back to the kitchen to see if I could find something else to eat in order to throw the "poisoned food" away.

All the food was gone. There was nothing else to prepare and eat that night either. I paced searching for a solution. I was hungry, literally starving. Also, I needed to take my medication before going to bed. I fasted all day and hadn't taken the medicine as prescribed.

Finally, I went and sat behind the table to negotiate with the Lord. "Papa, I am hungry. There is no food. What should I do? Were You not the One who said if we drank any poison it would not harm us? (Mark 16:15) Please, sanctify this food to shame the enemy. In Jesus's Name, I pray." I must have forgotten what happened in Ankamu.

I removed the lid off the food and asked the Lord to bless it, to nullify, to neutralize, and to sanctify the food again and again to satisfy my want without heeding His warnings. He didn't speak again. I thought He approved my so-to-say faith-filled prayers over the food.

I sat straight behind the table and began to eat. I swallowed the first spoonful, then another spoonful of rice. Fear suddenly gripped my heart. The moment I swallowed the third scoop of rice, my heart dropped within me. I began to perspire, shake, and see double. I dropped down on my knees, and crawled to my room praying in my heart for forgiveness.

Mawuto ran to me and asked, "Mama, what is wrong? Should I call Sister Philippine (Philippa)?" I nodded. (Sister Philippine is one of our spiritual children, and who was on duty that day at Clinic Biasa. She now resides in Germany with her husband). Within minutes, Philippine arrived. She transported me to the hospital. That was all I could recollect.

I regained consciousness with an awful migraine, sweating profusely, in an air-conditioned room. I felt as if someone was sitting on my head with a hammer, cracking my skull open. Visitors shivered because of the intense cold in the room but not me. I was perspiring all the time, but couldn't go to sleep. It was only by the grace of God that I survived. I spent about four and half weeks at the hospital. The Lord used Doctor Fiadjoe to flush all the bad stuff out of my body with I.V's and blood transfusions.

To the best of my knowledge, I was again only a stone's throw away from the grave.

Whatever happened were only the mercies of God that broke through my disobedience and protected the four innocent children I left in the hands of witches. The baby was only two years old, but Jehovah-Shammah kept my children from the evil one. I learned a huge lesson after this, that many times, the Lord, in His Sovereignty, allows us to go on with our stubbornness until we reap the consequences.

Our spirituality does not permit us to set aside God's commands and warnings. No matter how mature we think we are in the Lord, no matter how knowledgeable we are concerning God's promises, an obedient heart is all that matters when it comes to His dealings with us individually or collectively.

When I was discharged from the hospital, my heart broke when I saw my children for the first time in five weeks. Patty had starved the children ages 2 to 8 in my absence. She fed them only once a day. Since she couldn't kill me, she wanted to starve my children to death. She also refused to brush the teeth of the two year-old for the five weeks I was admitted. Edem's mouth was full of sores and he was emaciated.

My children looked like orphans. I had no relative in Togo. My family was in Ghana. But thank God, the angels of God surrounded them and kept them safe from being destroyed.

Geoffrey arrived from Singapore the week after I came home. But when Dr. Fiadjoe briefed him on what happened to me, it gave him a cause to praise the Lord and to remove Patty finally from the house.

"My brother," Doctor Fiadjoe said, "You were really fortunate. Your wife could have died on the spot. But, I believe God loves you so much He spared her life. You serve a mighty God."

Geoffrey also took the opportunity to witness to Dr. Fiadjoe. Dr. Fiadjoe came and visited our church a few times. I learned my lesson very well, not to challenge the voice of the Lord in any given command. Total obedience is what he requires. Disobedience is very, very costly. And what I feared happened.

At Heaven's Gate

Although Patty was out of the house, the effects of her spiritual attacks, verbal curses and physical abuse on the children remained a burden to struggle with. The children would wake up in the middle of the night screaming and calling out her name. There was battle after battle, but God was in it with us.

My own poor health was taking a big toll on me. With each monthly cycle, I had to go back to the hospital to receive a pint of blood, and with each transfusion came all kinds of complications. These were the days when donations of blood were not screened well for diseases. After receiving blood one time, all my joints became swollen. Later, I was told that donor had arthritis.

Another time after the transfusion, I shook unceasingly. My heart was racing faster than normal. I could not stand on my feet for three days. One way or another, something particular happened after each transfusion. We couldn't stop the transfusion, because they had become part of my survival. It seemed I was dying gradually, but I was standing on the promises of God. Because He promised me, the day the chariot came, that His grace would carry me through, and I believed it.

There was not a day without a group at the church crying out to God for my healing. The women were fasting and praying fervently for me. That reminded me of an event in the Bible. King Herod had arrested the Apostle Peter, "But the church was earnestly praying to God for him" (Acts 12:1-19). And Peter was miraculously released from prison by an angel.

Despite the prayers that were touching heaven for my sake, my condition zigzagged. At this time Dr. Fiadjoe tried a procedure to correct what was causing the unnecessary bleeding. Geoffrey took me to the clinic that morning, and waited in the room praying for the success. I was very weak that day, but I wasn't afraid to die. I had hope that I would live and fulfill my purposes on earth for His glory.

Sister Philippine and another beloved sister, Da Essi, who was the head-nurse at the clinic, were the doctor's assistants. Since they were Christians, they prayed with me before the doctor arrived. I was already hooked on to the I.V. The moment Dr. Fiadjoe came into the operation room, he said, "I don't know what is happening to you, but maybe this will help."

Maybe? I asked myself. No problem, I know the Lord would definitely heal me completely one day at His own time. If He restored Job, He will one day restore my health back for His glory. Amazingly, the moment I was given the anesthesia, I was lifted up to Heaven. It was an incredible atmosphere. The glory and the beauty of the environment were calm and appealing, oh, very blissful.

As I stood there at the gate, gazing at the majestic beauty of the environment. Someone walked toward me. With such an excitement, I called out, "Brother Paul, what a treat to see you here."

"Hello, Sister Monica," he also responded with such joy. "What are doing here?"

"I don't know. But please, I have a question for you."

"Go on, what do you want to know?"

"Brother Paul, I read in the Bible of your account on when you were taken to the third heavens, and you heard inexpressible things which man was not permitted to know. What was that? Can you tell me?"

"Oh, Sister Monica, are you going to stay?" he asked.

"Yes sir," I said with all confidence. "You see, those things I couldn't write down are Heavenly. They are not meant for the finite minds of people living on earth. If you go back, you will never remember it. It was kept from mortal men."

"No, Brother Paul, I think I have come to stay. I would love to hear it. Please, would you kindly tell me?"

He expounded on this revelation, which enveloped my whole being, as if my spirit was exploding with glory. I was rejoicing in the presence of this wonderful man of God whom I had not met or known in the natural world, but had read all the letters the Holy Spirit inspired him to write.

Suddenly, I felt the presence of a Mighty Being overshadowing me. The immensity of His presence was indescribable. At that instant, I asked, "Brother Paul, where is the Lord?"

"He is the One standing by your side," Brother Paul said with awe.

I looked up, and there He was. Jesus was so glorious beyond description. Oh my, He was magnificent, and beyond human understanding and description. "Lord!" I shouted with joy and elation and bowed to worship. I was like Peter on the Mount of Transfiguration. I had no words to describe what I was feeling.

The Lord looked at me with mixed emotions and said, "Monica, you can't stay. You are going back, because your time is not yet up. Geoffrey is calling you."

I knew immediately that He didn't want me there yet. My times are in His hands, and when the time comes, He will definitely take me home. But I wasn't satisfied.

"No, Lord," I said. "Please, I want to stay."

"Monica, Geoffrey is crying out for you. The children I gave you need you, and your time is not yet up," He said, with a love that surpasses human understanding. His love was so amazing.

Like a desperate and vulnerable child who doesn't want to let go of his or her father, I began to cry, "No Lord, please, don't leave me. Lord, don't leave me alone. I want to stay with You."

Before I could say another word, I heard, "No, Monica, go." The command was so powerful. But I held on to Him so tight, not wanting Him to leave me. In a flash, I was thrown into the thin air. All I could hear was the sounds of the sirens of heavenly ambulances everywhere, angels bringing me from Heaven to Earth. Instantly, I entered my body. I was still conscious of Heaven and its surroundings. My spirit was still holding on to Him and speaking in tongues.

When I regained consciousness, I was holding on to the rails on the bed and crying, asking the Lord to stay with me, "Please, do not leave me alone." I opened my eyes to a husband's sob. Geoffrey had cried his heart out. And with tears running down his cheeks, he scolded me like before, "Why do you want to leave me, Darling?"

Since I was still under the anesthesia, I could not answer his question. Later on, I told Geoffrey of my visit to Heaven, telling him how I talked to the Lord and the apostle Paul and what the Lord told me.

Now, I understood that the Apostle Paul and I have something in common, hence the messenger of satan was permitted to buffet him, and me too—too many visions, dreams, spiritual encounters and revelations. I think that might be a way to keep me humble and dependent on the Lord alone.

[29]

EXPOSED!

Geoffrey and the National Executive of our church, the Assemblée de Dieu du Togo, had scheduled a fund-raising trip to the United States in April 1989. And so, Dr. Fiadjoe scheduled me again for a complete hysterectomy in February so that Geoffrey could have the privilege of helping me before his departure. And although I wasn't afraid to die, I objected to the surgery at that time, because I had no peace about the scheduled date.

A few months earlier, the Lord brought Missionaries Richard Terherst and Audrey Ross from the United States to us. Audrey being a nurse, assured Geoffrey of her assistance in case of any emergency during his absence.

At the same time, the Lord also sent us another house-helper named Christie. She was a wonderful asset to our family. Although she did not know the Lord before she came to live with us, Christie accepted the Lord one morning during our devotions.

I was very grateful to the Lord for bringing me someone who loved us and was willing to be an older sister to my children. Today, Christie is married to Rev. Logossou, and she has a daughter named after me.

The Surgery

Geoffrey left as planned to the United States. But just a few days after his departure, I began bleeding profusely again, and breathing with difficulty. With these God-sent friends and helpers, I agreed to go in for the scheduled surgery.

No one was informed of the procedure with the exception of our missionary family. Aunt Audrey, as we called her, accompanied me to the hospital. I was admitted on the 13th of April 1989, because the surgery was due the following day at 11a.m.

After the normal routine tests and prep, I was told the surgery would take four or more hours. I wasn't scared, because all the near-death encounters had enhanced my faith in the Lord Jesus and given me enough hope of going to Heaven. After all, this Earth is not our final destination. So, I confidently entrusted my life into the Lord's hand to guide the surgeon.

Sister Essi, the head nurse, came and escorted me to the operation room. There, something marvelous happened. The Lord opened my eyes to see the presence of numerous angels in crystal white gowns around me. I literally saw the involvement of angelic doctors. Wow, what a treat! The sweetness of His presence overcame me. Yes, I was safe in His hands. That was all that I was aware of until that Saturday morning, when I overheard someone ask another person which day of the week it was. At that moment, I knew I was alive again.

Soon after I came home from the hospital, the Lord visited me again, but not without the powerful weapon of prayer and the assistance of Aunt Audrey. That very night, I felt the cold hands of death over me as I fought with two demonic forces. Audrey woke up and interceded on my behalf until I felt a release.

The Holy Spirit transported me into the realm of the Spirit, and showed me all the things that had been happening in the church before and after our arrival. Literally, I saw a full "video" of all the agents who were sent to the church, and who were rendering people impotent, causing miscarriage, killing people prematurely, and injecting people with the HIV viruses and other incurable diseases. Then I heard a voice resounding from Heaven saying, *"Monica, these will not get out except by prayer and fasting. These cannot be defeated except by prayer and fasting!"*

When I came to myself, I asked, "Lord, why should such things happen in Your house when the Holy Spirit is at work among us. Your Word is being taught and preached. We pray and fast all the time, so why?"

The Lord said, "Monica, the enemy you are dealing with is not flesh and blood. And so, spiritual warfare must be the lifestyle of the believer while on this earth. Just as a soldier is always prepared for action at any time, so should My children be, and much more, because the enemies you are dealing with cannot be seen, but they are very real. Spirits do not die. The earth is the domain of the evil one who wants to see My people destroyed. I promised you My presence, but you mustn't slack in resisting, rebuking, and casting him out.

"Monica, many mighty men and women of Mine have died young. Why do you think their lives were shortened? There was a cause, and the secret is with Me. When My people ignore that the enemy exists to destroy them; when My people do not put on the whole armor which I have given to them; when My people do not cherish My Word above all other things and live according to My principles and commandments, they fall prey to the enemy. When My people think that once I overcame the enemy for them, and that they do not have to do anything but to live their lives free of any combat, and to enjoy what I did for them at Calvary, they become easy preys. When My people have no knowledge of the evil they are dealing with, they sleep spiritually. Ignorance and self-deception are very dangerous. That was what happened to My disciples when they slept. They all deserted Me. Only the one who leaned on Me during the Supper really understood My heart. John stood the test and went with Me all the way to the cross. Good soldiers are always ready for action.

"Monica, I permitted you to go through these sufferings, so you can be a living testimony of My greatness, and teach My people these important principles. ..."

I grabbed a pen and wrote down what the Lord was saying with such an inspiration that was beyond myself. It was really unbelievable. I couldn't forget a word given. As I continued to pray in the Holy Spirit, the Lord made me aware that it's a lie fueled by the enemy for His children to think that there are no battles to fight, or else the Lord wouldn't have given us the spiritual armor in Ephesians 6.

The Lord Jesus overcame the enemy, and gave His people all the victory they will ever acquire in this life. He has given us all the power we need to overcome all the spiritual terrorists in this world. But just as a child or an inheritor has to preserve the inheritance given to him or her, so should we do whatever we can to preserve what He has given to us.

History reminds us that evil men and women are constantly planning and strategizing on how to destroy innocent lives. America has to fight terrorism at all cost. Israel must fight and protect its citizens. All free nations of the world must fight against terrorism of all forms. The same scenario applies to every believer. The Bible is very clear on visions and revelations. The Lord says, *"My people are destroyed from lack of knowledge" (Hosea 4:6).*

With the encouragement from the Lord, I made a call to the Women Ministries leader, Mrs. Rhoda Ndukwe, and narrated the revelations and the dream I had to her and encouraged her to call for a fast. She confirmed that the Lord woke her up and asked her to bring all the women together for a three-day prayer and fasting at the church, and they weren't going to leave without a breakthrough from the Lord.

After the ladies' three-days of prayers and fasting, a positive spiritual shift occurred in the church, but not until Geoffrey arrived home from the United States. It materialized when we received an unusual visit one morning.

The Confessions

Geoffrey had just come home from dropping the children at their school when someone knocked at our door. When I opened the door, I saw Patty standing there. She looked awfully sick. At first sight, I wanted to shut the door on her, telling her to leave us alone. But the Spirit of the Lord prompted me to be patient.

"Please, Mama. Please, don't close the door on me," she said. "I have come to remedy the situation."

I called out to Geoffrey, and left her still standing behind the door. We talked, prayed, and decided to listen to Patty at the church office. Once in the office, she said, "Pastor, I have come to confess all the terrible things I did or else I will die. I have come to ask your forgiveness for all the evil things I did to Mama (me) and to your children.

"Okay, speak," Geoffrey said.

"To tell you the truth, my aunt did nothing bad to me. I formulated the lie in order to gain access to your home. I was sent by the Lucifer to come to your house to lure you into sin and destroy the church. We hated you and Calvary Temple, because you were destroying our work. But when I came, I found out that it wasn't going to be easy because of the great spiritual gifts the Lord has given Mama. She is a strong spiritual backbone in your home and your ministry. So we decided to kill her first, and then it would be easier to deal with you. However, every step we took was revealed to her before we even implemented our schemes. That was when I attacked her. And even though I left your house, we've been in constant battle against her to kill her. I am sick today and dying, because God struck me and asked me to come and repent so that I will be healed. When I left your house, I joined with a group of witches to destroy your children as well, but it did not work. Anytime we came to kill them, there were angels around them. Finally, when Mama went to the hospital, the devil informed me of the surgery and sent me to kill her during the anesthesia. As I was flying in the spirit from where I was to the hospital to terminate her, an angel of the Lord struck me. I fell wounded. He told me to repent and confess it publicly or else I would die. This is the reason for my coming this morning. Everything that happened to Mama came from me, instigated by Satan. I was the one who came to the room and hit her lower abdomen. I was the one who poisoned her. …"

Geoffrey yelled out in anger, "We know that. Do not boast about it. Had the Lord not permitted it, you wouldn't have had any access to my wife. Shut up!"

Patty became terrified and began to cry, asking us for forgiveness again and again.

"And what did you and your agents do in the church? Tell me," I asked.

"Pastor," Patty said trembling. "Don't you know that the devil also goes to church? He sends his agents and demons to churches whether you like it or not. We maneuver our way through others and cause a lot of havoc, and many times we are not recognized by anyone. We come in to divide a church. We come in with sicknesses and diseases, untimely deaths, miscarriages, barrenness, and many other ills, even AIDS."

"I know that. Now, give me the names of all those who are involved in this church," Geoffrey commanded her.

At that point, Patty kept quiet and began to shake violently. We prayed in the Spirit, asking the Holy Spirit to break the power of the evil one over her so she could speak freely. After a while, she calmed down and said, "Please, Lucifer doesn't want me to reveal the truth to you."

What she said infuriated me. I stood up and said, "Satan, I command you in the Name of Jesus, shut up! You have no access in this place. Now Patty, speak out in the Name of Jesus. I know all the agents. The Lord revealed them to me even before you came here."

Patty confirmed that Lucifer informed her of his visit to our home, and how I had the boldness to command him to get out. "That really angered him, and he charged me to poison you," Patty emphasized. Then she mentioned names of people they infected with different diseases, even AIDS, and killed in the church, and promised to stand in front of the congregation to confess openly.

Interestingly, all the people involved were the ones the Lord had already revealed to us. It was really hard to swallow. But we forgave Patty and prayed for her. The Lord touched her immediately, and she began to recover.

That same week, we called for an emergency prayer and fasting. And the Sunday that followed became the Holy Ghost bazaar, when Patty stood in front of the assembly and confessed her involvement in witchcraft and how that she was initiated into marriage with Lucifer at a very young age in her village. (She detailed some disturbing matters boldly, stuff she wasn't able to do in our home, and how the power of prayer in our home almost killed her; things I am not supposed to conceal because of the families involved, and the sensitivity of the issue). After that, she named all those who were involved in their demonic schemes.

A fire was kindled. People ran forward to confess their sins. Some of the agents she mentioned repented, but others fled. Revival had begun in Calvary Temple.

From that moment, church attendance tripled. People came from all the neighborhoods to accept Christ as Lord and Savior. And the revival did not stop. We went from one service to three services on Sundays. Truly, all things really work together for good to those who love the Lord (*Romans 8:28)!*

You don't have to do anything for the devil to attack you. Being a Christian makes satan so nervous and angry, he has to do something to get you miserable and sidetracked. Why? He cannot be redeemed!

There is the belief that when a believer is living for the Lord, they will not encounter demonic assaults. That is a lie from the pit of hell. The stronger you are, the fiercest the enemy roars against you. Being armed with all the spiritual weapons the Lord provided for, does not exempt any believer in Christ from being attacked or assaulted by the enemy. The weapons are there to protect and to preserve us. The Bible declares: *"Many are the afflictions of the righteous, but the LORD delivers him out of them all" (Psalms 34:19).*

Why did the devil attack or tempt Jesus? Was the Son of God weak in faith and living in sin? The devil and his cohorts know who Jesus was and is. Jesus was and is Lord over them, yet they tried to tempt Him anyway. They could not inflict Jesus with diseases, because He is Lord over diseases. They could not oppress Jesus physically, because He is the Creator of the enemy himself.

The enemy incited others against Him. Satan even tried to use Peter to rebuke Jesus in order to divert Him from the purpose for which He came to earth.

> *But He turned and said to Peter, "Get behind Me, Satan! You are an offense to Me, for you are not mindful of the things of God, but the things of men" (Matthew 16:23).*

I know that no matter how the going might be, His grace will always be sufficient for me, and His power will be made perfect in my weakness. Because, when God permits the enemy to touch His children, it is for a greater cause, a blessing in disguise.

[30]

HOW SPIRITUAL TERRORISTS OPERATE

Let me give you some pictorial images that will help you understand what I have been talking about. First of all, why did Japan attack the United States of America at Pearl Harbor? Why did Al Qaeda attack America on 9/11?

I believe the enemy attacked us because there are now more Christians in North and South America than elsewhere, (although scattered throughout many nations). Secondly, we drifted away from God and dethroned Him from governing us, so we had no protection whatsoever, although we were armed physically. In addition, we ignored warnings, or we miscalculated the ability of our enemies to hurt us.

Before the attack on Pearl Harbor, small signs of imminent attack were detected, but they were either ignored or underestimated. The same scenario may have been played out in the pre-9/11 attacks. All warnings—both spiritual and physical were ignored, miscalculated, or underestimated.

The United States of America was the number one world super-power. The U. S. is armed to the teeth. The U.S. is fighting and liberating others politically and spiritually, which is worthy of emulation. United States was and is still one of God's instruments taking the Gospel of Jesus Christ to many lands. As a result, the U.S., apart from Israel, is the most hated nation in the world.

Also, what have the people of the Jewish faith done to their uncountable enemies? Bible history makes it so plain that when Israel served the Lord, the Almighty One (YAHWEH NISSI) shielded them against their enemies. But when they turned away from Him and ignored His warnings, they suffered the consequences. The Lord said to Israel,

> *"If you walk in My statutes and keep My commandments, and perform them, then I will give you rain in its season, the land shall yield its produce, and the trees of the field shall yield their fruit. Your threshing shall last till the time of vintage, and the vintage shall last till the time of sowing; you shall eat your bread to the full, and dwell in your land safely. I will give peace in the land, and you shall lie down, and none will make you afraid; I will rid the land of evil beasts, and the sword will not go through your land. You will chase your enemies, and they shall fall by the sword before you. Five of you shall chase a hundred, and a hundred of you shall put ten thousand to flight; your enemies shall fall by the sword before you. ... For I will look on you favorably and make you fruitful, multiply you and confirm My covenant with you. ... But if you do not obey Me, and do not observe all these commandments, and if you despise My statutes, or if your soul abhors My judgments, so that you do not perform all My commandments, but break My covenant, I also will do this to you: I will even appoint terror over you, wasting disease and fever which shall consume the eyes and cause sorrow of heart. And you shall sow your seed in vain, for your enemies shall eat it. I will set My face against you, and you shall be defeated by your enemies. Those who hate you shall reign over you, and you shall flee when no one pursues*

you. And after all this, if you do not obey Me, then I will punish you seven times more for your sins. I will break the pride of your power; I will make your heavens like iron and your earth like bronze" (Leviticus 26:3-19 paraphrased).

"Has a nation changed its gods, which are not gods? But My people have changed their Glory For what does not profit. Be astonished, O heavens, at this, and be horribly afraid; be very desolate," says the LORD. "For My people have committed two evils: they have forsaken Me, the fountain of living waters, and hewn themselves cisterns— broken cisterns that can hold no water. "Is Israel a servant? Is he a home-born slave? Why is he plundered?" (Jeremiah 2:11-14).

Also, the Church of Jesus Christ, which comprises individual members like you and me, is the most hated group of all the demonic terrorists groups seen and unseen—which are even greater and numerous than America's enemies.

I am not magnifying or exalting the enemy above my God and my King. He asked me to write and inform you. But if we underestimate the activities of the enemy and only dwell on what we know or are familiar with, we make ourselves vulnerable. The good news is, the God we serve, is the Greatest, the Creator, the Omniscient (All-knowing), the Almighty (All-Powerful), and Omnipresent (Everywhere present), who became flesh, and took upon Himself the sins of humanity. Jesus Christ redeemed us from our sins (Isaiah 9:6; Isaiah 53:3-6; John 1:1-6, 10-18; John 3:16-18; John 14:6-14; Acts 4:10-12; Colossians 1:12-20; Hebrews 1:14; 1 John 5), overcame the enemy and says, *"All authority has been given to Me in heaven and on earth" (Matthew 28:18).* Nothing takes Him by surprise. Nothing is beyond His reach, and nothing can overpower or conquer Him. Hence the reason we need to lean on Him rather than on our intellect. We need to listen to His heart and receive all the necessary information needed for the victory He had already given to us.

The Bible says in 1 John 4:4 that the One in me is Greater than the enemy. And who is the One in me? JESUS CHRIST! But I mustn't ignore the fact that Jesus cast out more demons than we could imagine. And He gave us the power to cast out demons in His Name (Mark 16:17). The disciples confronted the devil more often than most of us would (Acts 8:9-24).

The Apostle Paul had his share of combat with the demonic (Acts 16:16-24). And as the coming of the Lord approaches, every Christian must be aware of demonic terrorism, their operations, and their deceptive behavior and actions.

> *Now the Spirit expressly says that in latter times some will depart from the faith, giving heed to <u>deceiving spirits and doctrines of demons</u>, speaking lies in hypocrisy, having their own conscience seared with a hot iron, --- (1Timothy 4:1-2 Emphasis mine).*

If the enemy has the audacity to incite his agents to cry out "GOD IS DEAD", he can manipulate his way into their hearts for them to serve him. He also has the same audacity to sow lies into the minds of God's people that he (the devil) doesn't even exit. Why? He knows that ignorance and misperception are just a few of his weapons to lure people into spiritual slumber.

It is true that our focus mustn't only be centered on what spiritual terrorists are doing and forget the power we have in Christ over them, but we mustn't also underestimate their involvements in world and national affairs, in families and individuals, as well as in the ones they send inside our churches. Therefore, in order to understand how spiritual terrorists operate, we must remind ourselves of the meaning of terrorism and parallel its operations to nominal terrorists.

In its simplest meaning, we learned that terrorism is the systematic use of violence and intimidation to achieve some goal, or to bully someone into conforming to one's ideology.

We must also remember that terrorism comes in many forms—religious, economic, and of course, demonic. Now, here are a few examples on how spiritual terrorists operate.

❖ NON-HUMANS, BUT DEMONIC BEINGS:

Spiritual terrorists are not humans. But they operate within humans spiritually and in ranks. They have captains and high ranking wicked spirits who do their biddings.

For instance in the military, we have numerous levels of positions such as, private, private first class, corporal, specialist, several classes of sergeants, lieutenants, captains, majors, etc. The same ranking system plays out in the spirit realm as seen in the passage below.

> *For though we walk in the flesh, we do not war according to the flesh. For we do not wrestle against flesh and blood, but against <u>principalities, against powers, against the rulers of the darkness of this age, against spiritual hosts of wickedness</u> in the heavenly places (2 Corinthians* 10:3-4 emphasis mine).

According to the Bible, there are certain domains of the demonic we cannot operate in or touch without violating certain spiritual principles, which may be detrimental to our physical and spiritual wellbeing. Jesus Christ, our Lord, gave us power to cast out demons, but not the luxury to insult Satan and certain demonic behaviors we do not understand.

> *Likewise also these dreamers defile the flesh, reject authority, and speak evil of dignitaries. Yet Michael the*

archangel, in contending with the devil, when he disputed about the body of Moses, dared not bring against him a reviling accusation, but said, "The Lord rebuke you!" But these speak evil of whatever they do not know; and whatever they know naturally, like brute beasts, in these things they corrupt themselves (Jude 8-10).

Don't you think that if Satan and demons were physical, we would have been able to eradicate them just as we were able to kill Osama bin Laden? They are spiritual beings who do not die, and are constantly recruiting others. And so we Christians must really understand what we are dealing with, put on our armor, and stand strong in the Lord without wavering.

❖ SPECIALIZED AGENTS, LOCAL AND GLOBAL

Spiritual terrorists have special human agents they use in their spiritual activities (Daniel 10:12-14; 2 Corinthians 10:3-4).

These agents investigate into people's lives. They are always recruiting new combatants, and they are always training demonic suicide bombers to commit atrocious acts. These spiritual terrorists try to probe and scrutinize those who try to attack them in order to retrieve information concerning how their enemies operate against them.

When a person doesn't have time to serve God, these evil forces send in special agents to preoccupy their mind with all sorts of unhealthy thoughts, acts, and behaviors in order to destroy them. The Word of God says,

See then that you walk circumspectly (cautiously, vigilantly), not as fools but as wise, redeeming the time, because the days are evil. Therefore do not be unwise, but understand what the will of the Lord is (Ephesians 5:15-16 emphasis mine).

One night I had a dream. I have been a dreamer like Joseph since I was a child, and I am still. I do not take my dreams lightly at all, because they are all prophetic. I can say that 98% of my dreams come true.

In this dream, I saw two long cords attached to our house. The cords extended from our house in Togo to my hometown in Ghana. There were many agents of the devil walking back and forth on the cables, holding walky-talkies, communicating to one another. They were sending information to those on the other side concerning my family. I looked carefully to identify the people on the cables. Their bodily frames were strange. They were somehow transparent. They weren't normal human beings, but spirit beings. But when I looked closer, I recognized one of my cousins, the witch aunt, and another distant relative. And Patty was standing on the Togo side of the rope, which was attached to our house. My cousin was the middleman, while Patty was the connector between our home in Togo and the family in Ghana in the spirit realm.

The moment the cousin saw me, she sent a signal to her colleagues and yelled at the top of her voice, "Stop, she's seen us. Stop, we are in trouble."

At that point, I shouted, "In the Name of Jesus, I cut off this demonic connection into our home with the sword of the Holy Ghost." I prayed to the Holy Spirit.

All of a sudden, fire came down from heaven and consumed the cords. The cousin fell off and hit the ground. Then I woke up. I told Geoffrey, and we prayed.

Two weeks after, I received a letter stating that the cousin I had seen on the line with the walky-talky woke up one morning paralyzed and died a few days after. She was a priestess and a witch.

❖ INTERMINGLE SEXUALLY:

Spiritual terrorists mingle and intermingle with their human hosts to procreate sexually in order to dominate them. The Genesis 6 account of the Nephilim or the account in the Book of Enoch, which weren't canonized are worthy of study.

The demonic terrorists the world is fighting against have actually infiltrated into all our systems whether we like it or not. They are in every sector of our society. They are luring men, women, and young people, and are pouring in millions of dollars to overtake society. They are also intermingling with and marrying Christians and non-Christians in order to dominate the world.

In most parts of the world, mermaids are connected to the demonic and the spiritual realm. But in our western culture, mermaids have become objects of fun and an adventure. These mermaids are part of the demonic sexual seditions that occurred in Genesis 6:1-5, and which are literally infiltrating our homes.

Spiritual terrorists are seducers, and they have a world of their own in the spirit world inside the sea where they operate and intermingle with humans to procreate.

Geoffrey and I ministered to numerous men and women who had sexual encounters with these mermaids. These individuals couldn't get married, because the mermaids were very jealous of their relationship with them. Those who were married had unresolved marital difficulties, because their partners saw another man or woman in bed with them. Today, there are numerous people who have demonic partners who sleep with them.

Have you ever thought about why God instructed us in the 10 Commandments not to make any representation of anything under the sea and worship them? Under the sea? Yes, The All-knowing God knew what He was talking about.

You shall not make yourself any graven image [to worship it] or any likeness of anything that is in the heavens above, or that is in the earth beneath, or that is in the water under the earth; ⁵ You shall not bow down yourself to them or serve them; for I the Lord your God am a jealous God, visiting the iniquity of the fathers upon the children to the third and fourth generation of those who hate Me, ⁶ But showing mercy and steadfast love to a thousand generations of those who love Me and keep My commandments" (Exodus 20:4-6 The Amplified Bible).

I may be classified as being too direct and judgmental, but God didn't create half-human half-fish beings. The Bible makes it so clear that in the beginning, God created one man and one woman to procreate and fill the whole world.

So God created man in His own image; in the image of God He created him; male and female He created them. Then God blessed them, and God said to them, "Be fruitful and multiply; fill the earth and subdue it; have dominion over the fish of the sea, over the birds of the air, and over every living thing that moves on the earth (Genesis 2:27-29).

There was one Christian brother in our church I would name Guy. He was on the verge of death, because the female mermaid partner he married in the realm of the spirit, wanted to carry him to her home under the sea so he could help her take care of their children. It was the near-death experience he had that drove Guy into a deeper relationship with the Lord Jesus Christ.

Guy said to us, "Pastors, my mermaid female partner was so beautiful beyond anything I could imagine. I did not know that she was a mermaid. She would come in the form of a real woman each night and anytime I needed her. But one day, she took me into the sea world for our romantic date. I became awed by what I saw. She turned into a mermaid. It was really incredible to know that there is a world under the sea where these creatures live. The habitation of these beings inside the sea has no equal in comparison to our world. Over time, going under the sea for our dates became a routine. She took me there at night, and brought me back before daytime. I saw her pregnant. I saw her when she had the babies. My problems began when I could not agree with her to leave this world and go and live under the sea. Now she wanted to kill me."

Wow! Isn't that scary? We fasted and prayed for Guy. The Lord delivered when he severed that relationship in the Name of Jesus. Today, Guy is married with two children. This is just one example.

❖ AVID IMITATORS:

Spiritual terrorists have the capacity to imitate God in certain things that pertains to His creation. Do you remember Moses and Aaron's encounter with the magicians of Pharaoh in the Book of Exodus 7:8-13? When the Lord made Aaron's rod turn into a serpent, the magicians replicated the same. The only difference was that the God who asked Moses to perform those miracles was the Greatest, and He gave power to Aaron's serpent to swallow that of the magicians.

> *For such men are false apostles, deceitful workers, fashioning themselves into apostles of Christ. And no marvel; for even Satan fashions himself into an angel of light (2 Corinthians 11:13-14).*

❖ INTERFERENT:

Spiritual terrorists are able to interfere with God's plans and purposes for an individual.

The Lord Jesus had been training His disciples for three years. He knew His mission on earth was to give His life as a ransom for the sins of humanity. But one day, as He was rehearsing to the disciples of how He would suffer many things and then be put to death, it didn't resonate well with Peter. In response to what Jesus said, Peter took Him aside and rebuked Him.

> *And He began to teach them that the Son of Man must suffer many things, and be rejected by the elders and chief priests and scribes, and be killed, and after three days rise again. ³² He spoke this word openly. Then Peter took Him aside and began to rebuke Him. ³³ But when He had turned around and looked at His disciples, He rebuked Peter, saying, "Get behind Me, Satan! For you are not mindful of the things of God, but the things of men." (Mark 8:31-33 emphasis mine).*

What did Jesus say? *"Get behind Me, Satan! For you are not mindful of the things of God."* Was Peter the devil? No! Unbeknown to Peter, he was being used indirectly by the enemy to prevent Jesus from fulfilling His purpose on earth.

❖ KIDNAPPERS:

Spiritual terrorists kidnap people, brainwash them through acts of intimidation, and make them agents of theirs (2 Corinthians 10:3-5).

The demonic are always mimicking and the work of the Holy Spirit. When the Holy Spirit carried Phillip into the desert, he won the Ethiopian Eunuch for Christ and baptized him in Jesus's Name (Acts 8:26-40). While the Holy Spirit does a great work in an individual and transforms them when they are carried into the realm of the spirit, the demonic make those they abduct double agents of Satan.

And when he (evil spirit) comes, he finds it empty, swept, and put in order. [45] Then he goes and takes with him seven other spirits more wicked than himself, and they enter and dwell there; and <u>the last state of that man is worse than the first</u>. So shall it also be with this wicked generation (Matthew 12:44-45 emphasis mine).

One of my cousins was kidnapped one morning when she went to farm. The chief of the village sounded the gorgons around the neighboring villages to locate her. The local people went in search of her for many days. My family was devastated. Three months after, she appeared at the entrance of the village dressed like a typical Indian fetish priestess with all the ornaments and marks over her body. She was given witchcraft and became a fetish priestess until she died that fatal day when she fell from the rope in the dream the Lord gave me.

❖ POSSESS SUPERNATURAL ABILITIES, BUT ARE NOT OMNIPOTENT, OMNIPRESENT, OR OMNISCIENT LIKE GOD:

Spiritual terrorists are able to possess people with supernatural abilities beyond our understanding (Acts 16:16-19). Just look at how mediums and magicians operate. What most of them do and say are not just natural gifts. They are in connection with the demonic (Acts 8:9-24).

One of Mother's cousins *Ekua (name changed), went through a very difficult situation. While she was pregnant, she would feel every night about midnight as if her baby had been taken away from her womb. She would wake up with a flattened stomach. On the other hand, she would suddenly begin to feel the movement again around 4 a.m. Worried of what was happening to her, she told my Grandma.

You recall my Grandma, a real spiritual genius. Grandma laughed out loud, and told her niece, "Someone is removing the baby each night to fly and attend their demonic meetings. If you do not do something about it, your child will become a witch."

The niece became really scared and asked, "So, what should I do? And who is this person who is doing this to me?"

"I don't know who the person is. But it will be wise that when you wake up in the middle of the night, and you don't feel the movement of the baby, to move from where you normally sleep, and find yourself a different spot, but not in the same room. You will see what will happen the next day."

Too scared, she couldn't go to sleep the first night and nothing happened to her baby. The moment she fell asleep the second night, her baby was taken out from her womb. In fear and trembling, she hurriedly opened the door and ran to Grandma's house, which wasn't far from hers. She stayed with Grandma until evening and returned home. But the moment she opened her bedroom door, she met the unbelievable. Her husband was lying on the floor pregnant and groaning in pain.

What happened? Ekua had married a witch, who was taking the baby out for his demonic trips. And when he came and the wife wasn't around, he placed the baby in his own stomach. And since a man doesn't have a womb and cannot deliver a baby, the husband and the baby died a few days after. But where did he get the ability to remove a baby from someone's womb? A mystery, isn't it?

❖ TORTURERS & ABUSERS

Spiritual terrorists inflict their victims with all kinds of diseases and paralyses.

When they came to the other disciples, they saw a large crowd around them and the teachers of the law arguing with them. As soon as all the people saw Jesus, they were overwhelmed with wonder and ran to greet him. "What are you arguing with them about?" he asked. A man in the crowd answered, "Teacher, I brought you my son, who is possessed by a spirit that has robbed him of speech. Whenever it seizes him, it throws him to the ground. He foams at the mouth, gnashes his teeth and becomes rigid. I asked your disciples to drive out the spirit, but they could not." "You unbelieving generation," Jesus replied, "How long shall I stay with you? How long shall I put up with you? Bring the boy to me." So they brought him. When the spirit saw Jesus, it immediately threw the boy into a convulsion. He fell to the ground and rolled around, foaming at the mouth. Jesus asked the boy's father, "How long has he been like this?" "From childhood," he answered. "It has often thrown him into fire or water to kill him. But if you can do anything, take pity on us and help us." "'If you can'?" said Jesus. "Everything is possible for one who believes." Immediately the boy's father exclaimed, "I do believe, help me overcome my unbelief!" When Jesus saw that a crowd was running to the scene, He rebuked the impure spirit. "You deaf and mute spirit," He said, "I command you, come out of him and never enter him again." The spirit shrieked, convulsed him violently and came out. The boy looked so much like a corpse that many said, "He's dead." But Jesus took him by the hand and lifted him to his feet, and he stood up. After Jesus had gone indoors, His disciples asked Him privately, "Why couldn't we drive it out?" [29] He replied, "This kind can come out only by prayer and fasting" (Mark 9:14-29).

We see here in this passage, that Jesus identified the cause of this disease as being demonic. And He had to rebuke the demon to leave the boy. Then He gives directives to the disciples as to how they should deal with certain kinds of spirits—prayer and fasting. If Jesus were here today, He would have been ridiculed for labeling the young guy as being possessed by the enemy.

Another instance of connecting bodily infirmity with the demonic was with a woman Jesus met in the Temple one Sabbath day.

> *Now He was teaching in one of the synagogues on the Sabbath. [11] And behold, there was a woman who had a spirit of infirmity eighteen years, and was bent over and could in no way raise herself up. [12] But when Jesus saw her, He called her to Him and said to her, "Woman, you are loosed from your infirmity." [13] And He laid His hands on her, and immediately she was made straight, and glorified God. [14] But the ruler of the synagogue answered with indignation, because Jesus had healed on the Sabbath; and he said to the crowd, "There are six days on which men ought to work; therefore come and be healed on them, and not on the Sabbath day." [15] The Lord then answered him and said, "Hypocrite! Does not each one of you on the Sabbath loose his ox or donkey from the stall, and lead it away to water it? [16] So ought not this woman, being a daughter of Abraham, whom Satan has bound—think of it—for eighteen years, be loosed from this bond on the Sabbath?" [17] And when He said these things, all His adversaries were put to shame; and all the multitude rejoiced for all the glorious things that were done by Him (Luke 13:10-17 emphasis mine).*

❖ DEPRESS, OPPRESS, & TORMENT:

Spiritual terrorists torment people mentally and spiritually. They send threats to depress, demoralize, and torment anyone who does not believe in their ideology. It takes the power of Jesus Christ to defeat their torments.

> Then they sailed to the country of the Gadarenes, which is opposite Galilee. *27* And when He stepped out on the land, there met Him a certain man from the city who had demons for a long time. And he wore no clothes, nor did he live in a house but in the tombs. When he saw Jesus, he cried out, fell down before Him, and with a loud voice said, "What have I to do with You, Jesus, Son of the Most High God? I beg You, do not torment me!" *29* For He had commanded the unclean spirit to come out of the man. <u>For it had often seized him, and he was kept under guard, bound with chains and shackles; and he broke the bonds and was driven by the demon into the wilderness.</u> *30* Jesus asked him, saying, "What is your name?" And he said, "Legion," because many demons had entered him. *31* And they begged Him that He would not command them to go out into the abyss. *32* Now a herd of many swine was feeding there on the mountain. So they begged Him that He would permit them to enter them. And He permitted them. *33* Then the demons went out of the man and entered the swine, and the herd ran violently down the steep place into the lake and drowned (Luke 8:26-28 emphasis mine).

The man in the Biblical story had no control over himself. He was controlled mentally, spiritually, emotionally, and physically by these demons. Hence the Lord encourages His people to dedicate themselves wholly and daily to Him and to allow Him to renew our minds through His transformatory power.

> I beseech you therefore, brethren, by the mercies of God, that you present your bodies a living sacrifice, holy,

acceptable to God, which is your reasonable service. [2] And do not be conformed to this world, but be transformed by the renewing of your mind, that you may prove what is that good and acceptable and perfect will of God (Romans 12:1-2).

❖ INFILTRATORS:

Spiritual terror groups infiltrate the children's world by using filmmakers, Internet programs, books, violent films plus video games, and other avenues to promote their agenda.

Most of the science fictional films, books, and other related programs are indirectly being inspired and propagated by the head of the demonic. They sound really appealing to the world than the reading of the Word of God, but they are a way of opening the spirit of our children into the demonic. The Word of God says,

Be sober, be vigilant; because your adversary the devil walks about like a roaring lion, seeking whom he may devour. Resist him, steadfast in the faith, knowing that the same sufferings are experienced by your brotherhood in the world (1 Peter 5:8-9).

The Word of God encourages us to set our minds on things that would help us connect with God and His Word, and reject those "spiritual adventures", which actually open us up for all kinds of demonic activity.

Finally, brethren, whatever things are true, whatever things are noble, whatever things are just, whatever things are pure, whatever things are lovely, whatever things are of good report, if there is any virtue and if there is anything praiseworthy—meditate on these things (Philippians 4:8).

❖ SEXUALLY & MORALLY PERVERSED:

Spiritual terrorists possess people with immoral sexual spirit and seduce them sexually into illicit practices *(Genesis 6:17; Genesis 19; Romans 1:18-32; 2 Peter 2).*

> *Now a population explosion took place upon the earth. It was at this time that beings from the spirit world looked upon the beautiful earth women and took any they desired to be their wives. ³ Then Jehovah said, "My Spirit must not forever be disgraced in man, wholly evil as he is. I will give him 120 years to mend his ways." ⁴ In those days, and even afterwards, when the evil beings from the spirit world were sexually involved with human women, their children became giants, of whom so many legends are told. ⁵ When the Lord God saw the extent of human wickedness, and that the trend and direction of men's lives were only towards evil, ⁶ He was sorry He had made them. It broke His heart. ⁷ And He said, "I will blot out from the face of the earth all mankind that I created. Yes, and the animals too, and the reptiles and the birds. For I am sorry I made them." (Genesis 6:1-7 The Living Bible - TLB)*

Where do certain men have the power to abuse as many women as they desire, and sometimes murder them in cold blood? Why do you think God sent the flood in Noah's time and the fire to Sodom and Gomorrah? Sexual perversion had been perpetrated there by the demonic! Hence God demands that we honor Him with our bodies, which are His Temples.

A Christian must always live in sexual purity, a holy life that is pleasing to the Lord; whether married or unmarried, in order to avoid being wrecked physically and mentally.

> *Do you not know that the unrighteous will not inherit the kingdom of God? Do not be deceived. <u>Neither fornicators, nor idolaters, nor adulterers, nor homosexuals, nor</u>*

sodomites, [10] *nor thieves, nor covetous, nor drunkards, nor revilers, nor extortionist will inherit the kingdom of God. -- All things are lawful for me, but all things are not helpful. All things are lawful for me, but I will not be brought under the power of any.* [1] *Foods for the stomach and the stomach for foods, but God will destroy both it and them. Now the body is not for sexual immorality but for the Lord, and the Lord for the body.* [14] *And God both raised up the Lord and will also raise us up by His power.* [15] *Do you not know that your bodies are members of Christ? Shall I then take the members of Christ and make them members of a harlot? Certainly not!* [16] *Or do you not know that he who is joined to a harlot is one body with her? For "the two," He says, "shall become one flesh."* [17] *But he who is joined to the Lord is one spirit with Him.* [18] *Flee sexual immorality. Every sin that a man does is outside the body, but he who commits sexual immorality sins against his own body.* [19] *Or do you not know that your body is the temple of the Holy Spirit who is in you, whom you have from God, and you are not your own?* [20] *For you were bought at a price; therefore glorify God in your body and in your spirit, which are God's (1 Corinthians 6:9-10, 12-20 emphasis mine).*

[1] *Therefore gird up the loins of your mind, be sober, and rest your hope fully upon the grace that is to be brought to you at the revelation of Jesus Christ;* [14] *as obedient children, not conforming yourselves to the former lusts, as in your ignorance;* [15] *but as He who called you is holy, you also be holy in all your conduct,* [16] *because it is written, "Be holy, for I am holy." (1 Peter 1:13-15).*

Let marriage be held in honor (esteemed worthy, precious, of great price, and especially dear) in all things. And thus let the marriage bed be undefiled (kept un-dishonored); for God will judge and punish the unchaste (all guilty of sexual vice) and adulterers (Hebrews 13:4).

❖ NON-PREDICTABLE & DECEPTIVE

Spiritual terrorists are very deceptive. They promise negotiations, peace, and unity with their left hand, and with their right hand, they are always planning atrocious attacks against their enemies.

Spiritual terrorist are just like Shay and Patty who said they wanted to be delivered, when in actual fact, they had hidden agendas to deepen their roots in my family and destroy us. This is exactly what Pharaoh also did. He negotiated deceitfully with Moses numerous times when Moses spoke on God's behalf, "Let My people go." Pharaoh knew he wasn't going to liberate God's people, yet he promised their deliverance when a plague struck. Even after the Lord intervened through the death of their firstborns, Pharaoh still pursued the Israelites to the Red Sea until his army drowned (Exodus 5—15). What a tragedy! The devil doesn't give up easily.

❖ COUNTERFEITERS:

These evil beings can operate side by side with the gifts of the Holy Spirit, especially that of the Word of Knowledge. Without the gift of Discernment, it is impossible to detect their activities.

Then Micaiah said, "Therefore hear the word of the LORD: I saw the LORD sitting on His throne, and all the host of heaven standing by, on His right hand and on His left. [20] And the LORD said, 'Who will persuade Ahab to go up, that he may fall at Ramoth Gilead?' So one spoke in this manner, and another spoke in that manner. [21] Then a spirit came forward and stood before the LORD, and said, 'I will persuade him.' [22] The LORD said to him, 'In what way?' So he said, 'I will go out and be a lying spirit in the mouth of all his prophets.' And the LORD said, 'You shall persuade him, and also prevail. Go out and do so.' [23] Therefore look! The LORD has put a lying spirit in the mouth of all these prophets of yours, and the LORD has declared disaster against you (I Kings 22:19-23 emphasis mine).

These Biblical examples should serve as a warning to each one of us, because *"not all that glitters is gold."* Satan and his agents will always counterfeit God's gifts and enablement in His children in order to deceive them. The devil is a counterfeiter.

❖ HATER OF ANYTHING GOOD:

Spiritual terrorists oppose those who have a great future. They want to keep people under bondage, so they could have control over them. They hate free and successful people.

The devil and his demons do not know everything, but they have great knowledge of what an individual may become. And they do their job right by instigating others to either attack or destroy them before they rise in power *(Matthew 2:16-18; Jeremiah 31:15).*

The enemy instigated Pharaoh to kill all the male sons of the Israelis, because a deliverer had been born. But God used Shiprah and Puah, the two Hebrew midwives who feared God, to preserve the babies. Later on, God used Jochebed to preserve the life of her son, Moses (Exodus 1:15-22; Exodus 2:1-10).

Also, had God the Father not preserved His Son from being destroyed by Herod and his evil schemes, Jesus wouldn't have gone to the cross. And had Jesus not gone to the cross, we would have all perished.

> *However, we speak wisdom among those who are mature, yet not the wisdom of this age, nor of the rulers of this age, who are coming to nothing. But we speak the wisdom of God in a mystery, the hidden wisdom which God ordained before the ages for our glory, which none of the rulers of this age knew; for had they known, they would not have crucified the Lord of glory (1 Corinthians 2:6-8).*

We also know how God gave the devil permission to attack Job (Read the Book of Job). Yet, Job didn't see his suffering as something that was connected with the evil one. He cried out, and lodged his complaint with no comfort coming from anywhere. His friends condemned him for living in sin. His wife asked him to curse God and die. Yet, he maintained his integrity and devotion to the Lord until the Lord spoke.

I believe that if Job had had visions, dreams, and revelations such as the one the Lord gave me, he would have viewed his suffering differently. So, no matter what you may be going through, stay devoted to God.

Do not deviate or throw in the towel. God always brings out His purposes more beautifully even in trials and adversities. It took the determination and devotion of the afflicted person to God to bring about God's purposes for them.

> *Look, I go forward, but He is not there, and backward, but I cannot perceive Him; ⁹ When He works on the left hand, I cannot behold Him; when He turns to the right hand, I cannot see Him. But He knows the way that I take; when He has tested me, I shall come forth as gold (Job 23:9-10).*

If America had stayed on course with the God of the Bible, God would have fought our wars for us. The Lord God of Abraham, Isaac, and Jacob would have been our Shelter and Refuge. Didn't He do it in the past with all the wars we fought when we were dwelling under His shadows?

❖ HATERS OF THE GOSPEL OF JESUS CHRIST:

Spiritual terrorists oppose the Gospel and prevent people from believing in Jesus Christ.

The Word of God makes it so clear that, if the Gospel is hid, it is the fact that the god of this world has blinded the eyes so they wouldn't be saved.

> *And even if our gospel is veiled, it is veiled to those who are perishing. The god of this age has blinded the minds of unbelievers, so that they cannot see the light of the gospel that displays the glory of Christ, who is the image of God (2 Corinthian 4:3-4 emphasis mine).*

Spiritual terrorists spread hatred for the Gospel of Christ. Elymas was one of those who tried to prevent the proconsul (governor or administrator) of Paphos from hearing the Word Paul was preaching to him.

> *They traveled through the whole island until they came to Paphos. There they met a Jewish sorcerer and false prophet named Bar-Jesus, who was an attendant of the proconsul, Sergius Paulus. The proconsul, an intelligent man, sent for Barnabas and Saul because he wanted to hear the word of God. But Elymas the sorcerer (for that is what his name means) opposed them and tried to turn the proconsul from the faith. Then Saul, who was also called Paul, filled with the Holy Spirit, looked straight at Elymas and said, "You*

are a child of the devil and an enemy of everything that is
right! You are full of all kinds of deceit and trickery. Will
you never stop perverting the right ways of the Lord? Now
the hand of the Lord is against you. You are going to be
blind for a time, not even able to see the light of the sun."
Immediately mist and darkness came over him, and he
groped about, seeking someone to lead him by the hand.
When the proconsul saw what had happened, he believed,
for he was amazed at the teaching about the Lord (Acts
13:6-12).

In most of the stories I shared with you, you can deduce that
the fetish priests, witch doctors, and magicians who attacked us did
so because they were losing their clients.

Satan and his cohorts always oppose the work of God by
inciting others to attack God's servants in order to prevent
conversion. That is what we went through in the ministry.

❖ USURPERS & MANIPULATIVE:

Spiritual terrorists are manipulative, and they usurp
authority *(1Kings 21:25-26; 2 Kings 11:1-20).*

Certain kinds of civil disobedience and coups d'état have
their source from an old-aged leader—Lucifer. He wanted to be like
God. He wanted to take the place of the Most High, and God threw
him down here on earth. That is what a Luciferian spirit is all
about—rebellion.

How you are fallen from heaven, O Lucifer, son of the
morning! How you are cut down to the ground, you who
weakened the nations! For you have said in your heart: 'I
will ascend into heaven, I will exalt my throne above the
stars of God; I will also sit on the mount of the congregation

on the farthest sides of the north; I will ascend above the heights of the clouds, I will be like the
Most High.' Yet you shall be brought down to Sheol, to the lowest depths of the pit (Isaiah 14:12-15).

You were the seal of perfection, full of wisdom and perfect in beauty. You were in Eden, the garden of God; every precious stone was your covering: The sardius, topaz, and diamond, beryl, onyx, and jasper, sapphire, turquoise, and emerald with gold. The workmanship of your timbres and pipes was prepared for you on the day you were created. "You were the anointed cherub who covers; I established you; you were on the holy mountain of God; you walked back and forth in the midst of fiery stones. You were perfect in your ways from the day you were created, till iniquity was found in you (Ezekiel 28:12-15).

All terror groups do not respect others or leadership. They always want things done in their own way, or they want anarchy— no leadership at all.

And you He made alive, who were dead in trespasses and sins, ² in which you once walked according to the course of this world, <u>according to the prince of the power of the air, the spirit who now works in the sons of</u> disobedience, ³ among whom also we all once conducted ourselves in the lusts of our flesh, fulfilling the desires of the flesh and of the mind, and were by nature children of wrath, just as the others (Ephesians 2:13 emphasis mine).

❖ CALLOUS & CRUEL

Spiritual terrorists inflict physical pain and wounds on people (Matthew 8:28).

Terror groups of all kind, whether they are rapists, witches and wizards, witch doctors, or serial killers, et cetera, are all influenced and used by the demonic. And some of them go to the extent of dismembering another human being created in God's image, whereas the Bible makes it so clear that human blood is precious in His sight and shouldn't be spilled by another. Here is a specific command God gave to Noah and his descendants soon after the flood:

The Lord said to Noah: "And for your lifeblood I will require a reckoning: from every beast I will require it and from man. From his fellow man I will require a reckoning for the life of man. Whoever sheds the blood of man, by man shall his blood be shed, for God made man in his own image" (Genesis 9:5-6 English Standard Version).

There was one event that marked my life when I was in Primary 4. One of my classmates was kidnapped during recreation at school. When her body was found two days later, her heart and sexual organs had been removed. Such acts of cruelty were so rampant in Africa when I was growing up. Many children were lured with bonbons and food.

When terror groups invaded Ethiopia and other parts of Africa, they literally paralyzed Christians by cutting their limbs. Jesus said, *"The thief does not come except to steal, and to kill, and to destroy. I have come that they may have life, and that they may have it more abundantly" (John 10:10).* Cain killed his brother Abel, and God placed a curse on him.

And He (the Lord) said, "What have you done? The voice of your brother's blood cries out to Me from the ground. [11] So now you are cursed from the earth, which has opened its mouth to receive your brother's blood from your hand. [12] When you till the ground, it shall no longer yield its strength

to you. A fugitive and a vagabond you shall be on the earth"
(Genesis 4:10-12).

A week before the dedication of the new Calvary Temple we built for God's glory, I had a fight with someone in my dream. The person had a knife and wanted to cut through my throat. The Spirit of God aided me. I hit her hard with my right hand and overcame her. I woke up abruptly, perspiring. Geoffrey saw me struggling in my sleep. He laid hands on me and prayed over me.

By morning, my right arm was swollen to my elbow. Later on, the lady (name withheld) confessed to another pastor of her attempt to kill me. The pastor warned us of future attacks by this woman if care is not taken.

❖ CAMOUFLAGERS:

Spiritual terrorists transform themselves into all kinds of figurines to attack others. They can use the forms of cats, owls, roaches, et cetera. They disguise and mask themselves as angels of light to attack the unarmed.

For such are false apostles, deceitful workers, transforming themselves into apostles of Christ. And no wonder! For Satan himself transforms himself into an angel of light. Therefore it is no great thing if his ministers also transform themselves into ministers of righteousness, whose end will be according to their works (2 Corinthians 11:13-15).

Why do we believe the story of Eve being tempted by the devil through the serpent, but are not able to believe that the enemy can change into anything to harass God's children? Why do we believe Moses' account of the magicians of Pharaoh, and reject the notion that the enemy cannot go to such extents of using anything to manipulate and destroy the children of God?

Mother could not attend our wedding because of strange encounters she had with some roaches in her dream two days prior to the wedding. In the dream, she saw some roaches crawling in her covers. She hated roaches very badly, and so she jumped out of the bed to find something to kill them. She spotted a big strange cockroach by the window, looking at her as if it were human. She whipped the strange roach down with a piece of cloth and stomped her right foot on it. She then raced through the room to finish the rest of the band and went back to sleep (still in her dream). But when she woke up the next morning, her right arm and right foot were swollen.

Mother had killed lots of real roaches with her foot in the past, but this had been an attack from the enemy. Her encounter was very bizarre, but true. They were a kind of spiritual, demonic cockroaches she killed. Most Africans and Easterners know what I am taking about, an experience with demonic forces transformed into roaches. Geoffrey and I prayed for Mother the night of our arrival in Takoradi. The Lord miraculously healed her. It was at this time Geoffrey asked Mother to openly confess Jesus as Lord and Savior of her life. Years later, at the age of 85, Mother sang her favorite song, "How sweet the Name of Jesus sounds" to Heaven, while surrounded by her children and grandchildren.

Wherever you live, you should know that demons and witches are everywhere. They operate around the world, and their main aim is to destroy humanity. The Bible states:

> For our struggle is not against flesh and blood, but against the rulers, against authorities, against the powers of this dark world and against the spiritual forces of evil in the heavenly realms (Ephesians 6:12).

❖ SELF SEEKING & IMPOVERISHMENT:

Spiritual terrorists are able to bankrupt people spiritually, emotionally, and financially. They are selfish and ambitious. They care less about the welfare of others.

America has become war weary. Fighting terrorism is affecting everyone. Hence Christians are commanded to pray for their leaders and their nations.

I exhort first of all that supplications, prayers, intercessions, and giving of thanks be made for all men, ² for kings and all who are in authority, that we may lead a quiet and peaceable life in all godliness and reverence. ³ For this is good and acceptable in the sight of God our Savior, ⁴ who desires all men to be saved and to come to the knowledge of the truth (1 Timothy 2:1-3).

First of all, when Christians become nonchalant or lukewarm with their spiritual life, and do not necessarily pay much attention to their walk with the Lord, they can fall for anything. - And the enemy is more than willing to help bankrupt individuals spiritually, morally, and emotionally.

Be sober, be vigilant; because your adversary the devil walks about like a roaring lion, seeking whom he may devour. Resist him, steadfast in the faith, knowing that the same sufferings are experienced by your brotherhood in the world (1 Peter 5:8-9).

Secondly, when Christians refuse to pay their tithes and fail to give to support God's work, they remove themselves from the protection against the devourer of their finances. A lady came to me recently with her family and financial problems. During counseling, she said something about her finances that confirmed what the Lord had already told me.

She said, "Pastor, something is happening to me recently, which is really mind-boggling. I have been losing money from my account. I would go to the bank and report foul activities on my account, but they always dismissed my case, stating that they had receipts and my signatures on the withdrawn amount. Recently, there was a withdrawal of $200 on my account. When I contacted the bank, the guy said to me, 'You retrieved the money at 12.38 a.m. I have the receipt with your signature on it.'

"At 12.38 a.m. with my signature on it? I was sleeping. And who will go to the bank at that time of the day?" she asked the agent. She became bewildered and called her mum in Africa to inform her of her financial problems, but she heard something that shocked her.

"Oh yeah, your auntie told me she withdrew the money yesterday from your account, since you don't want to be helping us financially," her mum told her. "And we've been doing that for quite a while. I guess you are not seeing it."

At that point, I asked her, "Have you been a faithful tither?"

"No, Pastor, I haven't been a good tither and a giver at all. I have been thinking God understands that my income is minimal compared to that of others."

"Then, don't expect God to protect your finances. The Big Papa up there in Heaven knew of all these things before He gave us His prescription for financial security," I emphatically told her.

"But this is really mysterious. My mom and aunt are all in Africa. They don't know my account number, and I don't bank online. They do not have my bank card, but how are they able to withdraw money and sign my name?"

"They spiritually hacked into your computer. They have power to withdraw, because there is no protection over your finances. The devourer can only be rebuked by God Himself, because the devil is God's creation.

In the natural, this story may not make sense. But spiritually, it is possible. The Lord said in *Malachi 3: 8-12:*

> *"Will a man rob God? Yet you have robbed Me! But you say, 'In what way have we robbed You?' In tithes and offerings. You are cursed with a curse, for you have robbed Me, even this whole nation. Bring all the tithes into the storehouse, that there may be food in My house, and try Me now in this," says the LORD of hosts, "If I will not open for you the windows of heaven and pour out for you such blessing that there will not be room enough to receive it. And I will rebuke the devourer for your sakes, so that he will not destroy the fruit of your ground, nor shall the vine fail to bear fruit for you in the field," says the LORD of hosts; "And all nations will call you blessed, for you will be a delightful land," says the LORD of hosts (emphasis mine).*

❖ THEY CAUSE PHYSICAL HAVOCS:

Spiritual terrorists can cause a lot of family misfortunes and havocs—conflict in the home, miscarriages, and removal of babies from the womb for their demonic purposes.

Patty, the girl I fought with, confessed that many of the miscarriages that happened among our church members were all done by them. "When a lukewarm, careless, or weak Christian gets pregnant, we visit her in the form of her husband and have sex with her in the spirit," Patty said. "That kills the fetus, hence causing a miscarriage."

Now I understand why Jesus hates lukewarmness. He says: *"I know your works, that you are neither cold nor hot. I could wish you were cold or hot. [1]So then, because you are lukewarm, and neither cold nor hot, I will vomit you out of My mouth" (Revelation 3:15, 16).*

I have come to understand that spiritual carelessness is unacceptable and dangerous for a child of God.

❖ DEVALUE HUMAN LIFE:

Spiritual terrorists are instrumental in causing accidents, and ending lives prematurely. Spiritual terrorists do not value human life. They have prematurely eliminated countless innocent lives through demonic explosives, and crashes of all kinds.

I organized a national convention at Atakpame, Togo. Two days prior to the convention, the Lord gave me a scary dream. I saw a derailment of the train the women would be taken from Lomé to Atakpame and the uncountable casualties. The dream was so scary that I woke up shivering and screaming. Geoffrey and I fasted and prayed. I called all the women for an emergency prayer and fasting. The intercessory group we formed for the convention also stood in the gap for God's protection on all participants. After the prayers, the Lord told me that the forces of darkness would like to derail the train and bring shame to His Name. But He will give us victory if we prayed.

The day of the convention, the train left Lomé as planned to Atakpame. Arriving near Notse, something extraordinary happened. All the babies on board cried and moaned pathetically at once that the mothers had no choice than to cry out to the Lord. They didn't understand what was happening to their children. As they prayed, the Holy Spirit took over. The power of God came down, and two women on two separate coaches screamed and confessed that they were about to derail the train when the babies cried out.

What a mystery! The Lord, in His sovereignty, opened up the spirit of the innocent babies to feel what was about to take place. Their cries sparked prayers that overturned the wicked plot of the witches, because God reveals to deliver if His people would pray.

Our Lord Jesus clearly says that we shouldn't fear those who kill the body but cannot kill the soul.

> *And do not fear those who kill the body but cannot kill the soul. But rather fear Him who is able to destroy both soul and body in hell. [29] Are not two sparrows sold for a copper coin? And not one of them falls to the ground apart from your Father's will. [30] But the very hairs of your head are all numbered. [31] Do not fear therefore; you are of more value than many sparrows (Matthew 10:28-31).*

The Scripture makes it so clear that there is the possibility of such deaths, not only caused by martyrdom but also caused by accidental deaths and spiritual terrorists *(Luke 12:4-7)*. Most Christians forget that everything that happens physically originates spiritually.

One Sunday morning, I went to church sick to my stomach. I desired to stay home and sleep, but the Holy Spirit wouldn't allow me to. Dr. Ndukwe was leading the prayer session before the message. The moment I sat down, and began to pray, the Lord gave me an open vision, which alarmed me. I saw someone, holding the hands of two children, ages 4 and 6, and walking out of the church.

"What a weird vision," I said to myself.

Then the Lord said to me, "The woman who is holding the children wants to kill them right here in front of the church to bring shame to My Name. Tell the congregation to pray and snatch these kids from the hands of the enemy right now."

I called to relay the message and the vision to one of the ushers to give to the pastors. They didn't care about program interruptions. They called it to the attention of the congregation and we began to pray. Within a few minutes after prayer, we heard the screeching sound of car brakes in front of the church. The two children I saw in my vision were standing in the middle of the road, and almost got killed. The parents didn't know how their children got there, the ushers didn't see them walking out, and the children themselves didn't know how they got into the middle of the road. But the Lord knew it and showed it to me.

Truly, where there is no open-vision nor the word of knowledge operating in His house, the people of God become prey to the enemy's attacks. Think about what would have happened had Joseph not been given a vision of what Herod had planned to do against baby Jesus? Think on what would have happened had the king of Israel gone to battle without listening to the vision the Lord gave to his servant Elisha. We may not know everything, but if we are sensitive, God will preserve us through the gifts of the Spirit.

❖ OBSTRUCT PRAYERS:

Spiritual terrorists can intercept the prayers of God's people. Many a times, we become discouraged and stop knocking at Heaven's door when our prayers delay. But a Biblical example from the Book of Daniel should motivate us to pray harder and persistently until the answer comes to us. In Daniel 10, the prophet fasted for 21 days, praying for the deliverance of his people from captivity.

The Bible tells us that Daniel's prayers were answered the first day he began to pray, but the prince of Persia, which is the demonic, spiritual governor over that nation, withstood the angel who was bringing the response. And for 21days, a spiritual battle went on until another stronger angel, Michael, went and helped the courier angel.

> *Suddenly, a hand touched me, which made me tremble on my knees and on the palms of my hands. [11] And he said to me, "O Daniel, man greatly beloved, understand the words that I speak to you, and stand upright, for I have now been sent to you." While he was speaking this word to me, I stood trembling. Then he said to me, "Do not fear, Daniel, for from the first day that you set your heart to understand, and to humble yourself before your God, your words were heard; and I have come because of your words. [13] But the <u>prince of the kingdom of Persia withstood me twenty-one days</u>; and behold, Michael, one of the chief princes, came to help me, for I had been left alone there with the kings of Persia. [14] Now I have come to make you understand what will happen to your people in the latter days, for the vision refers to many days yet to come." (Daniel 10:10-14 emphasis mine).*

Our Lord Jesus commands us to prayer unceasingly without fainting (Luke 18:1-8). We also read in 1 Thessalonians 5:17, *"Pray without ceasing."* So when your prayers are delayed, pray persistently without wavering until the answer comes. God will always be on time.

❖ DISTORTION OF GOD'S WORD:

Spiritual terrorists are avid in distorting the truth of God's Word. They misquote, misinterpret, and use the Word out of context. In distorting truth, they are able to lure people into believing and pursuing lies.

Most people think that the devil is an idiot, who has no knowledge of the Word of God. That is far from the truth. He is rather knowledgeable of the Bible than most Christians. He believes in God and trembles (James 2:19).

The first thing the devil did in order to deceive mankind to disobey God was to use the commands God gave to Adam and Eve in a deceitful conversation, "Has God said?" And he is using the same tact today to entice humanity into questioning the viability, reliability, and the inspiration of the Word of God, which is the Bible. 'Has God said...? Did God really say that? The Word didn't really mean that … et cetera.' And the debate goes on and on.

When Angel Gabriel announced the birth of the Messiah to Mary, he emphatically assured Mary that the baby she was going to bear would be God's Son. And He was coming to earth for a greater purpose—to save mankind from sins.

> *Then the angel said to her, "Do not be afraid, Mary, for you have found favor with God. 31 And behold, you will conceive in your womb and bring forth a Son, and shall call His name JESUS. 32 He will be great, and will be called the Son of the Highest; and the Lord God will give Him the throne of His father David. 33 And He will reign over the house of Jacob forever, and of His kingdom there will be no end. … "The Holy Spirit will come upon you, and the power of the Highest will overshadow you; therefore, also, that Holy One who is to be born will be called the Son of God" (Luke 1: 30-33, 35 emphasis mine).*

And to doubting and confused Joseph, who did not know what to do with his espoused pregnant virgin wife, the angel affirmed to him in a dream saying,

"Joseph, son of David, do not be afraid to take to you Mary your wife, for that which is conceived in her is of the Holy Spirit. [21] And she will bring forth a Son, and you shall call His name JESUS, for He will save His people from their sins." [22] So all this was done that it might be fulfilled which was spoken by the Lord through the prophet, saying: [23] "Behold, the virgin shall be with child, and bear a Son, and they shall call His name Immanuel," which is translated, "God with us" (Matthew 1:20-23, Read also Isaiah 7:14; Isaiah 9:6-7).

Later on, Mary visited her cousin Elizabeth, who was also pregnant (Luke 1:1-25). But the moment Mary greeted Elizabeth, something miraculous happened. The baby in her womb leapt and Elizabeth was filled with the Holy Spirit and began to prophesy.

And it happened, when Elizabeth heard the greeting of Mary that the babe leaped in her womb; and Elizabeth was filled with the Holy Spirit. [42] Then she spoke out with a loud voice and said, "Blessed are you among women, and blessed is the fruit of your womb! [43] But why is this granted to me, that the mother of <u>my Lord</u> should come to me? [44] For indeed, as soon as the voice of your greeting sounded in my ears, the babe leaped in my womb for joy. [45] <u>Blessed is she who believed, for there will</u> be a fulfillment of those things which were told her from the Lord" (Luke 1:40-45).

All these Scriptures and interactions were given to affirm the deity and the Lordship of Christ, and to confirm the prophecies given concerning the coming Messiah in the Old Testament. Yet a few weeks before Jesus Christ began His ministry, the enemy's first tact was to contest His Son-ship, and to defy Him to use His power 'in the wrong sense', after a forty days prayer and fasting. 'If You are the Son of God,' was repeated in all the three levels of temptations he brought against Christ.

> *"If You are the Son of God, command that these stones become bread." [4] But He answered and said, "It is written, 'Man shall not live by bread alone, but by every word that proceeds from the mouth of God.'" Then the devil took Him up into the holy city, set Him on the pinnacle of the temple, [6] and said to Him, "If You are the Son of God, throw Yourself down. For it is written: 'He shall give His angels charge over you,' and, 'in their hands they shall bear you up, lest you dash your foot against a stone.'" Jesus said to him, "It is written again, 'You shall not tempt the LORD your God.'" [8] Again, the devil took Him up on an exceedingly high mountain, and showed Him all the kingdoms of the world and their glory. [9] And he said to Him,*
>
> *"All these things I will give You if You will fall down and worship me." [10] Then Jesus said to him, "Away with you, Satan! For it is written, 'You shall worship the LORD your God, and Him only you shall serve.'" [11] Then the devil left Him, and behold, angels came and ministered to Him.*

What do you think the devil used to tempt Jesus? The Word of God. He quoted different passages of Scriptures. But Jesus also overcame Him through the Word of God. *"It is written,"* Jesus quoted. Read Deuteronomy 8:3; John 6:35; Psalms 91:11, 12; Deuteronomy 6:13, 16.

Jesus warns us concerning false prophets and the addition or distortion of His Word. Spiritual terrorists are really avid in their schemes, and we must also be really careful in our walk with the Lord and in the study of His Word.

Jesus said, "Be wary of false preachers who smile a lot, dripping with practiced sincerity. Chances are they are out to rip you off some way or other. Don't be impressed with charisma; look for character. Who preachers are is the main thing, not what they say. A genuine leader will never exploit your emotions or your pocketbook. These diseased trees with their bad apples are going to be chopped down and burned" (Matthew 7:15 - The Message Bible).

But there were also lying prophets among the people then, just as there will be lying religious teachers among you. They'll smuggle in destructive divisions, pitting you against each other—biting the hand of the One who gave them a chance to have their lives back! They've put themselves on a fast downhill slide to destruction, <u>but not before they recruit a crowd of mixed-up followers who can't tell right from wrong</u>. They give the way of truth a bad name. They're only out for themselves. They'll say anything, anything that sounds good to exploit you. They won't, of course, get by with it. They'll come to a bad end, for God has never just stood by and let that kind of thing go on. ... There's nothing to these people—they're dried-up fountains, storm-scattered clouds, headed for a black hole in hell. They are loudmouths, full of hot air, but still they're dangerous. Men and women who have recently escaped from a deviant life are most susceptible to their brand of seduction. They promise these newcomers freedom, but they themselves are slaves of corruption, for if they're addicted to corruption—and they are—they're enslaved (2 Peter 2:1-4, 17-19 - The Message Bible).

You shall not add to the Word, which I command you, nor take from it, that you may keep the commandments of the LORD your God, which I command you (Deuteronomy 4:6).

For, I testify to everyone who hears the words of the prophecy of this book: If anyone adds to these things, God will add to him the plagues that are written in this book; and if anyone takes away from the words of the book of this prophecy, God shall take away his part from the Book of Life, from the holy city, and from the things which are written in this book (Revelation 22:18-19).

❖ DECEPTIVE MIRACLES:

Spiritual terrorists can perform extraordinary miracles to deceive people.

Mr. Afolabi and his friend *Komlan (name changed), a witch doctor, came to our house one morning with all his voodoo amulets. He had expressed the desire to accept Christ Jesus as his Savior, but he still thought his voodoos were more powerful than the Name of Jesus.

Before Geoffrey would ask Mr. Komlan to confess Jesus as Lord, Mr. Komlan decided to prove to us that his magical amulets were really powerful. We knew it wasn't a good idea, but he was insistent. As he charmed, his broom stood up and danced, while demonic voices came out of the pots.

Geoffrey and I prayed in the Spirit as he enchanted. When he finished his enchantments, Geoffrey prayed in the Name of Jesus and cast out the demons from the items and defied Mr. Komlan to enchant again. Mr. Komlan tried numerous times to no avail. His magical powers had left him, and the objects the devil used were lifeless as well. At that instant, he fell on his knees and accepted Jesus Christ as his personal Savior. We burnt all the juju amulets he brought, and he was set free.

This story reminded me of a Biblical story of Prophet Elijah and the priests of baal in I Kings 18:20-40. In this case, the prophets of baal enchanted from morning till evening, but their gods wouldn't respond. The Bible says that in the last days, demonic forces and false prophets would perform so many miracles to deceive God's children.

> *Then if anyone says to you, 'Look, here is the Christ!' or 'There!' do not believe it. For false christs and false prophets will rise and show great signs and wonders to deceive, if possible, even the elect. See, I have told you beforehand (Matthew 24:23-25).*

❖ PROUD AND ARROGANT

Spiritual terrorist are proud, haughty, and conceited. They do not listen to anyone. But the Word of God makes it really clear that it was pride and arrogance that led to the downfall of Lucifer. And he is empowers anyone who is full of themselves and leads them to destruction (Isaiah 14:12-15; Ezekiel 28:11-19).

God Almighty detests arrogance, and commands His children to walk in humility. Proverbs 16:18 says, *"Pride goes before destruction, and a haughty spirit before a fall."*

> *Everyone **proud** in heart is an abomination to the Lord; though they join forces, none will go unpunished (Proverbs 16:5).* Please, read also Proverbs 6: 16-19; James 4:6-8; 1 Peter 5:6-9.

❖ BRAINWASHERS:

Lastly, in trying to deceive us, these spiritual terrorists bombard the minds with negative thoughts about God and about ourselves.

These terrorists whisper comments such as, "God doesn't love you," "You are no good to anyone." "You are ugly." "Everyone hates you," et cetera. And when you buy into these lies, they gain ground in your mind, and they begin to suggest how you should deal with those comments. "Kill them," they whisper. Or, "Kill yourself, and life will be better."

No, life wouldn't be better without you, and you don't have to kill anyone to feel great. God loves you any way. The fact that you are living on God's beautiful planet shows how much God thinks of you. He had you in mind when He created this planet, and He has plans for you (Jeremiah 29:11-13).

The enemy told me I had no value hence God was punishing me. I wanted to die. But when I gave my life to Jesus, He turned my life around. And today, I know I am an asset in God's hands.

> *For I know the plans I have for you, says the Lord. They are plans for good and not for evil, to give you a future and a hope. Then you will call upon Me and go and pray to Me, and I will listen to you. And you will seek Me and find Me, when you search for Me with all your heart" (Jeremiah 29:11-13).*

> *Are not two sparrows sold for a penny? And not one of them will fall to the ground apart from your Father. ³⁰ But even the hairs of your head are all numbered. ³¹ Fear not,*

therefore; you are of more value than many sparrows (Matthew 10:29-30 emphasis mine).

People may say bad things about you. Disappointments may come, but those things said or done have nothing to do with who you are, and the love God has for you. Remember that spiritual terrorists are bullies, and they can play with your mind. But do not buy into their lies. You are loved and cherished!

These are just a few of the lessons the Lord taught me and is still teaching me in my walk with Him. And I hope you will make them yours as well and be vigilant in your dealings with spiritual terrorists.

[31]

GUARDING AGAINST THE DEMONIC

To be given foresight allows us to plan and arm ourselves against demons. Delving into the evil spiritual domain without the proper knowledge or protection from the Lord can expose someone to catastrophic encounters and sufferings. And so having a deep knowledge of what we cannot see is good. But knowledge alone does not keep someone from being terrorized spiritually. Knowledge plus the necessary spiritual armories and the weapons needed can aid or guard anyone from being destroyed by spiritual terrorists.

The Lord Jesus said something very important, which many Christians take for granted. He said, *"The ruler of this world comes, but he has nothing in Me" (John 14:20).* What actually does this statement mean? The Bible says that we have a great High Priest, Jesus, the Son of God, who was tempted as we are, yet without sin *(Hebrews 4:15).* Satan had nothing to accuse Jesus of, so he could not oppress Jesus.

We humans are sinful, filled with all kinds of stuff, which makes it easy for the enemy to place his foot inside our hearts. That makes the walk in the Holy Spirit a real priority for every believer in Christ Jesus. So in order to have total victory over these spiritual terrorists, we need to take certain things into consideration.

1. A PERSONAL RELATIONSHIP WITH THE LORD
(John 1:11-12).

Although we all are God's creation, we are not all God's children. One can only become a child of God when they believe in Jesus Christ as the Son of God, who came to earth, bore their sins on the cross, died and rose up again for their justification.

There is no salvation in any other, for there is no other name under heaven given among men by which we must be saved (Acts 4:12).

After dark one night, a Jewish religious leader named Nicodemus, a member of the sect of the Pharisees, came for an interview with Jesus. "Sir," he said, "we all know that God has sent you to teach us. Your miracles are proof enough of this." ³ Jesus replied, "With all the earnestness I possess I tell you this: Unless you are born again, you can never get into the Kingdom of God." ⁴ "Born again!" exclaimed Nicodemus. "What do you mean? How can an old man go back into his mother's womb and be born again?" ⁵ Jesus replied, "What I am telling you so earnestly is this: Unless one is born of water and the Spirit, he cannot enter the Kingdom of God. ⁶ Men can only reproduce human life, but the Holy Spirit gives new life from heaven; ⁷ so don't be surprised at my statement that you must be born again! ⁸ Just as you can hear the wind but can't tell where it comes from or where it will go next, so it is with the Spirit. We do not know on whom he will next bestow this life from heaven." ⁹ "What do you mean?" Nicodemus asked. ¹⁰⁻¹¹ Jesus replied, "You, a respected Jewish teacher, and yet you don't understand these things? I am telling you what I know and have seen—and yet you won't believe Me. ¹² But if you don't even believe Me when I tell you about such things as these that happen here among men, how can you

possibly believe if I tell you what is going on in heaven? [13]
For only I, the Messiah, have come to earth and will return
to heaven again. [14] *And as Moses in the wilderness lifted up*
the bronze image of a serpent on a pole, even so I must be
lifted up upon a pole, [15] *so that anyone who believes in Me*
will have eternal life. [16] *For God loved the world so much*
that He gave His only Son so that anyone who believes in
Him shall not perish but have eternal life. [17] *God did not*
send His Son into the world to condemn it, but to save it. [18]
"There is no eternal doom awaiting those who trust Him to
save them. But those who don't trust Him have already been
tried and condemned for not believing in the only Son of
God" (John 3:1-18 - TLB).

Jesus is the only Life, the Truth, and the Way to God (John 14:6). Religion doesn't make anyone a child of God. Good works doesn't make anyone a child of God. Although good works are good, they do not in themselves make anyone a child of God.

The Bible says, *"For by grace you have been saved through faith, and that not of yourselves; it is the gift of God, not of works, lest anyone should boast (Ephesians 2:8, 9).* To become a child of God, one needs to be born into God's family.

But as many as received Him (Jesus), to them He gave the
right to become children of God, to those who believe in His
name: [13] *who were born, not of blood, nor of the will of the*
flesh, nor of the will of man, but of God (John 1:10-12
emphasis mine).

Christianity is not a religion but a personal relationship with God Almighty, through His only Son, Yeshua (Jesus Christ). After believing in Christ, you must repent of your sins, and allow Jesus to be the Lord of your life.

Repent, and let every one of you be baptized in the Name of Jesus Christ for the remission of sins; and you shall receive the gift of the Holy Spirit (Acts 2:38).

If you confess with your mouth the Lord Jesus and believe in your heart that God has raised Him from the dead, you will be saved. 10 For with the heart one believes unto righteousness, and with the mouth confession is made unto salvation. 11 For the Scripture says, "Whoever believes on Him will not be put to shame" (Romans 10:9-11).

You can only be safe when you belong to the Lord. Your battle becomes His battle, and He fights to give you the victory. He gives you power and grace to live for His glory. And the devil knows those who belong to Jesus *(Isaiah 54:14-17; Luke 10:19; Mark 16:15-18).*

In the Book of Acts 19, we read the story of the four sons of one Mr. Sceva, a ruler of the synagogue. They thought that praying and casting out demons was such a pleasure they could meddle with *(Acts 19:13-20).* But the demons in the possessed man set the record straight. We read,

Then some of the itinerant Jewish exorcists took it upon themselves to call the name of the Lord Jesus over those who had evil spirits, saying, "We exorcise you by the Jesus whom Paul preaches." Also there were seven sons of Sceva, a Jewish chief priest, who did so. And the evil spirit answered and said, "Jesus I know, and Paul I know; but who are you?" Then the man in whom the evil spirit was leaped on them, overpowered them, and prevailed against them, so that they fled out of that house naked and wounded. This became known both to all Jews and Greeks dwelling in Ephesus; and fear fell on them all, and the name of the Lord

Jesus was magnified. And many who had believed came confessing and telling their deeds. Also, many of those who had practiced magic brought their books together and burned them in the sight of all. And they counted up the value of them, and it totaled fifty thousand pieces of silver. So the word of the Lord grew mightily and prevailed.

2. BE PRAYERFUL *(Psalms 91; Luke 18:1, 7-8).*

A prayer-less Christian is a weak Christian. Prayer is the spiritual breath of the believer in Christ. You stop breathing, you die. In my book, THE ENDTIME DAUGHTERS OF THE KING, I emphasized much on the importance of prayer and what prayer is to a child of God. Two of the points I mentioned in the book are that prayer is a rendezvous with His Majesty and a spiritual business agreement with the Almighty. And when you have this special rendezvous with God, and He has lavished you with His presence, you are in good hands. When you are in a business agreement with the Lord, who can destroy you? None! Because He is the Managing Director of your life. The enemy will try, but God will bring you out like a piece of refined gold that is worth a billion.

Although we prayed and fasted a lot together before our wedding, Geoffrey and I began a resolved binding spiritual practice the same day of our wedding, which we kept faithfully till death separated the two of us. This important spiritual practice began at four each morning with just the two of us in our bedroom, and it continued from five to six with our children and all those who lived with us. It was our divine encounter moments with our Heavenly Father through praise and worship, prayer and the reading of His Word.

So, right from the birth of our four sons, they learned to worship and praise the Lord. They were built in prayer and intercession for others, and they were anchored in the reading and memorization of Scriptures each morning before breakfast. We prayed and had family times and interaction with our children at meal times. And sometimes, we called for emergency prayer meetings besides the morning devotion to intercede for pertinent needs. This spiritual practice didn't diminish even after they all left the nest. I believe the presence of the Lord and the Word we inculcated into their lives was the Holy Spirit's glue that kept them in the faith, and held our family together throughout all the difficult times we encountered in the ministry.

The Apostle John wrote, *"I have **no greater joy** than to hear that my children walk in truth" (3 John 1:4)*. This is my joy as well, but it took a firm foundation of intimacy with our Christ Jesus our Lord and His Word through prayer.

The same spiritual passion and practice has never left me. It is my survival kit. I would always wake up at two in the morning to pray. But most of the time, the Holy Spirit would wake me up at His own time to seek His face and intercede for others. These moments of prayer and groaning before the Lord have strengthened me and saved lives numerous time.

Prayer is very important and vital to your spiritual life. Prayer makes you strong. But most importantly, when a child of God prays fervently, something happens in the invisible (James 5:16b). A powerful shift takes places in the realm of the spirit, which affects the physical. And the enemy knows those who are strong, and those who are weak. You need high spiritual energy to rebuke, resist, and cast the enemy out in Jesus Name.

> *Therefore let us approach the throne of grace with boldness, so that we may receive mercy and find grace to help us at the proper time (Hebrews 4:16).*

The LORD who made the earth, the LORD who forms it to establish it, Yahweh is His name, says this: Call to Me and I will answer you and tell you great and incomprehensible things you do not know (Jeremiah 33:2-3 HCSB).

3. BE ARMED *(Ephesians 6: 10-18; 2 Corinthians 10:3-6).*

God didn't leave us defenseless. He has given us everything we need in Him to overcome the enemy. Our weapons of warfare are not physical, but they are really powerful beyond all imaginations.

No soldier would ever go to war without being armed. Likewise, no believer in Christ can truly overcome the enemy without the proper spiritual ammunitions.

Stand therefore, having girded your waist with truth, having put on the breastplate of righteousness, and having shod your feet with the preparation of the gospel of peace; above all, taking the shield of faith with which you will be able to quench all the fiery darts of the wicked one. And take the helmet of salvation, and the sword of the Spirit, which is the word of God; praying always with all prayer and supplication in the Spirit, being watchful to this end with all perseverance and supplication for all the saints (Ephesians 6:10-18).

o   The helmet of salvation *(Exodus 15:2; 2 Samuel 22:3, 51; Psalms 18:36; Acts 5:12).*
o   The breastplate of righteousness—which protects your heart from all pollutants *(Proverbs 4:23; Philippians 4:8-9).*

- o The Sword of the Spirit—the Word of God *(Hebrews 4:12; Luke 4:1-13).*
- o The belt of truth *(John 8:31-36; Ephesians 5:1-9).*
- o The shield of faith, with which we extinguish all the darts of the enemy *(Hebrew 11:1-2, 6; 1 John 5:4).*
- o Prayer *(Luke 18:1-8; Philippians 4:4-6; Ephesians 6:18).*
- o The Blood of Jesus Christ *(Exodus 12; Revelation 12:11).*
- o The power and anointing of the Holy Spirit (Zechariah 4:6-7; Isaiah 61:1-3; Matthew 4:1-11; Acts 1:8).
- o By Revelation *(Joshua 6-8; Daniel 10:12-13).* Each combat and its strategy. The Holy Spirit will definitely reveal His secrets to you when you are open to listen.

I do not know what I would have done if I didn't have Jesus, and the weapons He gave us to fight the devil.

4. BE SENSITIVE AND OBEDIENT TO THE LORD.

The Bible says that the secret things belong to the LORD our God *(Deuteronomy 29:29).* The Holy Spirit desires to reveal hidden secrets of the enemy to us. And when the Lord reveals or speaks to you concerning something, do not argue with Him. Just be willing to obey Him in everything.

In 1 Kings 13, the story is told of a man of God from Judah, who was sent to Bethel to pronounce judgment on the altars Jeroboam had erected and to show God's displeasure against their idolatrous lifestyle. The man of God was very honest and unwavering in executing the command giving to him by God. He categorically refused king Jeroboam's invitation to go home with him, though he promised him a reward.

But the man of God said to the king, "If you were to give me half your house, I would not go in with you; nor would I eat bread nor drink water in this place. For so it was commanded me by the word of the LORD, saying, 'You shall not eat bread, nor drink water, nor return by the same way you came.'" So he went another way and did not return by the way he came to Bethel (I Kings 13:8-10).

The Lord had commanded him not to eat or drink in that town. Yet, soon after that, an old, wicked prophet was able to lie and persuade the man of God to eat in his house with what he called, 'the word of the Lord.' And that free dinner offered, cost the life of the man of God.

Now a certain old prophet was living in Bethel. His son came and told him all the deeds that the man of God had done that day in Bethel. His sons also told their father the words that he had spoken to the king. ¹² Then their father said to them, "Which way did he go?" His sons had seen the way taken by the man of God who had come from Judah. ¹³ Then he said to his sons, "Saddle the donkey for me." So they saddled the donkey for him, and he got on it. ¹⁴ He followed the man of God and found him sitting under an oak tree. He asked him, "Are you the man of God who came from Judah?" "I am," he said. ¹⁵ Then he said to him, "Come home with me and eat bread." ¹⁶ But he answered, "I cannot go back with you, eat bread, or drink water with you in this place, ¹⁷ for a message came to me by the word of the LORD: 'You must not eat bread or drink water there or go back by the way you came.'" ¹⁸ He said to him, "I am also a prophet like you. An angel spoke to me by the word of the LORD: 'Bring him back with you to your house so that he may eat bread and drink water.'" The old prophet deceived him, ¹⁹ and the man of God went back with him, ate bread in his house, and drank water. [20] While they were sitting at the table, the word of the LORD came to the prophet who had brought him back, [21] and the prophet cried out to the man of God who had come from Judah, "This is what the LORD says: 'Because you rebelled against the command of the LORD and did not keep the command that the LORD your God commanded you—[22] but you went back and ate bread and drank water in the place that He said to you, "Do not eat bread and do not drink water"— your corpse will never reach the grave of your fathers.'" [23] So after he had eaten bread and after he had drunk, the old prophet saddled the donkey for the prophet he had brought back. [24] When he left, a lion attacked him along the way and killed him. His corpse was thrown on the road, and the donkey was standing beside it; the lion was standing beside the corpse too (1 Kings 13:11-24).

We are responsible to God and accountable to instructions and visions He gives us. And we need to obey the Lord in all things, rather than listen to others who have no clue as to what the Lord requires from you. The consequences of neglected instructions are really great.

5. DO NOT FIDDLE WITH THE DEMONIC (Deuteronomy 18:10-14).

When the Lord set boundaries for His people, it was for a reason. He wanted His people to live free. The people in the land of Canaan did abominable things, and the Lord was sending His people Israel to destroy and possess their land. So the Lord gave them some rules and guidelines, and set strict boundaries for them to follow, if they would enjoy His blessings and protection.

There shall not be found among you anyone who burns his son or his daughter as an offering, anyone <u>who practices divination or tells fortunes or interprets omens, or a sorcerer or a charmer or a medium or a necromancer or one who inquires of the dead, for whoever does these things is an abomination to the LORD.</u> And because of these abominations the LORD your God is driving them out before you. You shall be blameless before the LORD your God, for these nations, which you are about to dispossess, listen to fortune-tellers and to diviners. But as for you, the LORD your God has not allowed you to do this" (Deuteronomy 18:10-14 English Standard Version – emphasis mine).

Boundaries are for various reasons. God sets specific boundaries,

- o To serve as warning to His children when we are about to err
- o To keep us in line with His Word
- o To keep us from entering into the domain of the unknown
- o To preserve the integrity of our relationship with Him, and
- o To help us live victoriously.

Where there are no boundaries, people live haphazardly and destroy themselves and others. It is very easy to think that when you cross the spiritual boundaries and open yourself up to fortunetellers, Ouija boards, readers of palm, or watch demonic films, and listen to occult programs, that they would not have effect on you. Sooner or later, they will catch up with you.

"Curiosity is the mother of invention," we hear. But curiosity without proper protection can lead to disaster. "The power of curiosity can be very productive and constructive, yet it has the ability to introduce you to a world of unknowns that can be very devastating," says Samuel Tomtania. "So, be careful how you play with what you do not understand or master. Always heed the word of your elders and parents who have had experiences and are God-fearing. They have great wisdom for your journey on this earth."

"I've always been very quiet, yet very inquisitive and always searching for answers to things around me, especially in the very existence of human beings, things visible as well as invisible," Sam says. "Growing up in Africa, I used to listen to a radio show that came on Sunday evenings. It usually narrated fictional experiences and unusual encounters of people with mystical forces. I had been warned by my parents to be careful about such indulgences. Yet, because the program was so fascinating with all the unusual stories and all the sound effects that brought them to life, I could not resist the temptation."

"One Sunday evening, after listening to the program with my younger brother and one of my cousins, we chatted about some of the unusual events in our own lives. Afterwards, the two of them left to do a few chores, so I decided to lie down on my bed for a few minutes. Out of the blue, I felt as if a force or some kind of presence was holding me down to the bed. I could not move, I could not utter a word and my whole body felt numb. It was a very scary instance. All I could do was to call on the Name of Jesus in my subconscious. I felt I was dying. I struggled with the demonic oppressive force for a while. All of a sudden, with the last shout of the Blood of Jesus, the oppression lifted off me, and I jumped out of the bed. It was beyond the word scary. I vowed never to listen to that show again. The scariest thing was that the same experience I had, happened to someone else as a result of that evening's show but with a much more bleak ending."

Friend, Sam's own experience is worth noting.

6. DO NOT TOUCH OR COVET ANYTHING DEMONIC
(Deuteronomy 7:25-26; Deuteronomy 12: 2-4).

The Lord told the children of Israel via the intermediary of Moses to devote all the wicked cities they would conquer to complete destruction, and not to touch or take anything for themselves. Achan ignored the instructions and took the accursed things inside his tent and hid them. No one saw him, but God did, and He removed His armor of protection from Israel. Israel was unable to stand before their enemies, and they were defeated in battle. One man's disobedience affected everyone, and so God commanded Achan and his household to be stoned. Why? Because Achan brought the accursed things into his tent and hid them *(Joshua 7:10-26).* Read also *Joshua 6 and 7.*

During our ministry in Kame, one of the voodoo priestess, a short middle-aged woman, whose name has escaped my mind, came to accept Christ. She was from Assrama. She was suffering from an incurable disease plus insomnia. She came to believe in Jesus, because the devil had turned against her. We prayed for her and the Lord miraculously touched her and healed her of the disease, which was about to kill her. Then we went to her home to destroy her idols, the voodoo house, including all the things she dedicated to the devil.

When we arrived, we saw new pots and pans she had dedicated to the enemy the night before she came to accept Christ. After we prayed, she brought out all her voodoo stuff to be broken and burned. Whilst we were about to burn the things, one of our members we named 'Kokouno" (meaning Kokou's mum), who is a cousin to the voodoo lady, spotted the new bowls her cousin bought but didn't use yet. She asked us if she could take them. Geoffrey refused categorically and told her that once the lady dedicated them to satan and brought them in the voodoo house, they belonged to the enemy and should not be used.

"Pastor, I am stronger than the devil," Kokouno said. "I will wash them with the blood of Jesus and use them. These bowls will be a waste if we burn them."

Kokouno was really zealous for the Lord and never thought there would be any problem. We did our job, burned the voodoo stuff that were there and went home.

A week later, Kokouno came to the house one early morning with her daughter. We knew something was wrong, because she lived three kilometers away, and had never been to our house that early. She looked pale, and the daughter was also sick. She was holding the bowls she took from the boots of the devil. After the normal African greetings, she bent over and said, "Pastor, I am so sorry for disobeying you. Here are the bowls. Please take them and destroy it. I don't want any part with the devil."

Geoffrey laughed out loud. We all joined in. It was serious but too funny in the way she presented it to us that day. She said in her dialect, "Aye, Pastor, this is not a joke oh. That guy is terrible oh. Nobody should try to bargain with him on anything that belongs to him. He is too bad, really bad oh."

Oh, my! Her expression was very funny. We giggled for a while. Then Geoffrey said to her, "Tell me what happened, Kokouno."

"Pastor, hmm, I went home, washed the bowls and placed them among my kitchenware. I had no problem the first night, and so I said to myself the following day, 'Aha, Pastor would have deprived me of these beautiful bowls.' The following night, I began to hear noises in my room. I got up, prayed and it stopped immediately, but it continued on for two days in row. And each time I rebuked the noise in Jesus's Name, it would stop but then resumed the next day even louder. Then my daughter became suddenly sick. I asked the Lord to tell me what was actually happening. Then last night, I had a terrible dream." She stopped and began to demonstrate her feelings in a way most Africans would, especially the Adjas, clapping and jumping around. "Chai, my God! That guy is really real oh."

"Pastor, in the dream," she continued, "I saw Lucifer in my room. He was very handsome oh. He came to me and said, 'I am Lucifer, and I am here because you have something that belong to me in your house. If you don't want me to destroy anything that belongs to you, give me my bowls. These bowls are mine, and you took them. They were given to me. As long as you continue to keep them here, I will be coming to your house.' Pastor, that's why I'm here today oh. I don't want anything from him. I haven't slept for days. Look at me, Pastor. Look at my daughter. I belong to Jesus oh. My children belong to Jesus."

She began to sing one of the native songs, 'Gbɔgbɔvɔ m'ateŋ awɔ nde o. Adjetɔ m'ateŋ awɔ nde na Mawu vio lo... Gbɔgbɔvɔ m'ateŋ awɔ nde'

We joined in and praised the Lord for giving her that particular dream to demonstrate to her that as Christians, we are not supposed to take our freedom in Christ for granted, or take part of what has been dedicated to the devil.

Paul the Apostle wrote, "*But I say, that the things which the Gentiles sacrifice, they sacrifice to devils, and not to God: and I would not that ye should have fellowship with devils*" (*1 Corinthians 10:20*).

We took the bowl from her hand, prayed for her and the daughter, and the Lord restored their health back to them. We destroyed the bowls in front of her and burned it.

Compromising and fiddling with anything that belongs to the devil is very dangerous. Taking or trifling with what belongs to the enemy will come back and bite you. Just as God takes care of those that are dedicated to His cause, in the same way the enemy claims back anything that has been dedicated to him.

The only thing the devil can't claim full ownership of, is the human spirit, because it belongs to God, the Creator of the human spirit. He oppresses and possesses the soul, so the person cannot function well spiritually, emotionally, morally, and physically. But if an individual is snatched from the devil's hand, the person must be careful not to open any other door through which the enemy may pass through to oppress you. The Bible says:

> *When an unclean spirit goes out of a man, he goes through dry places, seeking rest, and finds none. [44] Then he says, 'I will return to my house from which I came.' And when he comes, he finds it empty, swept, and put in order. [45] Then he goes and takes with him seven other spirits more wicked than himself, and they enter and dwell there; and the last state of that man is worse than the first. So shall it also be with this wicked generation" (Matthew 12:43-45).*

If an individual was dedicated to the enemy, signed a pact with Lucifer, or was involved in any type of occult practices, and he or she comes to Christ, there is the need for that person to rededicate and consecrate his or herself completely to God without turning back. The enemy will try to reclaim you. That is where deliverance comes in. Most western pastors do not believe in deliverance. That's okay for them. But for those of us who come from the other ends of the world, deliverance through the power of the name of Christ and the blood is what has kept many sons and daughters of God strong in the faith.

However, if you are still on the right track following God wholeheartedly and living Christian life without compromise, feeding daily on the Word of God, and not fiddling with the devil, be assured, God will not allow the enemy to overcome you.

Also, many Americans or Westerners travel to the third world and bring back home beautiful carved items and souvenirs. Please, be very careful. Some of the sources are demonic.

7. GUARD AGAINST DEMONIC TRANSFERENCE
(Numbers 11:16-27).

Another lesson the Lord taught us was transference. He taught us that demons or spiritual terrorist always want a habitation, something or somebody they can inhabit and use to accomplish their purposes. Physical laws and warfare are reflections of much bigger and elaborated spiritual laws and warfare. In the same manner, the warfare a believer encounters in the natural has a much bigger implications in the spirit realm. Hence the reason we need to protect ourselves and the ones we love from transference of any negative and destructive spirit.

In Numbers 11:16-29, we read a conversation God and Moses had concerning the provision that needed to be made for other leaders to assist Moses in leading the people. The Lord told Moses to choose 70 elders of whom He said, *"Then I will come down and talk with you there. I will take of the Spirit that is upon you and will put the same upon them; and they shall bear the burden of the people with you, that you may not bear it yourself alone."* And in verse 25, the Lord came down and literally transferred some of the Spirit He placed in Moses upon the 70 elders, and they began to prophesy.

> *Then the LORD came down in the cloud, and spoke to him, and took of the Spirit that was upon him, and placed the same upon the seventy elders; and it happened, when the*

Spirit rested upon them, that they prophesied, although they never did so again (Numbers 11:25).

A member's wife had serious spiritual problems. The brother brought the wife that morning to our house. The two older boys were at school. I called Geoffrey into the room and whispered into his ears, "Why don't you go into the chapel and pray for the woman?"

"No, we have to do this together," Geoffrey insisted.

"Where are we going to put Samuel and the baby?"

"They'll be with us."

"No! I don't want to expose these children to this intense demonic atmosphere."

"Nothing will happen to them."

"Have you forgotten what the Lord showed us? Then, you can do it alone. I can stay here with them and pray for you."

"Please, please Darling," he pleaded with me. "I want us to do it together, because her husband is not around. I don't want to encounter any negative problem with her."

"Okay," I accepted but not really excited about the idea. I had a plan in my head. I took the boys into our bedroom. I laid hands on them and covered them in the blood of Jesus for protection. I put Samuel on our bed and told him not to come out. Othniel was sleeping soundly in his cot.

I walked out, and we began to do the deliverance in one of the rooms. It was a tug-of-war at the beginning because of her deep involvement in the demonic. Then suddenly, the spirits began to come out. The possessed began to rumble and made different sounds like little piglets that have gone wild. They came out in a battalion. We felt the shock as well as they came out of her.

Suddenly, I heard a voice cry out, "Mama, they are going out to the kitchen."

Oh my goodness, what is Sam doing out there? I ran out to check on him and his brother. And here was Sam sitting by the dining table playing with his toys. None of us knew that Samuel had opened the door and come out.

"What are you doing here, little man?" I asked. "What is going out to the kitchen?"

"Mama, short, short people, going, going to your kitchen," he demonstrated with his fingers. He was only three and half years old.

"Where are they?"

"Look at them, they are marching like soldiers. They are short, short people. Mama, they are going through the window. They are gone, gone."

Chills went through my spine. "You foul spirits, go where you belong in the Name of Jesus Christ," I shouted and prayed. "You have no place in this house. Jesus is Lord over my family. In the name of Jesus, my Lord, I send you back to the abyss, to hell. You will not inhabit anybody again."

I called out to Geoffrey who was still attending the lady and narrated the incident to him. Together, we laid hands on Sam and prayed for him. Just imagine this picture. The worst-case scenario would have been demonic infestation of our sons had we not prayed over them before engaging in deliverance. Thank God they found no room in the children to inhabit, because the Bible says that when the demons in the man of the Gadarenes left, they went into the swine.

Then the demons went out of the man and entered the swine, and the herd ran violently down the steep place into the lake and drowned (Luke 8:33).

8. GUARD AGAINST THE SPIRIT OF RETALIATION.

The other thing the Lord told us about was **Retaliation.** This particular insight, I believe, is for the servants of God who are always leading, counseling, and praying for people. The Lord taught us that anytime we prayed and cast out demons from someone, we should immediately pray against the spirit of retaliation, and apply the blood of Jesus for our protection.

Anytime the Lord snatched a soul from the pit of hell through our witness, the enemy stirred up the hearts of his agents to cause commotion and attack us. The example taken from the Bible is that of Paul in Ephesus.

The Apostle and his collaborator, Silas, were preaching the Word of God in the Roman colony of Ephesus. A young lady who was a fortune-teller, (medium) or a psychic began to tell everyone of who they were. And for several days, she just wouldn't shut her mouth. Although what the girl was saying was true, the source of her insight and declaration was demonic. It wasn't bringing glory to God, but to the devil and her masters who were using her to gain money. Paul, having the gift of discernment and knowing the source of her pronouncements, commanded the spirit to leave the girl. That was when Paul and Silas were attacked by the agents of the enemy *(Acts 16:16-31).*

When we did not know much about some of these secrets, we experienced after effects and attacks on ourselves or on our children.

9. GUARD AGAINST REBELLION IN ANY FORM.

We destroy arguments and every lofty opinion raised against the knowledge of God, and take every thought captive to obey Christ, being ready to punish every disobedience, <u>when your obedience is complete</u> (2 Corinthians 10:5-6 emphasis mine).

King Saul was Israel's first king, but he had a problem with impatience and rebellion against hierarchy—GOD and instituted authority. He violated God's Word, and made a sacrifice in haste, which only prophets and priests were commanded to oversee. Although Prophet Samuel reprimanded him, I don't think he took the words of the Prophet serious. He should have asked God to forgive and restore him, but he didn't. He took things for granted (1 Samuel 13:11-14).

Another day came when Prophet Samuel instructed King Saul by the Word of the Lord to go and destroy the Amalekites. Saul went, but he did the prescribed job in his own way and disregarded the command to utterly destroy everything. That led to the Lord's rejection of his kingship. King Saul's rebellion against the command of God opened the floodgate of demonic oppression in his life (1 Samuel 16:14). Why? The Word of God states that rebellion is like the sin of witchcraft or divination.

Does the LORD delight in burnt offerings and sacrifices as much as in obeying the LORD? To obey is better than sacrifice, and to heed is better than the fat of rams. <u>For rebellion is like the sin of divination, and arrogance like the evil of idolatry.</u> Because you have rejected the word of the LORD, He has rejected you as king (1 Samuel 15:22-23 emphasis mine).

Allow me to insert a strange encounter Geoffrey and I had with a 27 year-old Christian man we would name Jacob. Jacob came to us for counseling. After we took him through the Word and emphasized on what Christ Jesus did for us at Calvary, we decided to pray for him. As we prayed in the Name of Jesus, and in the power of the Holy Spirit, Jacob fell to the floor and groaned, jerked and rolled his body like a toy, foaming and spitting out unusual yellowish saliva. The demons in the brother hissed and manifested like a serpent.

It was really scary beyond our understanding, because the brother was a Christian and was singing in the choir. When we commanded the spirit to leave, it identified itself as the spirit of rebellion and insubordination, and said it had inhabited the brother for six years and wasn't going to leave. But thank God for the power we have in Jesus's Name. The Lord set Jacob free after casting out that demon.

What happened? You may ask.

When Jacob came to himself, he confessed that he had had a hot argument with his parents over his then girlfriend, who was now his wife. His Christian parents were not in favor of him sleeping with his fiancée before marriage. But Jacob took their reaction negatively, and blew it out of proportion with anger, bitterness, and disrespected the parents over a Biblical issue, which he should have understood (I Corinthians 7:1-2; Hebrew 13:4).

Due to his rebellion against God's Word and that of his parents, the enemy found a loophole in his life for the six years he did not repent and make amend.

Although this may be a rare case, remember that rebellion in any form is the number one cliché of Lucifer.

10. YIELD ALL YOUR FACULTIES TO THE CONTROL OF THE HOLY SPIRIT.

I beseech you therefore, brethren, by the mercies of God, that you present your bodies a living sacrifice, holy, acceptable to God, which is your reasonable service. ² And do not be conformed to this world, but be transformed by the renewing of your mind, that you may prove what is that good and acceptable and perfect will of God (Romans 12:1-2).

Therefore do not let sin reign in your mortal body, that you should obey it in its lusts. And do not present your members as instruments of unrighteousness to sin, but present yourselves to God as being alive from the dead, and your members as instruments of righteousness to God (Romans 6:12-13).

When the negative voices in your head becomes louder and louder; when the tension in your head becomes painful and unbearable, and it seems you are going to explode, repeat this prayer over and over. And you will feel a lift in your spirit. The Holy Spirit will enable you to overcome all obstacles, so you don't yield to the enemy's pressure.

I bind my mind to the mind of Christ. I bind my body to the body of Christ. I bind my soul and spirit to the Spirit of Christ. My mind, my body, and my spirit are subject to the dictates of the Holy Spirit. I am bought with the blood of Jesus Christ, and His Blood is my covering. Satan has no power over me. I stand secure and protected in the mighty Name of Jesus, because Jesus gave me power over you and all your cohorts. I am an overcomer, more than a conqueror, and my life is hid with Christ and in God. In Jesus's Name, I pray. Amen.

11. DO NOT LIVE IN FEAR.

The Word of God urges us not to live in or with fear. Fear brings torments. The Lord wants you to enjoy the life He has given you. Yet, your adversary, the devil, knows how to come in with fear for everything. But the Lord has not given us the spirit of fear, but of love, of power, and of a sound mind (2 Timothy 1:7). This means that fear is a spirit. So, here are a few tips that can keep fear at bay in your life.

- o Love the Lord deeply, and love others sincerely from your heart, as you would have them love you.

There is not fear in love; but perfect love cast outs out fear, because fear involves torment. But He who fears has not been made perfect in love (1 John 4:18).

- o Set your mind on the Lord, and the peace of God will flood your entire being.

You will keep him (her) in perfect peace, whose mind is stayed on You, because he trust in You (Isaiah 26:3 emphasis mine).

- o Do the right thinking. What you meditate on can affect your spiritual life and engender fear.

Finally, brethren, whatever things are true, whatever things are noble, whatever things are of good report, if there is any virtue, and if there is anything praiseworthy, meditate on these things. The things which you have learned and received and heard and saw in me. These do, and the peace of God will be with you (Philippians 4:8-9).

The Lord Jesus encourages all of us to think about the victory He gave us on the cross and through His resurrection, and not on what the devil is doing. Yes, troubles and persecutions may come in this world. But we have a sure Word of encouragement from the One who is alive forevermore.

> *Peace I leave with you. My peace I give to you, not as the world gives do I give to you. Let not your heart be troubled, neither let it be afraid (John 14:27).*

> *These things I have spoken to you, that in Me you may have peace. In the world you will have tribulation; but be of good cheer, I have overcome the world (John 16:33).*

o Rejoice and give Him thanks at all times.

The Word of God commands us to rejoice at all times. Even when the going gets tough, and tears are streaking down your face, give Him praise and thanks in your heart. A joyful and a thankful heart gladden the heart of our Heavenly Father. So, let the joy of the Lord be your strength (Philippians 4:3-7; 1 Thessalonians 5:16: Nehemiah 8:10b).

Paul and Silas were arrested, beaten, chained and thrown into prison for casting out evil spirit from a medium. Although they were in pain, they sang and praised the Lord. Then a miracle happened.

> *As we were going to the place of prayer, we were met by a slave girl who had a spirit of divination and brought her owners much gain by fortune-telling. She followed Paul and us, crying out, "These men are servants of the Most High God, who proclaim to you the way of salvation." And*

this she kept doing for many days. Paul, having become greatly annoyed, turned and said to the spirit, "I command you in the name of Jesus Christ to come out of her." And it came out that very hour. But when her owners saw that their hope of gain was gone, they seized Paul and Silas and dragged them into the marketplace before the rulers. And when they had brought them to the magistrates, they said, "These men are Jews, and they are disturbing our city. They advocate customs that are not lawful for us as Romans to accept or practice." The crowd joined in attacking them, and the magistrates tore the garments off them and gave orders to beat them with rods. And when they had inflicted many blows upon them, they threw them into prison, ordering the jailer to keep them safely. Having received this order, he put them into the inner prison and fastened their feet in the stocks. About midnight Paul and Silas were praying and singing hymns to God, and the prisoners were listening to them, and suddenly there was a great earthquake, so that the foundations of the prison were shaken. And immediately all the doors were opened, and everyone's bonds were unfastened (Acts 16:16-26).

You see, what the devil meant for evil, God used it to save souls when Paul and Silas sang and praised the Lord (verses 2734).

12. GUARD YOUR HEART (Proverbs 4:22).

The writer of the book of Proverbs tells us to '*keep our heart with all diligence; for out of it are the issues of life' (Proverbs 4:22).* And the Lord Jesus, when interrogated by the Pharisees concerning His disciples who ate without washing their hands, also said:

Don't you see that anything you eat passes through the digestive tract and out again? But evil words come from an evil heart and defile the man who says them. For from the heart come evil thoughts, murder, adultery, fornication, theft, lying, and slander. These are what defile; but there is no spiritual defilement from eating without first going through the ritual of ceremonial hand-washing! (Matthew 15:17-20 Living Bible).

These instructions must be taken serious, because the heart is another important area in which many Christians become vulnerable to demonic attacks. And this list includes anger, bitterness, unforgiveness, and et cetera. What Jesus said is the multiple-play bundles of anything negative that is contrary to the Word of God.

The Christian life into which the Lord has called us is not always going to be easy. Painful demonic-orchestrated attacks, persecutions, and overwhelming trials can leave traces of anger, unforgiveness, bitterness, and a stronghold of emotional imbalances. These, if not given over to the Lord, may be used by the enemy against us.

Jesus Himself admonishes us to take up our cross and follow Him (Matthew 16:24-28). The Apostle Paul confirmed the words of Jesus with this:

We are troubled on every side, yet not distressed; we are perplexed, but not in despair; persecuted, but not forsaken; cast down, but not destroyed; always bearing about in the body the dying of the Lord Jesus that the life also of Jesus might be made manifest in our body. For we which live are always delivered unto death for Jesus' sake, that the life also of Jesus might be made manifest in our mortal flesh. -

For which cause, we faint not but though our outward man perish, yet the inward man is renewed day by day. For our light affliction, which is but for a moment, works for us a far more exceeding and eternal weight of glory; while we look not at the things which are seen, but at the things which are not seen: for the things which are seen are temporal; but the things which are not seen are eternal (2 Corinthians 4:8-11, 16-18).

Throughout his ministry, the Apostle Paul never failed to impress upon the new believers what they should expect in their walk with Christ.

And when they had preached the gospel to that city and made many disciples, they returned to Lystra, Iconium, and Antioch, strengthening the souls of the disciples, exhorting them to continue in the faith, and saying, 'We must through many tribulations enter the kingdom of God'" (Acts 24:21-22 emphasis mine).

Early disciples were aware of demonic assaults, persecutions, and the difficulties they were promised to face, and they did it with boldness in the grace the Lord had given them through the power of the Holy Spirit. They, through their perseverance and the victory they obtained in Christ, encourage us to stand strong, and not to harbor hatred, anger, or unforgiveness towards those the enemy used or is using to harm us.

We give no offense in anything that our ministry may not be blamed. But in all things we commend ourselves as ministers of God: in much patience, in tribulations, in needs, in distresses, in stripes, in imprisonments, in tumults, in labors, in sleeplessness, in fastings, by purity, by knowledge, by longsuffering, by kindness, by the Holy

Spirit, by sincere love, by the word of truth, by the power of God, by the armor of righteousness on the right hand and on the left, by honor and dishonor, by evil report and good report; as deceivers, and yet true as unknown, and yet well known; as dying, and behold we live; as chastened, and yet not killed; as sorrowful, yet always rejoicing; as poor, yet making many rich; as having nothing, and yet possessing all things (2 Corinthians 6:3-10).

Finally, when the Apostle Paul stood before Governor Felix in defense of his faith, he said, *"And herein do I exercise myself, to have always a conscience void of offence toward God, and toward men" (Acts 24:16).* Prior to this statement, we can all read Paul's resume in 2 Corinthians 6 and 11, and ask ourselves how he was able to have such courage and grace to live without offense. He says:

---In labors more abundant, in stripes above measure, in prisons more frequently, in deaths often. From the Jews five times I received forty stripes minus one. Three times I was beaten with rods; once I was stoned; three times I was shipwrecked; a night and a day I have been in the deep; in journeys often, in perils of waters, in perils of robbers, in perils of my own countrymen, in perils of the Gentiles, in perils in the city, in perils in the wilderness, in perils in the sea, in perils among false brethren; in weariness and toil, in sleeplessness often, in hunger and thirst, in fastings often, in cold and nakedness— besides the other things, what comes upon me daily: my deep concern for all the churches. Who is weak, and I am not weak? Who is made to stumble, and I do not burn with indignation (2 Corinthians 11:23-29).

Why did Paul have such courage? First of all, what happened to him was used by the Holy Spirit to advance the gospel of the kingdom of God.

> *Now I want you to know, brothers and sisters, that what has happened to me has actually served to advance the gospel. As a result, it has become clear throughout the whole palace guard and to everyone else that I am in chains for Christ. And because of my chains, most of the brothers and sisters have become confident in the Lord and dare all the more to proclaim the gospel without fear (Philippians 1:12-14).*

Secondly, the Apostle knew the deadly implications of a heart that is full of unforgiveness, resentment, bitterness, anger, and et cetera. Hence the reason he added: *"---Lest Satan should get an advantage of us: for we are not ignorant of his devices" (2 Corinthians 2:11).* These negative emotions and reactions can become stepping-stones for the enemy to walk on to terrorize you.

With all that I went through, the Lord gave me grace to forgive everyone else with the exception of Flora. The painful stomach ulcers and other health related issues I had were constant reminders of what the enemy used Flora to do to me.

In 1985, Flora paid us a surprise visit in Lome. It had been 8years since I last saw her. And since we weren't expecting her visit, her presence sent a negative signal to my mind and body. The next day, without any warning, I developed an unusual migraine, stomach, and chest pain. My cranium nerves throbbed painfully and unceasingly. It felt as if I was dying. I cried to the Lord to heal me to no avail.

The third day of this unusual sickness, the Lord spoke to me: "Monica, Flora's presence is the trigger point for what you are suffering from. Take the lid off the pain in your past. Dig deep into it and remove the unforgiveness and bitterness you harbored against your sister. Forgive her right now, and reconcile with her in your heart, and I will heal you."

The Lord's message cut through me, and the pain in my heart intensified. I sobbed and sobbed for a while and repented. It was hard to comprehend the depth of the unhealed wounds. Geoffrey and I prayed, and we talked with Flora. I reconciled with my sister, and the Lord healed me. We lavished her with gifts of clothing, food, and money that she happily took back to Ghana. Unfortunately, Flora passed away three years later. I wept bitterly for my loss, but I was grateful that I obeyed the Lord to break free from that yoke of bondage. How would I have lived without forgiven Flora before her passing?

CONCLUSION

As you could see, life is really full of mysteries, unresolved issues, and oftentimes terrors in different forms. Some are man-made, planned and implemented on the innocent and weak. Others are instigated by unseen forces beyond our scope to understand.

The Bible tells us that from the time our first parents, Adam and Eve fell from God grace, terror entered our world. "I was afraid and hid myself," was the first sentence Adam uttered in response to God's anguish and disappointed cry, "Adam where are you?"

Soon after that, Cain terrorized his brother and ended his life in cold blood. From that time, fear filled the hearts of every human being that would be born hereafter. Fear of the unknown, fear for one another, anxiety and emptiness due to man's inability to relate to its Creator, resulted from depravity. It opened the floodgates or all kinds of vices, and terrorism has become the norm for some people, whether physical or spiritual.

It is said that between 1941 and 1945, of the nine million Jews who had resided in Europe before the Holocaust, approximately two-thirds were killed.[4] A network of about 42,500 facilities in Germany and German-occupied territories were used to concentrate, confine, and kill Jews and other victims[5] and between 100,000 to 500,000 people were direct participants in the planning and murder of Holocaust victims. What wrong did they commit? Is that all that there is for the Jews and all the other victims with no vindications?

What about the thousands of Christian who were fed alive to lions, burned on stakes, pierced through with spears, or crucified? Is their story over? And the ethnic cleanse of the people of Angola, Sudan, and other parts of the world?

What about the Jones Town religious atrocities perpetuated against innocent lives? And the Columbine, Virginia, Fort Hood, Sandy Hook, Boston bomb victims, and countless atrocities committed against humans created in the image of God Almighty!

What about the slave trade that claimed countless lives in the Atlantic Ocean and plantations in the West? Is that all that there is for mankind?

All these point to the fact of intrinsic evil that is deeply imbedded in the hearts of humans. The Bible declares: *"The heart is deceitful above all things, and desperately wicked: who can know it? I the LORD search the heart, I try the reins, even to give every man according to his ways, and according to the fruit of his doings" (Jeremiah 17:9-10).*

Now, you may ask, 'Is that all that there is to life? Should evil triumph in their schemes against the innocent? Have all these victims mentioned above suffered in vain without vindication?'

The answer to this question is a big NO! Abraham also asked the same question, 'Shall not the Judge of all the earth do right?' The Lord says, *"Vengeance is Mine, and I will recompense; their foot shall slip in due time; for the day of their calamity is at hand, and the things to come hasten upon them" (Deuteronomy 32:35).*

The Almighty God will not be silent forever. A payday is coming when each one of us will give an account to God for how we served Him or yielded ourselves as instruments of destruction in the hands of the demonic to terrorize others. The Word of God is not silent on these issues. We reap what we sow.

> *Don't be deceived: God is not mocked. For whatever a man sows he will also reap,[8] because the one who sows to his flesh will reap corruption from the flesh, but the one who sows to the Spirit will reap eternal life from the Spirit (Galatians 6:7-8).*

Evil men and women will pay on the earth and hereafter for allowing themselves to be used as instruments of wickedness. Nothing go unpunished as phrased in French, 'Tot ou tard.' It is the law of nature, and the Lord never forgets. Only those sins that are confessed, forgiven, and washed with the blood of Jesus Christ are erased.

> *Then I saw a great white throne and Him who sat on it, from whose face the earth and the heaven fled away. And there was found no place for them. [12] And I saw the dead, small and great, standing before God, and books were opened. And another book was opened, which is the Book of Life. And the dead were judged according to their works, by the things, which were written in the books. [13] The sea gave up the dead who were in it, and Death and Hades delivered up the dead who were in them. And they were judged, each one according to his works. [14] Then Death and Hades were cast into the lake of fire. This is the second death.[15] And anyone not found written in the Book of Life was cast into the lake of fire (Revelations 21:11-14).*

The devil and his demons will also have their special payday, because their fate was already sealed when they rebelled against the Almighty.

'Depart from Me, you cursed, into the everlasting fire
<u>prepared for the devil and his angels</u>... And these will go
away into everlasting punishment, but the righteous into
eternal life (Matthew 25:41, 49 emphasis mine).

The devil, who deceived them, was cast into the lake of fire
and brimstone where the beast and the false prophet are.
And they will be tormented day and night forever and ever
(Revelation 19:10).

Oh, how I pray that mankind would heed this important
counsel from the wisest man of all time—King Solomon. He says,
"Fear God, and keep His commandments: for this is the whole duty
of man. For God shall bring every work into judgment, with every
secret thing, whether it be good, or whether it be evil" (Ecclesiastes
12:12-13).

Finally, these encounters I've written to you about are real
demonic assaults on my life and that of my children. The neardeath
experiences and the confrontational aspects of the satanic addicts
on my life were too severe and frightening. Their assaults on my
children were too intense I almost lost three of them. The
overwhelming revelation and dreams God gave to me and the
children themselves and the confirmations that followed, gave us
more insights and strategies to fight.

These were fearful sights, and manifestations beyond
description. I felt I was losing my mind through it all. But God was
on our side. The Lord gave us victory after victory, after a long
intense prayers and supplication, with fasting and spiritual warfare,
coupled with verbal and loud dialogue with God and proclamation
of His Word.

The truth is, terrorism in all forms and ideology will never
be eradicated from this world if mankind does not submit to its

Creator through His Son Jesus Christ. Our struggle against terror will never end until the human heart is changed. Our fight against terrorism of any kind, will never cease till when the Owner of this world, whose name is the Prince of Peace, step into the scene, and recreate His world anew *(Revelation 2:1-8)*. And that is what we are looking for. But as children of the Most High God, through our acceptance of His Son as our Lord and Savior, we have a sure word of encouragement and victory from the Commander-inChief, the Lord of Host—the God of Abraham, Isaac, and Israel, under whose wings we have found refuge. He firmly declares to you and me, *"No weapon that is formed against thee shall prosper; and every tongue that shall rise against thee in judgment thou shalt condemn. This is the heritage of the servants of the LORD, and their righteousness is of me, says the LORD" (ISAIAH 54:17).*

As good soldiers of the Cross, and faithful followers of Christ Jesus, I encourage you again not to live in fear, but to know who you are—the child of the Most High *(John 1:11-13; 1 John 3:1-2)*. Walk faithfully and humbly with the Lord as you wait for His coming *(Revelation 2:10; 1 Corinthians 15:58)*. Live at peace with yourself and with others *(Hebrews 12:12-15)*, and arm yourselves with the spiritual weapons the Holy Spirit has given you *(Ephesians 6:10-18)*. And remember: GREATER IS THE LORD WHO IS IN YOU THAN THE ENEMY WHO IS OUT THERE! And nothing shall separate us from the love of God.

> *Who shall separate us from the love of Christ? Shall tribulation, or distress, or persecution, or famine, or nakedness, or peril, or sword? [36] As it is written: "For Your sake we are killed all day long; we are accounted as sheep for the slaughter." [37] Yet in all these things we are more than conquerors through Him who loved us. [38] For I am persuaded that neither death nor life, nor angels nor*

> *principalities nor powers, nor things present nor things to come, [39] nor height nor depth, nor any other created thing, shall be able to separate us from the love of God which is in Christ Jesus our Lord (Romans 8:37-39).*

> *For whosoever is born of God overcomes the world: and this is the victory that overcomes the world, even our faith.*

> *Who is he that overcomes the world, but he that believeth that Jesus is the Son of God? (1 John 5:4-5).*

However, if you are not a child of God, through faith in Christ Jesus and your acceptance of Him as your Savior and Lord, you are actually entertaining a dangerous roommate, who can destroy you in no time. You have no protection whatsoever. I encourage you to seek refuge in the only One who can save your soul, and preserve you from demonic destruction, and the damnation of your soul in the fires of hell with the devil and his cohorts.

This book is not an end in itself. It is just an eye-opener and an instrument the Lord will use to inform, instruct, and help protect His people. The real deal is God Himself. So do whatever you can, and in the capacity giving you, to stay closer to the Lord as much as you can, and be alert. He will fight all your battles and ultimately win this war over evil. But remember, "All that glitters is not gold". So, *"Hold fast the pattern of sound words which you have heard from me, in faith and love which are in Christ Jesus. That good thing which was committed to you, keep by the Holy Spirit who dwells in us" (2 Timothy 1:13-14).*

GLOSSARY

1. **A witch:** A sorcerer, enchanter, a magician, a medium. A witch comes out of his or her body and is able to travel to places to cause havoc, kill others, inflicts diseases. They are able to speak to the dead, which is against Biblical command (Deuteronomy 18:9-14).

2. **Adept**: Followers or students of witch doctors, fetish priests, mediums, and devils.

3. **Agouti:** A tropical African or South American mammals about the size of a rabbit.

4. **Amega:** Literally means "A boss" or "A big man".

5. **Concoction:** A mixture of different kinds of herbs and water fetched from where their idols or gods are situated. Demonic incantations or oracles are cited on the concoction before bathing the sick in.

6. **Demonic presence:** A strange, villain presence or appearance relating to, or characterized or inspired by the demonic or wicked spirit, using witches in an out of body appearances beyond human ability. These are possessed by a demon, or seemingly associated with evil spirits.

7. **Fetish:** The word *fetish* is derives from Latin *facticius* *("artificial")* and *facere ("to make")*. A fetish is an object believed to have supernatural powers, or in particular, a

man-made object that has power over others. Essentially, fetishism is the attribution of demonic value or powers to an object. Fetishes can be amulets, idols or images, talisman, which have supernatural powers to speak, move, or communicate with their adepts concerning an individual, a people group, or a nation as well.

8. **Fetish priest:** A fetish priest is the guardian of the fetish (as mentioned above), and serves as its spokesman or representative. He or she practices occultism, and oppresses people, making them helpless and hopeless if they do not know Christ.

9. **Forefathers:** Progenitors or ancestors, family line or lineage. Mediums and witches have received power from the devil to invoke the dead.

10. **Idol:** An idol is an image or other material object representing a deity to which religious worship is addressed, or any person or a thing regarded with blind admiration, adoration, or devotion. (Exodus 20:1-3)

11. **Incantations:** Enchantments, invocations, spells and charms done through the medium of the demonic to destroy or gain access in to the spirit of an individual.

12. **Occult powers:** [1]The occult (from the Latin word *occultus* "clandestine, hidden, secret" or "hidden knowledge". In common English usage, occult refers to "knowledge of paranormal", as opposed to "knowledge of the measurable", usually referred to as science. For most practicing occultists, it is simply the study of a deeper spiritual reality that extends beyond pure reason and the physical science. The Bible is against the practice of occultism (Deuteronomy 18:9-14). [1]Webster Dictionary.

13. **Praying in the Spirit:** Groaning and praying in an unknown language (Ephesians 6:18).

14. **Serpent spirit:** This speaks of demonic occult practices that are in link with the same spirit that tempted and deceived Eve to disobey God's command. However, they go in depth into using those practices to connect to families and individuals in order to destroy them through the medium, witch doctors, and fetish priests.

15. **Tam-tam**: African drums or instruments usually played with a softer beater, or played wild rhythms to praise God or the devil depending on the player's connection.

16. **Tongues:** Unlearned known or unknown language given to Christians as a prayer language when baptized in the Holy Spirit (Acts 2:1-4; 1 Corinthians 12:10; 1 Corinthians 14:1-2, 18).

17. **Voodoo:** The usage of magic, potions, ashes, amulets, casting of spells et cetera, and other practices which Satan's adepts use to destroy others. There are many different kinds of voodoo spells.

18. **Witchcraft:** Witchery, magic, sorcery, necromancy etc… A witch practices witchcraft and bewitch people through

19. **Witch doctors:** These are experienced in witchcraft. They operate in ranks as well. Witch doctors are very wicked, because they are possessed. They hate Christians, and they have the capacity to operate in the demonic realms from where they live against another person hundreds of miles away.

NB: *Some of the names have been changed for privacy sake.

BIBLIOGRAPHY

1. Charles L. Ruby, "Online Etymology Dictionary". Etymonline.com. 1979-10-20. Retrieved 2009-08-10.
2. Encyclopedia Britannica, "Non-Jewish Victims of Nazism".
3. Eric Lichblau (1 March, 2013) "The Holocaust Just Got More Shocking" – The New York Times.
4. Geoffrey Nunberg (October 28, 2001). "Head Games / It All Started with Robespierre / Terrorism: The history of a very frightening word." *San Francisco Chronicle*. Retrieved 2010-01-11.
5. Kim Campbell (September 27, 2001). "When is 'terrorist' a subjective term?"
6. Lucy Dawidowicz, "The Holocaust" 1975 p403 (Holt, Rinehart and Winston, ISBN 003013661X).
7. Merriam Webster on-line Dictionary.
8. Michael Berenbaum, "The World Must Know," The United States Holocaust Memorial Museum – pp 125ff.
9. Pamela Radcliff. P104—107. "Interpreting the 20th Century: The Struggle over Democracy, The Holocaust" Retrieved (2 March 2013).
10. William Safire, New York Times columnist: *Christian Science Monitor*. Retrieved 2010-01-11.

ENCOURAGEMENT TO THE READER

The truth of the matter is that the whole human race missed the mark of being in right relationship and having direct communication with God when our first parents, Adam and Eve, disobeyed God (Romans 5:12-21). The moment Adam and Eve sinned, they broke faith; thereby, the entire human race was cut off from enjoying all that they were endowed by God to live by.

> *Therefore, just as through one man sin entered the world, and death through sin, and thus death spread to all men, because all sinned—(Romans 5:12)*

Sin, depravity, sickness and diseases, death and judgment became our lot. But God, who loved us so much, made a way for every human being on earth to come back to Him and connect their broken link (life of sin) to His communication line. And God did this through the death and resurrection of His One and Only Son, Jesus Christ.

> *For when we were still without strength, in due time Christ died for the ungodly. For scarcely for a righteous man will one die; yet perhaps for a good man someone would even dare to die. But God demonstrates His own love toward us,*

in that while we were still sinners, Christ died for us. Much more then, having now been justified by His blood, we shall be saved from wrath through Him. For if when we were enemies we were reconciled to God through the death of His Son, much more, having been reconciled, we shall be saved by His life. And not only that, but we also rejoice in God through our Lord Jesus Christ, through whom we have now received the reconciliation (Romans 5:6-9).

And although we are all God's creation, we do not become God's children automatically. We have to be born into the Kingdom of God in order to become God's children and enjoy all that God has for His children; those who are in right relationship with Him through Jesus Christ our Lord.

So then, how can someone become a child of God, you may ask? It is so simple and very easy. First of all,

1) Recognize that you are a sinner, who has missed the mark and is separated from God. (Romans 3:23; Romans 5:12-13).

Without accepting your sinfulness, you make yourself righteous before a holy God. That cannot be. God is the only righteous one. All our goodness and so-called righteous acts are like filthy rags before God's holiness.

For since the beginning of the world men have not heard nor perceived by the ear, nor has the eye seen any God besides You, who acts for the one who waits for Him. You meet him who rejoices and does righteousness, who remembers You in Your ways. You are indeed angry, for we have sinned—in these ways we continue; and we need to be saved. But we are all like an unclean thing, and all our righteousness are like filthy rags; we all fade as a leaf, and our iniquities, like the wind, have taken us away (Isaiah 64:4-6).

You cannot have a relationship with a holy God, whose very nature cannot abide with sin.   You don't do everything right because we are sinners by nature.

For all have sinned and fall short of the glory of God, and are justified freely by His grace through the redemption that came by Christ Jesus. ... For the wages of sin is death, but the gift of God is eternal life in Christ Jesus our Lord (Romans 3:23; Romans 6:23).

2) Accept God's unconditional love. God loves you so much and does not want you to perish.

For God so loved the world that He gave His one and only Son that whoever believes in Him shall not perish but have eternal life. For God did not send His Son into the world to condemn the world, but to save the world through Him. Whoever believes in Him is not condemned, but whoever does not believe stands condemned already because He has not believed in the name of God's one and only Son (John 3:16-18).

3) Believe on the Only Son of God, who came to die for our sins so that you might be saved, and be connected and reconciled to God once again. Jesus Christ is the only way to God.

...Jesus Christ the Nazarene, the man you crucified but whom God raised from the dead. For Jesus is the One

referred to in Scriptures, where it says, 'The stone that you builders rejected has now become the cornerstone.' There is salvation in no one else! God has given no other name under heaven by which we must be saved (Acts 4:10-12 summarized).

He then brought them out and asked, "Sirs, what must I do to be saved?" They replied, "Believe in the Lord Jesus, and you will be saved—you and your household'" (Acts 16:31).

Whoever believes in Him is not condemned, but whoever does not believe stands condemned already because he has not believed in the name of God's one and only Son (John 3:18).

Jesus said to them, "I am the Way, The Truth, and The Life. No one can come to the Father except through Me" (John 14:6).

4) Repent and confess your sins to God, and ask the Father to forgive your sins.

Then Peter said to them, "Repent, and let every one of you be baptized in the name of Jesus Christ for the remission of sins; and you shall receive the gift of the Holy Spirit. [39] For the promise is to you and to your children, and to all who are afar off, as many as the Lord our God will call" (1 John 1:7-9).

5) Confess Christ Jesus as your Lord and Savior, and invite Him into your heart.

*That if you **confess with your mouth**, "Jesus is Lord," and **believe in your heart** that God raised him from the dead,*

*you will be saved. For it is **with your heart that you believe**
and are justified, and it is with your mouth that you confess
and are saved (Romans 10:9-10 emphasis mine).*

6) Now live your life every day to please the Lord and read
your Bible every day. The Bible says,

*If any is in Christ, he/she has become a new creation (right
relationship with God and right living is now the option).
Old things have passed away, and now all things have
become new (2 Corinthians 5:17).*

*Through whom (Jesus Christ) also we have access by faith
into this grace in which we stand, and rejoice in hope of the
glory of God (Romans 5:2).*

The Word of God says, *"... To all who received Him and
accepted Him, He gave the right to become Children of God. They
are reborn—not with physical birth resulting from human passion
or plan, but a birth that comes from God" (John 1:12-13).*

Now pray this prayer sincerely from your heart:

"Dear Heavenly Father, I come to You in the name of Your
Only Son Jesus Christ. I recognize that I am a sinner. I
believe that Jesus Christ died for my sins on the cross. I
believe He rose again and lives forever. I sincerely repent
of my sins, and invite the Lord Jesus in to my heart. I make
Him the Lord of my life. Wash me in His blood and make
me new again. Connect me to Yourself, so that I will have
confidence to commune with You day by day in order to
receive from You. Thank You very much for accepting me
just as I am and making me Your child. Today, I declare

that I am born again. Today I declare that I am a child of God. Today I believe that by His stripes at Calvary, I am healed spiritually, emotionally, and physically. Thank you Father, in Jesus name I pray. A-men"

If you prayed this prayer sincerely from the depth of your heart, you are now born again into the kingdom of God. What a Privilege! The broken communication line between you and your Heavenly Father is now connected. Praise the Lord!

Now, let these important principles guide your life. When you take them to heart, you will definitely grow and enjoy fellowship with your Lord and Savior all the days of your life.

1. THE WORD OF GOD: Feed on the Word of God, which is your spiritual food, every day. Read the Bible every day, starting with The Gospel according to John. The Word of God will keep you in line with the will of God (Psalms 1; Psalms 119).

2. PRAYER: Keep the communication line open through Prayer. It is your spiritual breath. A prayerful Christian is a victorious Christian (Jeremiah 33:3; Luke 18:1-8; 1 John 5:14-15).

3. ADORATION: Praise and Worship the Lord every day (Psalms 148 through Psalms 150).

4. WITNESS: Share your faith with others. Allow God to use you to bring others into the kingdom of God (Mark 16:918; John 3:16-18; Acts 1:8).

5. FELLOWSHIP: Find a Bible Believing Church and attend church regularly (Hebrews 10:22-25; Acts 2:42-47). You

need to Fellowship with other children of God, who believe in the Bible. We are not perfect, but as we fellowship together, feed on His Word, and worship in His presence, His power changes us from day to day.

6. WATER BAPTISM: Seek for water baptism (Matthew 28:18-20; Acts 2:38-41). Although water baptism in itself does not save, it is imperative for any believer in Christ to seek to be baptized. Because water baptism is the believer's identification with Christ in His death, His burial, and His resurrection into a new life (Romans 6:3-4).

7. WALK IN THE SPIRIT. Walking in the spirit means, you do not live after the dictates of your flesh. Living after the dictates of your flesh, is very, very dangerous (Galatians 5:16-26). Since you are a tripartite being; that is body, soul and spirit, and you have now been joined together with the Father through Christ Jesus our Lord, You need to allow the Holy Spirit to control your life by living in obedience to God's Word. The reason is, your body is just a vehicle that carries your spirit (The connector to God) and your soul; which is your will, your mind, and your emotions.

8. LIVE THE CHRISTIAN LIFE IN ACCORDANCE WITH GOD'S WORD (Hebrew 12:12-28; Psalms 1): Pattern your life after the Word of God. Psalms 119:11 says, "Your Word have I hid in my heart, that I might not sin against You (God)."

When in doubt as to what to do, get down on your knees and call on the Lord. "Call upon Me, and I will answer you, and show you great and mighty things you do not know" (Jeremiah 33:3). He will definitely come to your aid, and direct your path. Start your day with Him in prayer, and end the day with Him as well. GOD BLESS YOU.

A Word from the Commander in Chief: JESUS CHRIST

And He (Jesus Christ) said to them, "I saw Satan fall like lightning from heaven. Behold, I give you the authority to trample on serpents and scorpions, and over all the power of the enemy, and nothing shall by any means hurt you. Nevertheless, do not rejoice in this, that the spirits are that the spirits are subject to you, but rather rejoice because your names are written in heaven ... And these signs will follow those who believe: In My name they will cast out demons; they will speak with new tongues; they will take up serpents; and if they drink anything deadly, it will by no means hurt them; they will lay hands on the sick, and they will recover. ... And they overcame him (the devil) by the blood of the Lamb (JESUS CHRIST) and by the word of their testimony, and they did not love their lives to the death" (Luke 10:18-19; Mark 16:17-18; Revelation 12:11 emphasis mine).

RESOURCES

[1] GOD STILL SPEAKS – Published by Xulon Press

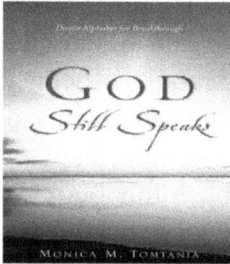

Book Summary

Have you ever wondered whether God speaks to men audibly today or not? Have you ever wondered whether God is still with you or has abandoned you?

Have you ever questioned the Lord for all the ills in your life, and even blamed Him for allowing such things to happen to you? Has life's problems diminished your view of His greatness? You turn toward heaven in desperation and then leave without any feeling of His presence. You cry and wait for exact answers to your questions. But God turns around to give you instructions instead of answers and responds contrary to your expectation. Life isn't fair, but God is still on the throne. He is the Reason for

our being. He knows the end from the beginning, and He will take care of all things. Remember, God still speaks in different ways, and He will speak peace to your situation if you let Him. He is still the Great I AM!

Why I Published This Book

I had numerous personal encounters with the Lord, of which I wrote down. I wrote most of these encounters down as a legacy for my own children and grandchildren to know God as Someone, who not only sees us through difficulties, but that He is a personal God, who communicates with His children concerning His purposes for our lives, even in our fiery trials. I wanted to keep these encounters with my family, but the Lord had a different plan. He unceasingly dealt with me to publish this book, which He said would bless His children, especially those who are going through difficult times, and think He has abandoned them. All the arguments of my inabilities and shortcomings did not stop Him from bugging me. And so He made a way for me to self-publish this book for His glory. As men and women of God, we must leave behind not only the history of our sufferings to our children, but also the precious times we had with God, and the testimonies of His provision, His protection, and of His faithfulness during those moments.

What Others Are Saying About The Book

"Great scripture reference; powerful book! *I came across this book inadvertently, while cruising thru new Christian books on line. The content is solid for a generation that already hears too many voices, but not the voice of God. The book is rich with scriptures....it is a must read!" Ryan Ogle*

"This book came from the heart of one who truly loves and trusts the Lord! Through Monica's fiery tests and trials, her love for God never wavered. She's an inspiration and strength for other women....." Betty Collins, CA

"This book is really amazing. We are thankful to the Lord that HE brought you into our lives. You have been a GREAT BLESSING to us though you may not even realize it, you have. We have

confidence in the ministry God has given you and are blessed by God to know you. ... " Don and Faith Magallanes, MS

"I lost hope, thinking God has forgotten and even forsaking me. But when you sent your book to me while I was incarcerated, God literally used you book to bring me freedom; and not only to me, but my fellow prisoners as well. I began now to share my faith with others. Thanks for igniting faith in me again to believe that God loves, and I can do all things in his name. .... " Michael Elkins, MS

"Had it not been this book, I would have committed suicide. But when I read what you went through, and yet you have the love of God still flowing through you, I believe God is for me and not against me ..... " Randa, MS

"Why the Lord took my young husband away while I was pregnant with our first child was unbearable. I thought life was over with. Filled with all kind of unanswered questions, someone gave me your book. It was like a mirror to my soul. All the questions I had asked were in your book, and I thought, 'God, you told her to write this book just for me.' Thank you very much for obeying the Lord to publish this wonderful book.... " Sarah, New York

(2): *THE ENDTIME DAUGHTERS OF THE KING* –
Forwarded By Pastor Pat Chen

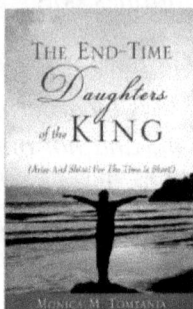

EzineArticles.com:
http://EzineArticles.com/featured/

The End-Time Daughters of the King Published by Xulon Press

Book Summary

The Lord is raising up a mighty army of women, valiant, warriors, conquering women from all walks of life into positions man has never dreamt of ... They are rising up from every tribe and tongues, from all the corners of the world. ... They will be Presidents, Ministers, and whatever they desire to become. ... "They are My mighty army of warriors that I'm going to use to ignite revivals in the lands. They carry on their hearts and spirit deep wounds and scars, bruises and ashes of their past. My Daughters will lead many sons and daughters into the Kingdom. ... Yes, they have been refined. ... But I have given them My heart to snatch this generation from hell," says the Lord.

BOOK REVIEWERS
Reviewed by Richard R. Blake
richard330@yahoo.com

A Call to Revival, Restoration and Healing

Monica Tomtania shares from her life experiences in her new book

"The End-Time Daughters of the King." Her message is significant and timely. Monica skillfully uses the scriptures to relate a testimony of inner change and response to the voice of the Holy Spirit in her life. She encourages the reader to be attentive to the voice of the Lord as she fervently prays for revival and restoration. Thought provoking "Quotable Quotes" add to the validity and urgency of Tomtania's revelation. Monica writes with clarity and displays the heart of a minister in an attitude of servant leadership. I appreciated her use of summary statements throughout lesson learned from the lives of Biblical examples:

those who have gone through God's refining fire. Tomtania urges women today to become torchbearers and igniters like the Biblical examples of Rebecca, Jochebed, Miriam, Deborah, Jael, Ruth, Abigail, Mary and Anna. Monica proclaims that New Testament women like Priscilla, Lydia, Dorcas, and Phoebe are all a foretaste of what the Holy Spirit is planning for end time women who are willing to become vessels that will pay the price of fire, refining, and cleansing which produces holiness and seals the God's covenant.

The process of maturity, transformation, healing, and the importance of the Bible, as the word of God, are all recapped for the reader. Monica invites the reader to go with her into the King's chamber to experience intimate communication, and revelation in His presence. She gives examples from Scripture of some who had time alone with God. Monica explains the importance and the relationship of prayer as the access to God's presence and described this as rendezvous with His Majesty, the King of the Universe. "The End-Time Daughters of the King" is a clarion call to women to respond to the opportunity to arm themselves in preparation for spiritual battle today - a time appointed by God.

[3] A MUSIC ALBUM: PASSION FOR HIS GLORY:

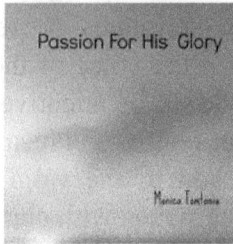

Passion For His Glory

Monica Tomtania

This Album came out of desperation for more of the Lord after a fiery test that took away all that she had in a real house fire. It may not sound as all the albums you've listened to, but it certainly will take you deeper into Christ and Who He is and birth a deep passion for more of God's Glory. The songs on this Album came directly from the throne room into the spirit of His handmaiden. As you listen to the words of this piece, allow the Lord to take you into a passionate journey of knowing Him deeply. The Apostle Paul said, "That I may know Him and the power of His resurrection, the fellowship of His suffering, being made conformable unto His death." Moses, a man who spoke to God as man would speak to a friend cried out, "Lord, show me Your Glory!" That's the cry of my heart, and I hope that is yours as well. Thanks.

www.ingramcontent.com/pod-product-compliance
Lightning Source LLC
Chambersburg PA
CBHW060239100426
42742CB00011B/1577